DATE DUE

Medieval Worlds

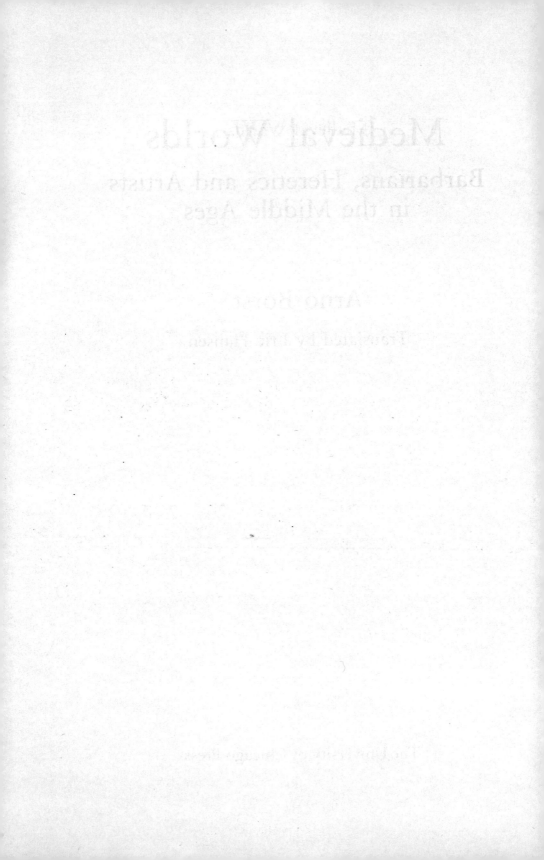

Medieval Worlds

Barbarians, Heretics and Artists in the Middle Ages

Arno Borst

Translated by Eric Hansen

The University of Chicago Press

The University of Chicago Press, Chicago 60637
Polity Press, Cambridge, UK, in association
with Basil Blackwell, Oxford, UK
English translation © Polity Press 1991
All rights reserved. Published 1992
Printed in Great Britain

00 99 98 97 96 95 94 93 92   1 2 3 4 5 6

First published as *Barbaren, Ketzer und Artisten.* © R. Piper GmbH
& Co. KG, München 1988

ISBN: 0-226-06656-8 (cloth)

Cataloging in Publication data are available from the Library of
Congress

This book is printed on acid-free paper.

Table of Contents

Preface

No, the Middle Ages have nothing more to say, the era has closed its mouth forever. All that remain for us are fragments, and not even the experts can coax more than a fraction of these to speak. Unless we can devise a terminology capable of illuminating associations, those remnants will reveal nothing new. That terminology would have to interpret the entire Middle Ages without foisting anything modern upon them, and at the same time motivate modern man to listen, instead of interrupting. I have attempted to foster just such a negotiatory mode of language since experiencing both sides of the coin in my own life: that preoccupation with the past can distract from the demands of the present, yet that it can also contribute to a fuller life. If you would not blindly follow every new whim of the present, you will gain perspective only by looking beyond our time: but to comprehend ages past, you must first determine where you stand yourself, and what issues relate inescapably to your life. Thus, developing a perspective that lets us examine both the Middle Ages and our own age is a task hindered by obstacles from both sides.

The Middle Ages were an era of inquisitorial questions and imperialistic declarations, hardly an age of patient listening and consideration. Abnormal phenomena were interpreted as nothing less than precursors of the end of the world. A mere minority remained open to fresh insights, and because I like to think of myself as one of them, in the following pages I will quote them more often than the influence they had on their contemporaries would normally allow. Furthermore, it is not solely due to their abstruse Latin, the universal language of the Middle Ages, that testimonies of the age cannot be easily understood. In comparison with the hectic and talkative present, we tend to view the past as even more rigid and monosyllabic than it already was. And to make the matter even more difficult, medieval historical research, like every modern discipline, has developed its own methodological and terminological rules which only specialists can use to communicate.

The present age is adept at hiding its own dominant influence behind sociological jargon; it tends to ignore objections raised against its own prejudices, and when its presumptions lose their foundations, it reacts by conjuring up visions of doom. It was hardly more than luck that, for the greater part of my life, history had yet to attract the public eye. Thus, the quiet voices I was listening to were not drowned out by public chatter; when I discussed the things I believed to have understood, experts lent only a distracted ear. Of course, within the past decade the entire world has begun talking about history, and more and more excitedly about the Middle Ages, in a pandemonium that makes it next to impossible to differentiate between what we do have in common with the Middle Ages and what we do not. While the scrupulous try to protect the medieval era against this storm of topicality, others, more fashion-conscious, are declaring a 'New Middle Ages'. Both cover their ears to the broad diversity of oscillations between past and present, both consonant and dissonant.

This collection is an attempt to make that interval audible. It comprises the yield of my teaching occupations from 1952 to 1987 at the universities of Münster, Erlangen and Constance. During those periods, the task of combining research and teaching provided me with the opportunity of attempting long-term and diversified ventures. Almost all subjects expounded here were initially discussed with students in seminars; most were then presented orally to specialists or laypersons; subjects thus finalized were presented to experts in journals or to the public in newspapers; those less acceptable were discussed anew from a different angle. Some pieces here have not been published previously, for lack of final polishing; others, still unfinished, have been omitted completely. All essays included here, despite multiple drafts and rewriting, will, I hope, reveal of themselves when and where they were completed and to whom they were directed; this method of examining history demands that the varying circumstances as well as the recurring leitmotifs be made obvious to the reader. I will exclude the use of footnotes this time; there are enough references in the text and bibliography for the expert to verify statements more closely and for the layperson to investigate relationships further. I would like to open this discussion to both parties.

I have already explained my aims and concerns once in 1978, when history was first becoming a post-modern amusement, but I will repeat myself here. I see the process of history as man's attempt, in an always confusing present, to form his social existence in a way that will let it withstand the constantly threatening future, and also to come to terms with a repeatedly insurmountable past. Those involved directly never see what eventually becomes of society's attempts to 'find itself', since they never live long enough. How much their efforts succeed cannot be determined until a practical state of reality materializes out of the fluctuating range of potential human behaviour. By then, however, later generations have become aware of some undesirable side-effects that have appeared along with those intended, and the longer one is aware, the more oppressive the side-effects become. Trying to dispose of one historical development, they get involved in a new one with different aims, but similar results. This process binds together memory, perception and expectation as it does past, present and future: not with solutions, but with problems. Our problems are hidden by the dust of the archives, and our solutions are questioned by the dead.

This is the reasoning to which most of the dead subscribed so absolutely while alive: it forced them to accept the solutions of the ancients. In the Early Middle Ages, they hardly had opportunity to look for their own answers; vexed at every turn by the treacheries of an overwhelming natural environment, they had no choice but helplessly to endure the whims of historical process. The weak derived two types of guidance from the Christian religion of salvation: the example of the early martyrs' unyielding resolution and the consolation of eternal peace in a life to come. This comforting world view, which could help one cope with any kind of adversity, gave birth to an agonizing dilemma in the High Middle Ages, when nature had already been to some extent tamed: either God's absolute truth could be forced upon the contemporary human world, or this material world was not worth making artificially livable in. This irreconcilable pair of options drove society and science to superhuman achievement on the one hand, and to inhuman brutality on the other. Caught in a vice between the dreams and oppressions of the Late Middle Ages, the collective view of the world, framed by religion, shattered. Simultaneously, however, a polymorphic, fluctuating, earthy lifestyle established itself, not somewhere out on the secularized fringe, but in the very centre of the source of tension between God and the world; this lifestyle became the seed of modern society. How did this astonishing transformation cause medieval man to look at language, power and history? What types of religious, social and intellectual movements did it bring forth, what varied experiences with art, nature and mortality did it inspire? These are the questions at the core of the following propositions.

This medieval development, only briefly sketched here, was given momentum by three main types of behaviour, which I label respectively 'barbaric', 'heretical' and 'artistic'. Framed by words like those, these behavioural types sound more shocking than their practical historical effect ever was. Let us first consider the objective results of all three mentalities. It was the barbaric vitality of the Early Middle Ages, a tendency to react to anything foreign by either subjecting or repulsing it, that saved society from the most atrocious wars, which would have pitted all against all and that forced man into crude, pre-eminently military and political social structures. This is the subject of the first third of this book. The legal refinement of these structures nearly paralysed the High Middle Ages into a self-congratulatory routine. Meanwhile heretical sensitivity, which made every individual responsible for his own salvation and happiness, helped to open closed systems, especially religious and social ones. The second part of this book discusses these. The dogmatic callousness of such movements ruptured the Late Middle Ages so completely that the age threatened to sink into chaos, most especially a chaos of intellectual and cultural systems. What kept the period above water and held it together was an artistic virtuosity that created elbow-room amid the many contradictions for intellectual activity. The final third of this book illuminates those quests for alternatives that prepared the way to a new beginning.

Let us now consider the subjective meaning of the three terms 'barbarians', 'heretics' and 'artists'. Most attractive to the historian is the fact that all three originate in the Middle Ages themselves; there is no need to force modern terminology upon the period. Nevertheless, the words carry certain preconceptions that should be examined more closely. All three are what Reinhart Koselleck called asymmetrical opposites. Hardly anyone would use them of himself, but almost everyone likes to apply them to enemies. And, all in all, they never characterize anyone we know well: they assign attributes of unacceptable behaviour to 'others' in general, to groups of people 'not worthy of our interest'. At the present, catchwords like these may stir up more sympathy than earlier, but hardly less animosity. The medieval world did not take these expressions lightly at all, for reasons of survival. Ostensibly superior, they accused outsiders of the same behavioural patterns that were in fact subversively destroying their own domestic relationships.

The precedence of a regulated domestic zone over unpredictable outer regions, dictated by experience, was unquestioned. The medieval world thought of itself not as barbaric, but as Roman, and this it believed most passionately. In the sixth century it even borrowed the expression *barbari* from the political thought of the ancient world and applied it to the neighbouring nations against whom they were marching to battle. Since European nations were organized into states and Christianized in the eleventh century, the range of the catchword was extended more widely, to the pre-supposed savagery of Asians, Africans, Byzantines and Muslims; at the same time it was extended more deeply, to political enemies and their supposed lack of restraint. Thus, the Europeans of the Middle Ages could hardly have been aware of how much vitality they gained from their own barbaric upheavals.

The people of the Middle Ages were even more zealous in defend-ing the precedence of law over coincidence within the community of their own beliefs. They saw themselves as Christian, and decidedly not heretical. The word *haeretici*, borrowed from the Greek be-ginnings of Christianity, applied not to unorthodox societies like Byzantine 'schismatics' or Islamic 'pagans', but to 'eccentric' move-ments within Catholic Europe. It was not until the eleventh century, in the face of newly arising religious movements, that the expression gained enough topicality to capture the imagination. The catchword verbally diabolized those 'sects' of the faithful which the hierarchical church, especially during the thirteenth century, was trying physical-ly to eradicate. In this way, growing persecution of heresy was also capable of breaking resistance to hierarchical ties. But as a result, the Christian Middle Ages were unable to recognize the fullness of life that their own heretical deviations provided.

Within the Latin intellectual world, a more exclusive self-definition established itself: this protected the precedence of content over form. The difference was incomprehensible to laypeople, who were satisfied with a single label for all people who created culture of any kind, including craftsmen, artists and scholars: the word *artiste*, *artista*, 'artist', which is still used in all Romance and Anglo-Saxon languages. On the other hand, the Latin word *artistae*, which came into use in the thirteenth century, was limited to members of universities who studied the 'trivial' language-oriented fields of the *artes liberales*. Since Latin formalistic instruction in grammar, rhetoric and dialectic was meant only as preparation for the higher sciences, theology, law and medicine, the term carried a taint of superficiality. In German, this still has not changed: the noun *Artis-ten* refers to circus or variety performers who entertain with physical skills; the adjective *artistisch* means showing formal ability, if not contrived. Because the scholars of the Middle Ages tended toward depth and gravity, they could not accept the joy their own artistic embellishments could provide.

Later, the enlightened age discovered not the life-giving side of these three terms, nor even the dynamic tension between negative definition and positive results; rather, it demanded even more asymmetrical and static distortions. They seemed to unmask the entire emptiness of the dark Middle Ages, which obviously had not seen through the blind barbaric frenzy, heretical stubbornness and artistic hair-splitting, and thus became hopelessly bogged down. Not until the end of the twentieth century did we lose our faith in our ability to perceive our own efforts progressively more clearly. The present, influenced by post-modernism, is confronted by a new process of history, one which appears to begin in the middle of the old with the question of how we can shape our lives together most meaningfully: should we hold tight to our inheritance like barbarians, dissect it like heretics or gamble it artistically away?

However, only those who disregard history are damned to repeat it. Nowadays we know that it did not turn out the way our ancestors wanted; they yearned for something unconditional, which they did not achieve in their lifetimes. Because they continued trying anyway, an alternative process of history eventually evolved, our modern one. We can hardly afford to relinquish their larger aims: personal freedom and a regulated society to live in. However, we do not necessarily have to cling to their secondary goals, especially the economic and technical ones of the time. Should we continue to overrate these, as we have until now, the result will probably be not merely a future different from the one we imagine: if nature becomes depleted, there may be no future at all for coming generations. Potential survivors would truly find themselves in a 'New Middle Ages'.

To use that term today, however, one must define it, for the twentieth century has given it three contradictory meanings. Beginning in 1924, the Russian philosopher Nikolai Berdyaev predicted the coming of the 'New Middle Ages'. He hoped for an ideological absorption of global revolution, for a progress toward the irrational, enthusiastic and religious, which would absorb the traditions of both antique and modern worlds. Berdyaev's New Middle Ages promised a Messianic future for the coming era that had never been achieved before and would outdo the old world. In another vein, the American Walter Miller prophesied in 1955, with his science-fiction novel *A Canticle for Leibowitz*, a coming age of atomic disaster. In it, mankind is able to survive thanks to the institution of monastic orders, which had earlier helped the Christian church, Latin culture and the Roman state survive the decline of the ancient world. Miller's New Middle Ages imitated fictitious fragments of the old one in order to ward off the absolute modern age and its demise. Since 1972, the Italian semiotician Umberto Eco has warned against just such reactions. He knows enough of the period to feel less comfortable 'living in the New Middle Ages' (see his book of essays, *Travels in Hyperreality*) than did Berdyaev and Miller. He invented a 'hypothetical Middle Ages project', reduced the diversity of the former age to a few structural terms and projected them into a miserable and absurd future. For Eco's fiction science, the New Middle Ages personified, even more than did the old, a monster of irrationality, a breach with rational history.

To keep the future open, we must avoid judging it by the ideologies, fictions and abstractions of the present, as well as by the traditions, institutions and patterns of the past. Therefore, I propose a fourth interpretation of the expression 'New Middle Ages'. My interpretation will evaluate the epoch that might be coming no differently from the one that is doubtlessly gone, namely, according to how it deals with the mainstream and extreme situations of human society. People who lived in Europe more than a thousand years ago experienced Roman, Christian and Latin traditions neither as stable institutions nor as fragmented structures, but as alternate poles of a dynamic field of tension, compounded by barbaric, heretical and artistic contradictory forces. Such a multi-faceted complex does not simply arise of its own accord, and cannot be fully comprehended as an isolated subject. The strength of the Roman state, Catholic denomination and Latin profundity of thought have since forfeited their potential for integration as much as barbaric self-assertion, heretical consciousness or an artistic world view. The only thing that could create a new medieval culture is an intertwining of totally different yet similarly intense forces. In a paralysed or disjointed future, however, only the elemental part of a European development more than a thousand years ago would be repeated: the destruction of a carefully nurtured society in a fight for existence with inflamed, greedy and malicious creatures. Estimating the future results of this 'New Middle Ages', which would be far less humane, imaginative or rational than the old, requires more than our human abilities, creative imagination and scientific rationalism allow. The most reasonable and empathetic way to avoid a repetition of the Middle Ages is to listen to speakers of the age and consider what they had to say. If we do not wish to abandon both past and future, but to live with history and deal carefully with nature, the Middle Ages will have more to tell us than it could have imagined itself.

Part I
Interpreting Language

1

Barbarians: The History of a European Catchword

I

To understand Europe, one must first explore its history, for Europe is a thoroughly historical continent. And in order to discover what holds this part of the world together, one has to investigate what divides it, for this is where a multitude of conflicting views have ruled for ages, and to this day Europe has been easier to unite in resistance of enemies than in agreement on a common history or in achievement of a common future. Thus, the term 'barbarians', used to strike out at and injure others, is a term for Europe. It is as old as Europe itself, and lives on unchanged in all European languages. It is impossible to expurgate, but we have to ask ourselves why this particular word has been so central to the tension-filled history of Europe, and whether we really want to continue to live with it. The reason Europe's historical diversity has brought mankind so much restlessness and suffering till now is exposed by the history of the word. When we use it, we betray the way we imagine the individual's relationship to society, how we see the position of our own society in the community of nations and what we think of the past and future of the human race. Tell me whom you call a barbarian and I will tell you who you are.

II

The origin of the word *barbaros* is early Greek, and it gained three central meanings in the course of classical antiquity which it has retained to the present day: an ethnographical, a political and an ethical definition. In the oldest, the ethnographical meaning, the word refers to a basic feature of European thought, the aggressive curiosity that needs to define and intellectually subsume anything foreign. Homer used it in the *Iliad*, referring to the Carians in Asia Minor; he said they 'spoke barbarically'. The Carian language is wholly non-Greek, and its origins still have not been clarified. Homer, the Greek, could not understand the Carians when they spoke, but he would not refer to them as 'mute', as other peoples would often label foreigners. The word *barbaros* simply imitated the sound of an incomprehensible word, as baby language does: 'baby', *bambino*, *balbus*. Therefore, incomprehensible language was none the less human language for the Greeks, not at all comparable to the twittering of birds or barking of dogs, as it was for many cultures from China to Spain. Homer appreciated the masculine power and refined culture of the barbarians; he praised the bravery of Carian warriors and the beautiful jewellery of Carian women. That kind of idealizing admiration of foreigners has remained, from Homer to the present day, a predilection of intellectuals and men of letters; in ancient Greece it was thwarted by the less compromising attitude of politicians and the military, who preferred another definition of the word.

The Persian Wars pitted the small Hellenic city-states against a world empire and forced them, who were themselves divided by constant conflict, into an alliance. This is how they learned to see themselves as the ideal people and their enemies as lesser beings, as also happened with the Eskimos and Indians. In 472 BC, Aeschylus derogatorily labelled the Persian national enemies 'barbarians' not only because they spoke like horses, but because of their military power and political traditions; they appeared to him as slaves subjugated to an oriental military tyrant. On the other hand, the Hellenes of Europe considered themselves champions of political freedom. 'Europe' as opposed to 'Asia' became a slogan of war, 'Hellenes' as opposed to 'barbarians'. Under Alexander the Great, the Hellenes turned their defence against the Persian barbarians into offence and forgot a part of their domestic tensions during their first major European expansion. This us-or-them pattern became a second major characteristic of European behaviour, and has turned the originally neutral term 'barbarian' into a word of passion, an insult. Yet it was precisely the result of Alexander's triumphs, the development of a Hellenistic community throughout the Mediterranean, that led to a new, third meaning in the history of this word.

In this community of cities and states, in the synthesis of Greek culture and Roman government, and beyond logic and prejudice, the differences between various languages and political structures faded; man began to judge one another by their humanity, according to their ethical and social habits. Even amid the sharp-witted Greeks and powerful Romans there arose 'barbarians', raw, uncultivated and cruel men: that is the application Cicero and the Stoics had for the word *barbarus*. Inhumane, animal-like stupidity is not a characteristic of foreign nations, but of all of us; something that must be moulded into civilization by cultivation and education. Civilization is not an outgrowth of urban dwelling, subtle scholarship or efficient authority; uneducated nations can be highly civilized. Thus Tacitus could glorify Germanic tribes that did not belong to the Roman Empire and, as a 'foreign nation', were termed barbarians: these 'wild people' were nevertheless the better people. Out of this constellation of terms and values grew a third feature of European expectations: a man should not be judged initially according to his cultural or political situation, but rather according to his ethical conduct; not as a collective being, but as an individual.

These three antique uses of barbarism did not mix well, and in many ways even contradicted each other. But at least in one period during late antiquity, they were united and reconciled: early Christianity. When the apostle Paul was stranded off the coast of Malta and got drenched wading to shore, the natives lit a fire so he could warm himself; the Acts of the Apostles calls their conduct *philanthropia* in Greek, *humanitas* in Latin. Barbarians are capable of behaving in a cultivated and sociable manner. In fact, such races are not that alien to us at all; at most, they simply speak differently from us. In Corinthians, Paul's use corresponded to Homer's: when I talk to someone who cannot understand me, he is a barbarian to me and I am one to him. The diversity of human possibilities can be easily reconciled by charity. Political and social differences pale when one looks to Christ as an example for all. Thus Colossians says: '...there is neither Greek nor Jew, [...] Barbarian, Scythian, bond nor free: but Christ is all, and in all.' This new religious and universal example for mankind was not able to gain historical acceptance in that form, however, for Hellenic-educated intellectuals, as well as Roman rulers, opposed it. Both groups maligned the Christians, calling them primitive, enemies of the empire, barbarians. The early fathers of the church, however, were the first in the history of the world not to shun that title and to regard it as an honourable one: 'Yea, we are barbarians,' said Clement of Alexandria. That robbed the term of its cutting edge, and it began to look as if the victory of Christianity in the Roman Empire would soon relieve it of importance altogether.

III

But it did not go that far. The reason has much to do with the Germanic Migration of Peoples which overran the newly Christianized Roman Empire in the fifth century. This made the us-or-them scenario modern once more, this time for a millennium of the Middle Ages; the political term 'barbarian' was revived and ideologically intensified with religious implications, then magnified into the satanic. Just as the assailed Hellenes labelled their enemies barbarians in the Persian Wars, so did the Latin nations. The advancing Germanic tribes spoke incomprehensible dialects, had military power, were as robust as peasants and disdained urban civilization; and their pagan superstitions rejected Christianity. It was a defensive instinct that moved the Christian Roman Cassiodorus to make a hair-raising definition around 550, probably referring to the hated Vandals: he pronounced that the word *barbarus* was made up of *barba* (beard) and *rus* (flat land); for barbarians did not live in cities, making their abodes in the fields, like wild animals. The opposite, positive image is easily imagined: the shaved monk, a *litteratus* and *clericus* bent over scholarly manuscripts in cathedral chapters. A division was established here that would never be fully rectified in Europe again, a national gap between Latin and Germanic peoples, a social gap between Latin-versed clergymen and dialect-speaking peasants.

It was to develop into an inner-European fissure, for in the sixth century the Germanic invaders eagerly adopted Catholic religion from the culture they had subjugated and Latin literature from the Roman government. Yet, because Franks and Anglo-Saxons were learning these traditions as pupils instead of applying them as masters, they were haunted by feelings of inferiority. Frankish and Germanic writers had to suffer being mocked as 'barbarians' by Latins throughout the entire Middle Ages. The layman Einhard, proud friend and biographer of Charlemagne, wrote bitterly in 830 that he was little more than a barbarian, ill-practised in the Roman tongue. As late as 1926, a French historian summarized the global history of the Early Middle Ages as an epoch sandwiched by the Germanic and Turkish invasions and dismissed it in his heading as *Les barbares*. The Frankish and Saxon conquerors were belittled by the Byzantines even more than by Latin peoples, because they had barbarously destroyed Rome's ingenious order of government: true urban culture could only be found in the court of the Eastern Roman Emperor in Constantinople. The western military victors themselves became convinced that they were culturally inferior, and the 'barbarian' trauma drove them to even more aggression.

One claim to glory remained their own: the Germanic peoples had adopted the correct faith, the Catholic one, and had thereby forsworn all barbaric idol worship and overcome the hair-splitting and heresies of the Byzantines. The Franks and Saxons had the true faith; thus the 'others', the pagans and heretics, became the actual barbarians. And they were given more than just the abusive nickname. The aggression of the Great Migration continued in the form of the violent expansion of Catholicism, and the contemporaries of Charlemagne called this proselytism 'suppression of barbaric nations'. The Carolingians' image of themselves as missionaries was fortified in the course of the ninth century, as their empire was torn apart by invasions of Saracens, Normans and Hungarians. All these invaders were non-Christians; this let the defenders see themselves as God's people. It became the duty of Christianity to force these barbarians to their knees, so in the tenth century, the Germanic nations went from a defensive position to an offensive one, which became especially merciless in the Ottonian battles against the Slavs. Their goal was achieved in every way; the word 'slave' is a witness to how it was realized, for it originates in the word 'Slav'. From the eleventh century on, no unenslaved communities of non-Christians, no barbarian peoples, existed in the Catholic Occident.

No one, however, neither Pope nor Empire, was capable of politically uniting the religiously uniform West. Instead, national monarchies sprouted up everywhere, fighting with each other for pre-eminence, and that is where the old prejudices continued to thrive. In the early twelfth century, the French Benedictine abbot Suger of Saint-Denis compared the Germans to Muslims; he called for the pious French to slaughter these barbarians mercilessly, and leave their corpses for wolves and ravens to feed on. During the same period, the German bishop Otto of Freising reminded his contemporaries that the ancient Greeks and Romans had despised all foreign peoples as barbarians, considering themselves superior both in intellect and the beauty of their tongue; for his time, he called all nations 'barbarians' who lived outside the borders of Frederick Barbarossa's Holy Roman Empire, including the Greeks. At the same time, the oldest chronicle of Poland complained about Germans calling the rulers of Poland barbarians; the same chronicler, however, considered the neighbouring nations, the Lusatians, Prussians and Lithuanians, of course, barbarians. The Middle Ages believed in a west–east gradient of civilization, starting

with the old Roman cities on the Rhine and Rhône and declining
towards the newly colonized lands on the other side of the Elbe and
Vistula Rivers; they believed barbarians generally lived in the East.
Tension like this between European nations was not enough; the
twelfth century records how people of the same nation, the same
city, the same family behaved barbarously. The German Emperor
Henry IV complained in 1106 that his own son treated him more
abusively than any barbarian would a slave. Although men of letters
preached chivalrous self-discipline or monastic self-denial as a cure
against such suicidal behaviour, a more efficient way out of the
internal dilemma was renewed consolidation against an external
enemy.

When Pope Urban II called for the first Crusade against the Holy
Land at Clermont in 1095, he painted a properly classical picture of
the barbarous Seljuks; he even lent them the antique, anti-Hellenic
name 'Persians'. He spoke of them as an alien people, strangers to
God, who desecrated Christian churches and tortured the Christian
faithful, an almost inhuman nation; to destroy them was a Christian
duty. This common goal caused the nations of Europe to forget
domestic feuds. When the Mongolian invasion of 1241 alarmed the
Hohenstaufen Emperor Frederick II, he set the Mongolian hordes in
contrast to Christian nations, calling them bestial and lawless barbarians. Again, in 1453, when the Turks conquered Constantinople,
the humanistic Pope Pius II applied the same method in his attempt
to unite the quarrelling Renaissance lords: the Turks, he wrote, were
a completely wild nation, enemies to any kind of culture and learning. They stemmed from the barbarity of Scythian lands, had no
history and practised innumerable depravities; what they ate was
abominable and they were complete strangers to wine, grain and
salt. His picture of barbarity could only be preached to those who
had never seen Seljuks, Mongolians or Turks before; the international conspiracy of hate shattered quickly, once the Crusaders
settled into the Near East. Merchants travelling overseas from
Italian port cities discovered trading partners of an advanced material culture in the Muslims of the Middle East and Mongolians of
the Far East; Franciscan missionaries soon discovered that the
Oriental religions, Islam and Buddhism, were not primitive at all.

When the bourgeois Later Middle Ages spoke of barbarians, the
image of distant pagans came to mind less and less; there were
enough other enemies that were closer. In the thirteenth century,
the scholastic St Thomas Aquinas no longer defined barbarians
religiously, as one might expect from a saint, but socially: a barbarian was one who did not live according to the rational rules of

a civil society, of a *civitas*, and who did not speak a systematic language. Translated, that meant barbarians were the high-handed provincial aristocracy and their crude peasantry. For the poet Dante Alighieri as well, the antithesis of peasant barbarism was *civilitas*, bourgeois virtues and breeding. It is not difficult to understand why the Peasants' Wars of the later fourteenth century were rejected by the bourgeois as barbaric, and for them, the wars of the aristocracy were barbaric as well. In the Hundred Years' War of the fourteenth century, West European mercenary troops were often called *barbari*. In Italian, Spanish and French, the word was quickly shortened to *bravi*, and in Italian the word *bravo* still refers to a paid murderer. (It was not until much later that it developed into the German word *brav*, which means good as in 'good boy': a man who thinks of himself last, and whose conduct a spectator might applaud with the word 'bravo!') Parallel to these social tensions, the national quarrels continued. Starting with Petrarch, the humanists boasted of their Roman, Latin past, looking down their noses at all non-Italians as barbarians, Germans most of all. Ulrich von Hutten gave the Italians their own medicine, and it was Erasmus of Rotterdam who finally put an end to the squabbling.

Once again, however, it was not humanism that triumphed, but the religious image of the enemy. The humanist Lorenzo Valla applied it to the internal situation in 1440, turning against the Christian origins of Europe. He castigated the 'raging, vehement, barbaric government of priests', the tyranny of a medieval papacy that manifested itself in foolish claims and crude rhetoric, and which above all suppressed religious freedom. In an attempt to settle Europe's internal strife, the sixteenth century once again conjured up the medieval idea of Crusades against barbaric nations, this time on the occasion of the overseas expansion that was just beginning, during the early phases of exploratory travel and colonization. In 1493, Pope Alexander VI divided up the New World that Columbus had discovered among the kingdoms of Spain and Portugal, 'so that the barbaric peoples should be subdued and returned to the faith'. But in an age of European religious wars, the label of barbarian lost its religious power of persuasion for good, and, with it, its uncompromising negative meaning. As early as 1525, Luther harked back to Paul, writing to Erasmus: 'I have always lived barbarically, among barbarians and in the midst of barbarity.' In 1543 he called it plain blasphemy for a man to boast of not being a barbarian. The Middle Ages had ended, and immediately the antique concept of barbarians began to reappear, this time tempered and diffused by scepticism.

IV

The evolution of the word 'barbarian' was allowed to roll on and
was even lent an explosive new potential by the need of a modern
age to portray itself as historically progressive, compared to its
origins and traditions. Europe took everything the world had to
offer, bad and good, diseases and delicacies. That same sixteenth
century gave the name 'beri-beri' to the East Asian, South American
and African disease resulting from lack of vitamins; that was also
when we began calling the tasty plant imported from China and
Tibet 'rhubarb', and both names recall exotic barbarians. But did
the Europeans bring only advantages? The Spanish missionary Las
Casas energetically denied this in 1559, when he wrote that the
Indians had good reasons to call their new Spanish masters barbarians, for it was the Spaniards who had ruined life there with their
ill-considered intrusion. Not much later, the French essayist Mon-
taigne added that the original naïveté of the natives was becoming
corrupted by European vices, and that it was nonsense to equate
primitive peoples with barbarians. Critical voices like these constituted the beginning of a modern ethnology that has often, as had
Tacitus, pointed to noble savages of primitive periods as positive
examples for decadent Europeans to learn from.
    But was barbarity a product of the historical process, or was it
more a timeless anthropological problem? Could a natural barbaric
tendency be denied in every individual? To subdue it, humanistic
scholars argued the power of moral cultivation, as had Cicero. In
1647, the Spanish Jesuit Gracián wrote, 'Man is born a barbarian
and only refinement can free him of his bestiality.' But the self-
discipline of the individual was not enough; the age of absolutism
understood that man was a social animal, and they hoped to find the
solution to the anthropological problem in a regulated society where
man's brutish impulses could be repressed. In 1670, the philosopher
Spinoza formulated the concept thus: 'And so we see that all people
living without the structure of government live like barbarians,
leading a miserable, almost animal-like life, and even they are nevertheless capable of obtaining the little they possess, as miserable and
crude as it is, only with co-operative aid of some kind.' In 1798,
Immanuel Kant reduced the need for enlightened compromise
between personal freedom and civil law to this succinct formula:
'Power without Freedom and Law: Barbarism.' Social order
appeared a feature of the kind of humanity that could overcome any
historical restriction. But was it really? The eighteenth century began

to entertain doubts, for in the states of the *ancien régime* there were still many who led a primitive, barbaric existence. To overcome this barbarism, one had not to search out past origins, but look forward, to a future yet to be planned, and to merge the humanistic idea of moral education with the political idea of a communal society: the education of man, Enlightenment, progress.

Now, anything backward or obsolete was called barbaric, especially the Middle Ages and religion. Voltaire, Gibbon and Schiller, using almost identical words, called the period of the Germanic Migration of Peoples a triumph of religion and barbarism; they pitted it against the catchwords of reason, and above all against civilized culture. Already, St Thomas Aquinas and Dante had called for cultured breeding; the new word 'civilization', introduced by Comte de Mirabeau in 1757, included the material refinements of life. This battle-cry of the bourgeois revolution echoed in the pages of the *Communist Manifesto* of 1848, which bourgeois global society praised as a triumph of progress over locally isolated barbarism. Such an exultant leap into the future, however, simultaneously threatened the roots of human existence, as became obvious during the bloody development of the French Revolution. Some, looking far into the future, took the cruelties for granted; such a man was Jules Michelet, who, as late as 1846, enthusiastically declared: 'This word pleases me, I shall adopt it as my own – barbarians! Yes, that means filled with new juices, vivid and rejuvenating; barbarians, that means travellers on the road to the Rome of the future.' This was meant to justify, answering the criticism of Victor Hugo, for example, who in 1838 had called the terror of the revolutionary troops a relapse into ten centuries of medieval barbarism. There were other opponents too, like the English conservative Edmund Burke, who regretted as early as 1790 that France was changing from a noble, chivalrous nation to a people of crude, stupid and wild barbarians, impoverished and filthy in addition. History as a political argument had become modern. Yet, in a way, the consequences of the Germanic Migration of Peoples were reappearing: the victors could not enjoy their victory; their guilty conscience sought and found a new us-or-them scenario, domestically and internationally.

The proletarians were chosen to be the new bogey-men. The July Revolution of 1830 caused the Prussian historian Barthold Niebuhr to prophesy that a barbaric age would soon reappear; in 1846, the Swiss historian Jacob Burckhardt feared that the barbaric plebeians would exterminate every form of intellectual nobility, and with it, Old Europe. Even in France, the proletarians were often called barbarians. It was a late response when Lenin returned the insult in

1913: he called the proletarians the only protection against Asian backwardness, barbarism, slavery and the degradation of men. This last comment hits the bull's-eye better than any show of stubbornness; the degradation of man was one result of the bourgeois faith in progress, of the division of labour and of the dream of endless potential. Not only the socialists were aware of this: Hölderlin predicted this form of nineteenth-century barbarism as early as 1799, when he called his German countrymen 'barbarians since ages past, and for all their diligence and science and even their religion, all the more barbaric...you see craftsmen, but no human beings; thinkers, but no human beings; priests, but no human beings; lords and servants, young and settled, but no human beings...'

Nietzsche, too, after 1870, protested against this stupefying atrophy, though in a more desperate expectation of new barbarism from without. The blond beasts would wipe out fossilized bourgeois culture and begin a new one, 'Barbarians in every terrible sense of the word, predatory men, possessing unbroken strength of will and a craving for power'; their vitality would also squash our weakened Christianity. Nietzsche was not alone in criticizing civilization; most prophets of doom in the later nineteenth century imagined the new barbarians not to be blond, but yellow, foreign blood from the Far East, the 'Yellow Peril' from Japan or from the nations of the Mongolian Steppes, following a new Genghis Khan. Much of this doom-prophesying was designed to justify European imperialism, the superpowers' race for the last remaining colonies. At the core of it, imperialism was the final attempt of European nations to prevent civil war by expanding. In 1904, Anatole France warned against this illusion; he called European colonial politics the newest barbarism, as well as the end of civilization, for the highest human value was always man. In 1914, he warned once more against war, which would pit Europeans against each other and reduce a common historical civilization to barbarism.

But politicians and military leaders would not listen to the warnings of intellectuals, and they carried out their fraternal strife in the form of a global war, in which both sides called each other the barbarians. In the meantime, it had long since become clear that the real threat was less in certain barbaric peoples than in the barbarism of man himself, and that war between nations was but one, superficial side of the problem. The other side was best characterized by the Netherland historian Johan Huizinga in 1935; he foresaw the advent of a barbarism of creeds, in which the magical and fantastic would rise up in a blur of hot desires, and where myth would stifle logic. Adolf Hitler himself confirmed such fears in a conversation in

1933: 'You call me uneducated, a barbarian. Yes, we are barbarians, it is what we want to be. It's a title of honour. We are the ones who will rejuvenate the world. This world has reached its end.'

V

With the experience of two world wars, the twentieth century gained an understanding of barbarism that helps explain not only Europe's present, but a good part of its past. What confused and darkened the past was not the variety of eras abdicating to one another, nor the diversity of conflicting opinions. Dialogue and compromise could have clarified and gratified this fullness, had war and myth not repeatedly interfered. War as the father of all things: that predictable aggression that, since the Greeks, has furthered science and the triumph over nature, but also permanent hatred between men. Myth as the foundation of society: that authority that, since the Greeks, has tied the individual to his country and origins, yet degrades outsiders to animals. War and myth are ancient, yet they are the barbarism of our century. For the last two and a half thousand years, we have changed the earth in every way, but we have estranged mankind in every way, too. If we believe in the myths of our own society, we will have to make war against other societies; this correlation is so simple that it has seldom been grasped until now, much less resolved.

If it is ever to be surmounted, I see only one alternative, one that is not new, but nearly as old as war and myth themselves: Stoics and early Christians, Sceptics and leaders of the Enlightenment have proposed it again and again, but until now it has always been in vain. It is simply the attempt to consider the entire individual, not as a member of a group, not as a tool of an institution, not as a functionary in an organization, but as a whole person. And it is the attempt to live together, not only with business colleagues, with fellow party members, with compatriots, but with other human beings. The challenge is difficult and has often failed throughout European history, but the most important tool is always available: dialogue with one another. All of us can talk with strangers who speak foreign languages, who are formed by a different past and hold other convictions; if we cannot understand them, then we are the barbarians. Much would be gained if this definition were the only one left, in all languages around the globe. For as long as that term applies, vaguely and collectively, to 'someone else' instead of to each of us personally, we will not be free of barbarians.

2

The History of Languages in the Flux of European Thought

I

Man has been actively thinking about language not since he began speaking, but since his own intellect and understanding of life first became questionable to him. Since that time, he has continued enjoying the miracle that lets him express himself, talk to others, name things and relate events, but is already brooding over the puzzle that despite it all, the nature of humanity and the world has not been revealed to him. Thus, he has turned to examining the core of the language that has been given him but which has fallen short of giving him what he ultimately desires. The idea of searching language itself for answers pleases him; he isolates it from his own fragile existence, even referring to it as a hidden, sheltering *Haus des Seins*, a 'house of being'. It was Martin Heidegger who wanted *die Sprache als die Sprache zur Sprache bringen*, to make language a subject of language; like Heraclitus of Ephesus, he circumscribed the never-changing mystery with pondering, enigmatic word games. History was hardly capable of solving the riddle, for history was the 'recurrence of the possible'; the past would always accompany us, the enigma of language would never change. Thus was Heidegger justified in reviving the methods of Heraclitus. True, two and a half thousand years lie between Heraclitus' Greek and Heidegger's German, and those years have left deep scars in the thought and speech of man; but Heidegger withdrew himself from the range of these influences by creating his own language. It is an anti-social language, difficult to comprehend; it disdains one purpose of speech to examine its essence. By reversing the procedure, by using language as the tool with which to master one's historical world with all its inhabitants and circumstances, one must pay another price, which is

hardly less high: unquestioning dependence on predetermined expressions and historical events, and these are limitations.

People of less philosophical consciousness, too, come across
limitations like those: whenever experiencing their larger environment. It bothers them that foreigners cannot understand them; they
feel alienated by the incomprehensible heritage willed on them by
their ancestors. Then they do begin asking about the history of
language, about the mental structures that differ from one another
and change constantly. It is in the roomy museums of knowledge, in
inaccessible, technical systems of facts and data that they find their
answers. Linguistics, for example, as with Jacob Grimm, examines
the historical evolution of speech forms, revealing phonetic shifts,
related tongues and linguistic structures. History, as with Leopold
Ranke, examines historical material passed down in writing, revealing events 'in their human conceivability, their unity, their fullness'.
But what do dusty books and dead processes comprehensible only to
specialists say to the living who question their own language? And is
there no difference at all between the specific and the universal,
between a single language and language itself, between the
events and their historicity, the creations of man and his substance?
Might the solution to our riddle of language lie somewhere in this
discontinuity?

Wilhelm von Humboldt addressed that question long ago, and
only today are we beginning to understand his answer: the general
can be realized only in the specific. Linguistic formations originate in
the consciousness of man; they are historical structures that embody
man's will. Every unique statement is part of our inner selves; every
linguistic phenomenon is, as a historical experience, part of us. Thus
the riddle of language becomes the riddle of man, though the actual
subject does not change, for man is the historical being that can
speak. Our speech and our past, everything we say or do, comes to
us as a distant legacy; no one can fabricate one's own language, no
one can choose one's own historical position. Traditions and situations limit our inspiration; the mother tongue and the environment
determine to a great extent how we see the world. Yet we are free
just the same, and we use our inheritance as though it were our
own; for an instant, we hold it in our hands. Then it escapes from us
and will never return; what we have said or done is irrevocable and
has its effect in a future that we cannot determine. Our linguistic
and historical life is thus specific and fragmentary; it gives us no
chance to experience the whole and enduring truth. But we can
approach it – by a different route from Heidegger's – by relating
events to each other and collecting fragments, by consulting those

who are a part of a past that belongs to us yet lived their own lives. It is thinkable that not every possibility of human existence has yet been realized in history, but at least a larger variety has than any one person can imagine. Therefore it is possible that history has more to yield about the role of language, if not about its essence, than has solitary meditation, and even more can be gained by examining a variety of interpretations of the history of language, all of which have been made in a specific tongue and in a specific situation and were determined by a historical process. Then we can grasp both form and concept, period-specific and continuous, diachronic and synchronic, evolution and essence of a single language as well as of language itself.

The selection I offer here is specific and fragmentary, though not arbitrary. I will consult here no more than six witnesses from differing periods, nations and fields of influence; only in this way is it possible to provide a look into the entire spectrum of historical achievement. Each of these men possessed world class in his field and stood on the threshold of a new era. Behind each statement stands a life; what they said about the history of language was once reality, and the influence of their arguments exceeded their time. Thus, I would like to let them speak largely for themselves; I will refrain from censoring them even when I disbelieve them. Understanding alone is enough; it is also difficult enough.

II

It is about 600 years after Christ, and a provincial Roman named Isidore has just been ordained bishop in Seville. He speaks Latin, has dedicated himself to the heritage of the classical period and to the dreams of the global Roman empire that is reincarnated in the Catholic church. But his Latin spirit is confronted by overwhelming Germanic power; Isidore's Spain is ruled by the Visigoths, who, until lately, have championed a non-Roman Christianity, still speak a foreign tongue and mistrust Latin ways. Their raw strength threatens to crush higher culture. None the less, Isidore leaves the ivory tower; he accepts recent events and attempts to reunite that which has been divided. He approaches the Visigothic kings, becomes their friend and teaches them to embrace the Roman language, culture and church. Simultaneously, he learns from them to renounce the authority of the Roman state, to believe in the greatness of Spain within its borders and in an enduring world order. Isidore of Seville does not use the Gothic language when he writes;

he sticks to Latin, but it is a different Latin from Cicero's. Under his guidance, the finely tuned and complex-structured literary tongue becomes a form of communication based on clearly arranged sentence structure and frugal vocabulary, more appropriate to clarity than elegance, a welcoming hand stretched out to the barbarians. It is a tongue that offers predetermined realities; every word has a fixed position and reflects a fixed facet of the world. A word's sound reveals its meaning; if you listen closely, you can hear in language the voice of the creator and the meaning of life. The Latin word for 'language', *lingua*, comes from *ligare*, to connect: language ties words together with articulated sounds. *Sermo*, the speech, came from *serere*, to merge: conversation binds speakers to each other. Thus, the true achievement of language is present in the words for 'language': speech binds together. This is why, a thousand times over, Isidore couples the sound of the word with its meaning, using language like a ribbon to wrap up the natural, historical and spiritual universes that he describes in his encyclopaedia.

This great achievement, *Twenty Books of Etymologies or Origins*, which Isidore left uncompleted at his death in 636, was meant to preserve antique knowledge for barbaric times and, again, use language to forge a path for the present back to its origins. Isidore the Christian trusts fully in the history of salvation: in the consonance of words, he discovers their origins, and if you have the word, you have the thing itself, for both come from God. Does that imply that God set down the harmony of sound, meaning and object during Creation? Not at all: language is the responsibility of man. In Genesis, the Bible says that God led the animals to Adam for him to name. It was the first man who created language, for he was wise and grasped the nature of things; he infused Hebrew with the whole of nature. Certainly, men renamed things later, inspired less by insight than by chance; for the owner can name his possession as he pleases. Language is not merely a reflection of the world, but also a tool of man. But does that explain the variety of languages? No, for Hebrew is not the only expedient language; in this age, if you want to express yourself precisely, you have to speak Latin. Every age has its appropriate and unique tongue. Furthermore, the individual is capable of learning any conceivable language, but can fully command only one: his own, which must suffice. This provision of history is good, and is no accident: it originates in God. Moses tells how the entire world had a single language before it began building the Tower of Babel; in order to stop that act, God confused the world's language, thereby scattering the people. The single Hebrew *lingua*, which had bound all words, objects and people together, gradually became divided, and with it mankind; for nations are built on languages. But it was God who divided the tongues; for that reason, there are exactly seventy-two, corresponding to the ancient, cosmological symbolic number. Thus, despite their divergent designations, they say the same thing. Every language allows access to an eternal truth, and that is something even the course of history cannot change.

Isidore stresses that contemporary Latin is becoming diluted and corrupted by the barbarians of the Great Migration. But even then, it is possible to make out God's work and providence in the Latin vocabulary. In God's eyes – that means in their structures – every language has equal status. Of course, Hebrew, Greek and Latin are especially holy, since they are found on the cross of Christ, and were used in writing the Bible; furthermore, they represent the natural foundation of all articulation: Hebrew is guttural, Greek palatal and Latin dental. But only their spiritual content is sacred, not their natural form, for language as form is merely human. God and the angels do not speak: God's word created the world soundlessly. And when the end of the world comes, languages will be silenced once more: in heaven, the saints will not sing in Hebrew. But no matter what priority the eternal takes over the created, God blesses all languages and the entire universal course of history; man is given the right to glimpse the glimmer of truth in all things. None the less, there is plenty of room for man and his widely-spread history, for sovereign peoples and diversity of tongues. The eternal is contained within the temporary; language and history are tangible, but lead to the intangible, like stairs into the clouds. With this philosophy, Isidore helps found the synthesis of Germanic statesmanship, Latin culture and Catholic faith that characterizes the Western Middle Ages; his encyclopaedia becomes an elementary text for the Middle Ages, and for a thousand years, medieval peoples will discover the miraculous work of God named and described in that book. Long afterwards, as late as the time of Cervantes, a belief will continue to prosper in Isidore's Spanish homeland that language mirrors the universe, and that men, especially poets, who listen and restate, only reiterate the divine creation. The spoken word itself becomes etymology, a manifestation of truth.

III

It is 1302, and Dante Alighieri has just been banished from Florence, his childhood home. He is caught between the forces of his time: the clerical and political universality of the medieval papacy and empire on the one hand, and the autonomy of the modern bourgeois classes on the other. By staying in exile and by uniting those parties intellectually, he remains unhappy but gains immortality. He does not seek worldly happiness in urban freedom or clerical power, but in a profane emperor of the world. It is in ecclesiastical scholasticism that he finds spiritual support, and he is taught in Latin. With its help, he creates a new kind of language for the cities, the Italian language of literature, and he founds it on his home dialect in Florence, the one in which working women chat and parents learn to love each other. A tongue like that, however, is neither the earliest nor the best, as anyone would prefer; even Florentines consider the whole world their home, as fish do the whole sea. Thus, to reach the audience of the entire world, Dante's book *De vulgari eloquentia (Concerning the Vulgar Tongue)* is written in Latin. The ideal language, indeed, the oldest and most expedient, is neither the mother tongue nor the one learned in school, but Hebrew; that is what we would all speak, without the aid of mother or school, if our kind were still as it was in the beginning. The sacred language was planted in the nature of man at the time of creation: its vocabulary, grammar and pronunciation were a loan of eternal truth. Admittedly, it was man who initiated it. Immediately, however, and of his own free will, he turned it over to the Creator; Adam's first word, whether a question or an answer, was a joyous '*El*', the Hebrew word for 'God'. Language is dialogue with God, prayer on one hand and grace on the other; the heavenly word enables the blessed poet to simulate the cosmos.

But eventually the original gift was lost; we ourselves forfeited it. When arrogant humanity built the Tower of Babel, it fell prey to its own selfishness; as it neglected prayer, the hand of God let it forget the Hebrew tongue of nature and grace. The various occupations during the construction of the tower – architects, masons, stone-carriers – created, each for themselves, their own dialects according to their specific needs; they became specialized, imprecise and therefore different. The very first word to come forth from these was 'Woe!': they were the fruits of sin and covetousness. Dante believes names were originally meant to be derivatives of objects, but they are not so any more. No matter how highly Dante praises Isidore, his etymologies do not convince him; he avoids games with words. Neither truth nor nature dwells in language today. Those who know the truth, like angels, stand above words; and those who act out of instinct, like animals, remain speechless. Only man, lost on a path between facts and norms, needs language, as a rider needs a horse, to make contact with oneself and with fellow men. History has made the situation even more difficult; since Babel, time and place have further altered the dialects, and God no longer watches over them. A symbolic order of seventy-two languages no longer exists; experience alone reveals to Dante more than a thousand dialects in Italy. And each new language says something unique, especially those poetically formed dialects: Homer and the Psalms, for example, cannot be adequately translated into Latin. This limitation is a kind of dignity as well, if only in the restricted circle of the native country. The colloquial tongue is neither sacred nor common, but Dante's modern Tuscan is nobler than any dead dialect. The foreigner cannot comprehend it, nor would the ancient citizens of our cities, resurrected, understand their modern descendants. On top of that, the vernacular cannot mirror the pure and unchanging truth without the personal effort of the poet. But precisely that makes it incomparable.

In *The Divine Comedy*, Dante lends Italian this position. Like Isidore's encyclopaedia, the work concerns cosmic nature, the spirit and the course of history. Yet, at the same time, it tells the story of the salvation of an individual, that is, of Dante himself. The path the poet takes encircles the universe, which is revealed via his language. Doubtless, language was provided by nature; but man makes out of it what appeals to him, *secondo che v'abbella*. That is how it always has been; even Adam's dialect was playfully altered, and it perished long before Babel. Perhaps Adam did not speak Hebrew at all; his first word was the emotional shout of joy 'I'. The change in Dante's convictions is anchored deep. Language has become an expression of the soul, beauty and art; therefore, its origin is no longer sinful transgression: every man must speak his own language, as every man also has his own story. Even in the hereafter, the human character will not be erased, dialects will not be wiped away: in *The Divine Comedy*, Dante meets his contemporaries there and is identified as a Florentine by his accent. The only thing he cannot find there is Italian countrymen, for all men are equal, united in punishment, penance or rejoicing; they understand each other, as long as every man confesses to being what he is. Only men who cannot decide stutter unintelligibly: the cowardly angels who stood aside while Michael battled with Lucifer, or Nimrod, whose idea it was to build the Tower of Babel and who ended up alone. He could be heard screaming '*Raphèl maÿ amèch zabì almi*', words no one could understand. Language and history determine man in his uniqueness and mortality; God's will lends this temporariness an eternal significance. Every human characteristic is a part of the divine plan, every event a sign; the physical sound suggests human fate and spiritual origins.

Thus, Dante's Italian is sensual, visual, drawn from the daily lives of the people and at the same time remains Latin-scholarly, spiritualized, profound; musical motion permeates the strict verse form of the *terza rima*; poetic images accumulate to reveal a deeper meaning behind the words. But the relationships are not static equations, as with Isidore, they become shifting metaphors. The poet does not pick them fully created from the tongue, he creates them for the first time; he creates a new world of art with his language. As before, it reveals the cosmos of creation, but already it is concealing it a little too; at last, the Renaissance will elevate man to the position of creator. Then, poets will draw strength from Dante's synthesis of reality and thought, topicality and poetry; the Italians will have Dante to thank for their faith in the enduring harmony of the articulated sound. Linguistic form will become poetry, the proclamation of beauty.

IV

It is October 1517, and Martin Luther, a man whose soul is searching for God, is just beginning his great protest against the materialistic theology of the Later Middle Ages, which, up to that time, the monk and professor had preached but had been unable to bring to life. The world now seems less a static system, or a harmony set in motion, than a hurdle keeping the prayerful soul from a merciful God. No additional power should be allowed to step between man and God, neither the Catholic church nor the Latin tongue. Luther's dialect is that of a powerful speaker, filled with the vibrations of his soul; it reveals the word of God directly from the Holy Scriptures. Passionately urgent, his native German reveals personal experience in graphic, flowing phrases. Luther visits *die mutter ihm hause, die kinder auff der gassen, den gemeinen man auff dem marckt* ('the mother in her house, children in the alleys, the common man in the marketplace'), he takes language *auff das maul* ('from the horse's mouth'). Paradoxically, however, it is just this robust dialect that does an about-face, rejects the world and calls on the Spirit of God. The impact of Luther's translation of the Bible becomes the foundation for early High German, the nearly universal German dialect, but that is not Luther's intention: instead, all he wants is to make the way back to God easier for the faithful.

In the beginning was the word, but it was not the word of man, nor of the world. True language proceeds from God and calls to man; we can only answer. An endless abyss yawns between God's original tongue and the speech of man, a division that Isidore overlooked and Dante concealed. True, the first man named the world, but without God's authority, and therefore non-committally. *Wys man nent, alßo ists genent*: a thing's name is the one man gave it. Language is the privilege of man, and what Adam did we can do too, for 'Adam' means 'man', and all men are *ein kuch mit Adam*, like Adam. The oldest language itself has little authority. Hebrew is perhaps the simplest of all languages, 'the very best and most rich in words, and purest', but it soon fell victim to time's deterioration. And what little had remained valid degenerated fully at the Tower of Babel; it was here that man selfishly assumed a divine role and thereby lost his original tongue completely. Since then, our speech has been allowed to wander astray; Babel reoccurs each time God's word is independently interpreted, every time man is newly estranged from God. Thus, the Tower of Babel becomes a metaphor for the world: for the clerical world with its papacy and monastic orders, for the political world with its tyrannical princes and Turks. Such human defiance of God's plan is punished today as it was in Babel, by war, hunger and the degeneration of the true faith. The confusion can no longer be contained in a symbolic number, 'as though there had to be exactly seventy-two of them'. Until the material world holds its own tongue in the face of God's word, speech will deteriorate into further confusion.

Ein ittlige sprag hatt ir eigen art, every language has its peculiarity. But forms of language pass away, only content remains. Blessed alone is the speech that comes from God or seeks Him out: the languages of the Bible and of prayer. The language of the Bible: we must honour Hebrew and Greek 'above all others', for they give us the Old and New Testaments; they are the 'sheaths in which these knives of the spirit rest'. The deeper meaning of the history of language, therefore, is the importance of spreading God's word. It was He who let the Romans make their language a global one, so that the gospel could bear fruit everywhere; He also let the Turks conquer Constantinople so that the fleeing Greeks could bring the New Testament to the West. The miracle of Pentecost allowed the apostles to understand all languages, so that they could comprehend God's word and preach it to all peoples. In this way, a united people of God can arise from the many diverse tongues, a people that knows *unsers Gottis sprach und wort*, the language and word of our God, and speaks no differently of God as He does of Himself. Because Christ speaks to all men in all tongues, we should praise Him in all tongues; the German in prayer should call on his God in German. The language of prayer: 'I thank God that I can hear and find my God in my German tongue, as I have not found Him before, neither in Latin, in Greek nor in the Hebraic tongue.' Luther loves his 'mother tongue' (and introduces the term into High German), but to him it is not sacred, since it is unstable and restricted. In the past, it might have been related to Greek, which sounds so full and so beautiful; with its simple love of truth and intimacy, German might still be the most perfect language: if something is obscure, Luther says it is *nicht wol deudsch geredet*, not spoken in good German. But that applies only to the spirit of language. Its structure diffuses into dozens of dialects; the coarse Bavarians cannot even understand one another. Luther is happy that Emperor Maximilian and the electoral Saxon chancery have 'pulled into one' the diverse dialects, using as the standard that spoken in Meissen, which Luther's Bible then helped become the universal 'High German'. Yet this earthly union only partially imposes order upon the world, for the people of Meissen, Bohemia, Poland and Silesia remain strangers yet.

Historical coincidence rules the earth: the Babylonian Captivity completely corrupted the purity of Hebrew; if Hannibal had defeated the Romans, the scholarly world would be speaking Punic instead of Latin. But what does that matter? True, *Gottis wunder und werck*, the miracles and work of God, are visible in the history of man as well, in tremendous examples of faith and disbelief; but the course of history is material and temporal and must therefore remain forever corrupt and beyond salvation. The etymologist cannot impose order upon the world, neither can the poet transfigure it; even in the holy sacrament, word and symbol merge with one another only under the power of inner faith. The soul disdains the world which God has separated from it. But when the soul faces God's revelation, it cannot mumble ecstatically, it must explain itself and call out to an incomprehensible God in comprehensible, well-chosen words. Then the soul can hear His voice, His judgement and promise, silently but perceptibly. Of language in the after-life, Luther has nothing to say. His example will guide later theology towards an inner word, which cannot consume itself; Luther will teach Germans to love their mother tongue, though only in order to attend to the spirit and disdain the form. Spoken expression is theology: confession before God.

V

It is February 1689, and a ship bringing John Locke and the consort of William of Orange from Holland has just landed in England. The king and the philosopher complete the Glorious Revolution; they replace the divine, absolute right of kings with a parliamentarian constitution, hegemony with balance, religious battles with liberal tolerance, rationalism with empiricism. One year later, in 1690, Locke's *Essay Concerning Human Understanding* lays the foundation of change. The book is not puzzled out in solitude, but discussed repeatedly with friends; Locke would rather be blind than deaf, he is a man who needs conversation. This is clear from his speech. It is sober and conversational, verbose in order to be exact, inexact in order to remain polite. Using neither learned etymologies, poetic images nor spiritual intensity, Locke speaks as a layman, as one who would rather lend the world a listening ear than trust his own theories. The style is the man: Locke, doctor by profession, believes in the evidence of the senses alone, not in the postulates of religion and reason, not in the providence of salvation, not in language's ability to impose order. After all, God created man with the gift of language to make him a social being; community is a result of communication. But the faculty of speech that binds society together can only communicate ideas; it cannot reveal eternal concepts. There is no inborn concept or language, no tradition of truth in man: he labels things arbitrarily. The names of things touch their own essence only in a limited way; they are far more useful in determining the origins of our ideas. Language, then, originates in mental perception; people with faulty perceptions may simply be inexperienced.

How, for example, was Adam, the first giver of names, supposed to have gained experience? It was imagination he had, nothing more. His descendants share and develop this ability, refining language by forming more abstract terms from visible processes. At first, 'spirit' had nothing to do with spirituality, it meant merely the exhalation of breath; the word 'angel' originally meant 'messenger'. The foundation of our thought and speech, therefore, is sensual experience, yet we cannot follow even that without question. Often, we confuse words with the things they designate, sometimes we do not think of anything while talking. Phonetic speech cannot attain moral and mathematic-physical certainty; if it could, it would be comprehensible to the Japanese, the deaf and the dumb as well as to the English. Since language is arbitrary, languages are mutable and diverse, formed by historical forces and by the lifestyles and customs of a country. There is hardly one out of any ten words that can be adequately translated; a 'pound' is something completely different for the modern Englishman and for the ancient Roman. Foreign tongues and times create different ways of seeing things; that is why we cannot understand them. We must conclude that the individual speaks according to personal experience. 'Gold' might be something yellow and sparkling for one person, but might in addition connote something heavy for another, or again, something mutable for the third; no one can entirely describe the object 'gold' with only that single word. This theoretical autonomy and inaccessibility of language was referred to as a confusion of tongues in the Bible: in Babel, a man could only understand himself, speech was no longer conducive to conversation. On one hand, this Biblical event reveals the basic structure of language; on the other, it was merely a confusion of terminology, not the birth of new languages. For diverse tongues might be less imperfect than speech itself, but they have been established by the practice of communities.

The social purpose of language diminishes its inadequate capacity for imparting knowledge; 'the convenience of communication' restricts the arbitrariness of naming and renaming. Speech cannot be true, but it must be comprehensible. Its history is largely a social history, but that acts only in closed and concurrent groups, it forms no pattern. The course of history is the playground for free experimentation; though we can learn liberal wisdom, we can never extract an obligatory inheritance. Why, for example, should all descendants of Adam be damned with original sin because of a transgression that most people have never heard of? There exists no historical process of salvation, and hardly a history of the world at all. Antique authors are inscrutable, their historical messages have been preserved inadequately, falsified or fraudulent and at the very least difficult to interpret. It is not these past worlds we need to aid us with our modern lives, but the future world; it is not Latin, which – a thousand to one – adults never use in daily life, but our native English tongue; and if you want to learn additional foreign languages, French is the best, for it is the language of our current neighbours. And another thing, you do not gain a language by learning grammatical or rhetorical rules; the best way is to write and speak it: these are external activities that express the internal activity of your soul. In the future as well, man will extract knowledge from his environment, will educate himself from it and not rely on his restricted mind. It would be foolish to try to reform the languages of the world with a Pentecostal universal tongue. One's native language must remain as it is, formed more by the use of the masses than by the insights of thinkers, for thinkers are few, but speech is for all; the people determine the spoken and national norms, always based on practice.

Language will never become a storehouse of human knowledge to be filled progressively, for it must remain democratic and mediocre; the great world emperor Augustus had no more power over language than a babbling child. Not Adam, the Tower of Babel nor the miracle of the Pentecost can change the constant of human averageness. Let us try to 'live at peace with our mediocrity', for the truth is not for us. The link between truth, speech and history becomes broken; more definitely than Luther, Locke separates history from God, and man from nature. We glimpse the eternally true, silent speech of God and nature, but we cannot translate it into our human tongue, for it no longer has God and the world as partners in conversation. Language, any language, remains limited to mental existence and can reveal no more than psychological truth; language offers more impressions than knowledge, more the moment than the sequence of tenses. It is these teachings of Locke's that will teach the eighteenth century to prefer the sentiment, to trust in nature, have faith in experience and mistrust traditional doctrine; Locke will guide Anglo-Saxon philosophy toward practical, technical usefulness, he will reaffirm the illogical materialism of the English language and motivate an entire epoch to come to grips with this world devoid of illusions, devoid of the need to overcome, understand or improve it. The word is psychology: the doctrine of the soul of man.

VI

It is the spring of 1794, and Marquis Antoine de Condorcet has just been thrown into a provincial French prison; that is where, a day later, poison puts an end to this far more typical than ingenious mind, a mind hardly famous throughout the ages, but certainly in his own time. Having achieved acclaim with his treatises on integral calculus and the theory of comets, the mathematician turned to the theory of the French Revolution; the aristocratic Condorcet preached the Republic of a sovereign people. In 1792, he becomes president of the National Assembly and tries to ensure the future of the Revolution by reforming the schools. To be sovereign, a people must be unified, must speak a uniform tongue. Aristocratic education until now has used the Latin classics to provide the privileged with a pompous and abstract 'cultivated' language that remains incomprehensible to the uneducated. In the future, all men will learn an identical tongue in common schools, rejecting the old books and grammars that are still full of errors; and like Latin, France's backward peasant dialects must be relegated to historical museums. The French of the future will be a modern, indivisible and clear tongue. Condorcet will not live to see that future; when the radical Jacobin reign of blood overpowers the intellectual global reformers, their president has to flee the guillotine, taking refuge in the countryside. In the three-quarters of a year between his overthrow and suicide, in 1793/94, Condorcet completes in his country refuge his *Historical Survey of the Progress of Human Understanding*. It is not the most original, but probably the most consequent instance of a revolutionary interpretation of history and language; even Condorcet's choice of words is typical. His style reflects a colourless man and a passionate partisan; plain but animated, it sketches out a social algebra that is easy to understand and highly dynamic, devoid of intimacy and laced with inhuman precision.

Man, we read, did not invent language arbitrarily, for he is a product of nature; this is what Rousseau also taught. Thus, speech was formed by the impression of natural phenomena upon the receptive soul; the first paradisiacal tongue drew its poetic metaphors from nature; it was a natural, concrete speech the first men used: a handful of hunters and fishers long before the formation of political groups, for language is the foundation and origin of every *ordre social*. Locke thought similarly; but with Condorcet, speech and history become united as parts of an unremitting process that pushes social forms from one improvement to the next. As the hunters and fishers gradually banded together to form larger herding groups, their language became more malleable and diverse, without expanding its basic imagery, limited to the concrete and dependent on nature. When agriculture created a diversity of environments, social groups were divided and speech erected its Tower of Babel; each group developed another, specialized tongue. This changed during the course of time, as groups interchanged with each other in business or war. But speech, like the social orders, began dividing and subdividing, even within the various nations, as priests began suppressing the working classes. These sly foxes improved language until it became an arbitrary and nearly mathematical system of abstract symbols, capable of reflecting the higher truth of one's thoughts. The clerical class jealously guarded the secret of such an important improvement. Thus two classes arose, and language gained dual purposes: a reflection of nature on one hand, and a symbolization of thought on the other: poetic expression and scientific instrumentality.

In this regard, language structures, like social classes, remained separated in classical antiquity. Of course, the cultivated speech of education was spread by Roman global dominion and, at least among the rulers, stimulated intellectual dialogue. That ceased during the Middle Ages under the barbaric rule of the priests; progress was forced to a halt. The discrepancy between scholarly Latin and the crude vernacular continued to thrive. Dante was the first to break the chains of the pious; humanism and the printing press shaped the vernacular into an instrument of thought for all races and classes. And such is the status of our present situation; the progress of imagery to thought, of impression to expression, has become universal. The speech of scholars and free nations, the speech of the English and the French are the most refined and therefore the most widely spread. French is already on its way to becoming the common language of Europe.

When revolution and Enlightenment finally spreads to all countries, the 'language of one great people' will rule the entire world; this Pentecostal tongue will be French, the purifying and unifying of which Condorcet has just begun. But as soon as reason itself begins ruling directly, progress will accelerate as irresistibly as the law of gravity, and no longer will a single nation with its language dominate: all nations will be fraternal equals, their perfection complete. Together, they will replace the vague and obscure tongues of the poets and thinkers with a true *langue universelle*, the precise language of algebra and chemistry. It will be a language capable of defining nature itself, wholly free of error; it will encompass and unite all other tongues, and will easily be translated into them. Then history, and perhaps even death itself, will be defeated by a universal society without class distinctions, which will make the after-life superfluous. Condorcet's concept is a quite accurate imitation of the Christian interpretation of the salvation of the world, but one that no longer requires God; reason itself becomes religion, with mathematicians as its historians and prophets. Condorcet considers himself a priest of progress, and his faith cannot be shaken even when the mechanics of the Revolution threaten and eventually extinguish his own life. The foreseeable future, full of constantly developing alliances, is one that will necessarily overwhelm and consume the individual; the progress of each race to its optimum cannot pause to consult the individual, nor can it leave any product of the past, whether it be language or nation, untouched. It is the French belief in reason that gives birth to Condorcet's unlimited trust in progress, which is more a hopeful dream than scientific deduction. His influence on the sociology of the nineteenth century will be strong; that his spirit lives on, undiminished despite the many disasters, will be confirmed again and again, for example when the Americans construct translation machines or program computers to design a universal language; he will inspire dialectical materialism to imagine a society without class distinctions as being paradise on earth. The spoken word becomes sociology: the product of a group.

VII

It is 1950, and from 20 June to 2 August, Moscow's *Pravda* prints a series of five letters from Joseph Stalin, which are then published as a brochure under the title *Marxism and the Question of Linguistics*. In those sixty pages, the Communist dictator and chief ideologist will topple the current materialistic view of society and history. It is no coincidence that linguistic theory provided the impetus. Language manipulates thought; thus, it is an important means to power for an ideologist. As early as 1904, the young Stalin made it a useful weapon in his battles. Later, he would sanction the fact that, until 1950, the official historical doctrine of the Soviet Union was based on the theories of a linguist. This man, Nikolai Marr, had formulated his theories to a large degree in the spirit of Condorcet: the foundation of history is the social evolution of mankind in all its phases. During the paradisiacal stage of primitive Communism, where all men performed physical labour, there was no need for a social order or for anything but the language of gestures; the spoken word was developed by religious suppressors who needed it to defend their exploitation ideologically. Similarly, modern national languages are designed to sustain the capitalistic system. A future society devoid of classes will give birth to an entirely original, universal tongue, concrete and uniform in spirit, one that can overcome the barriers of class; as in the primitive period, it will wholly relinquish the use of sound. Speech and intellect are ideological products of the class system, they form a superstructure that gains value only in relation to other structures; they slavishly adapt to the abrupt but portentous changes in the economic base, and therefore cannot evolve linearly themselves. At any given stage in evolution or production, languages form a purposeless chaos of overlapping and intermingling, similar to the Babylonian confusion of tongues. Their form, history and implications are hardly worth considering. For all practical purposes, they result in a barbaric speech riddled with the abbreviations, foreign expressions and constantly repeated propagandistic formulas so familiar in the experience of the German people, and which still thrive today in the western world as the side-effects of materialism.

In 1950, when the situation changes, Stalin changes too. The 'patriotic' war against Hitler awakened Russian national feelings: the same thing that aided Mao Tse-tung in China. True, by now Bolshevism governs many states, but despite that (or because of it), Stalin cannot turn history around as he planned to. Not even in Russia has the goal of a society without class distinctions been achieved. Now the 'revolution from above' has shifted the accent from hoping for the ideal to historical achievement. Stalin idolizes history; even Marxist dogmas are to be weighed historically, no longer accepted blindly. The patterns of dialectical materialism are scattered throughout history, and so the past must be studied, it cannot be divined by casting bones in the backyard. Intellectual freedom is accepted, for language is free. It is no longer an ideological superstructure lacking importance in and of itself; it is no longer a slave of the economic base; it remains unaffected by erratic dialectical class revolutions. Russian, for example, has remained unchanged from Pushkin's time until today, a time during which Russia went through two social upheavals, one capitalist and the other socialist; nor did the French Revolution overturn French. For language is not created by an ephemeral class, but 'by the whole course of society', by 'the efforts of hundreds of generations'. Speech affects every human activity, 'without exception', and human beings themselves; they need it to get along with their peers as well as with their enemies. History gives us what we need: man has always possessed the spoken word. It evolved in the society of primitive communism; as primitive and lacking as it was, it became the basis of modern speech 'during remote antiquity'. Stalin does not deal with the question of a primal tongue, probably because he has no wish to exalt a language to an eternal or spiritual level, but for him it is still a primal phenomenon.

Where, then, lies the origin of the diversity and transformation of tongues? Obviously, in progress. Divergences in the social, economical, political and intellectual phases separated one tribe from the other, but at the same time the growth and exchange of experience enriched their various tongues. The rich diversity, therefore, cannot be seen as deviation from the ideal. True, the Babylonian confusion of tongues has not vanished despite the dynamism of these systems; Babel is formed by the reactionary Great Empires of Roman slave-drivers and medieval feudalism. Via their imperialism, they scattered races and confused language borders without creating larger units capable of survival. In recent history, the chaos of feudalism has been overcome by peoples with national languages. It was not capitalists who created these, they are based on a more primal foundation; the bourgeois shopkeepers have ravaged it with their jargon, but they have not ruined it. National tongues will retain their validity into the socialist era, and Russian will be one of them. For that reason, Stalin's language is meant to sound Russian: he avoids foreign terminology, makes it flow and keeps it correct. Stalin even defends the current diversity of languages against the Anglo-Saxon ideology of progress: their secret imperialistic intention is to suppress the naturally developed languages with a global English tongue. True progress, like the Russian dream of global salvation, becomes a long-range goal. Not until the final victory of socialism can the nations with their hundreds of languages work freely together; that is when national languages will turn to regional dialects, slowly combining to form a single international tongue. This will be 'neither German, nor Russian, nor English, but a new tongue that will assume the best elements of all national and regional languages'. It will not be a mathematical system of symbols either, as Condorcet and Marr believed; without the spoken word, men will never understand each other.

Stalin extols speech as a characteristic of man, as an important entity in its own right of 'nearly limitless' influence. It is limited neither to economical reality nor to ideological thought; it is, as Karl Marx formulated, 'the immediate reality of thought'. With language, thought becomes a historical, world-changing power. The influence of Stalin's thoughts may have been checked by his death in 1953, but has not yet disappeared. For in the twentieth century, independent of Stalin and his ideological camp, many will come to a similar conclusion: that language is an entity, a whole. It derives from the human soul, but turns outward and shapes our world, and it cannot exist independently from man. The investigation of speech leads to anthropology: the awareness of the essence of man.

VIII

These six interpretations, only briefly outlined here, depict radically different perspectives on life and language; they have no common denominator except for the human one. This, then, is the one level that unifies them: the language theories of all these men are fused together with theories of history, as their forms of speech are conditioned on their place in history; theory cannot be separated from reality, nor thought from form. Perhaps, as some philosophers claim, one could cut away all elements dependent on historical circumstances, not to mention all erroneous ones; but then you would cut out the quoted figures themselves, and rob them of life. They have to be seen as they were: they were men who saw existence as a whole. None of them disregarded their periods, despite the errors; they viewed past and future from very definite standpoints, and meant to use their standpoints to turn the world around. Their natures were active, these were not desk-bound scholars; what they wrote, they wrote under the primacy of the practical over sheer rationalism. Our selection, therefore, is one-sided, and it has to be. There were and are enough influential thinkers who consider language to be a self-contained system or an ageless game; in their reasoning and their results they are strict in separating content from form, language from history. But people who isolate the various problems from one another usually isolate themselves from their own time, perhaps not as completely as they intend, but usually so much that they have nothing of importance left to say.

For our six witnesses, however, language is not a clinically compounded phenomenon, but in form a confession that all men recite, in content an appeal that concerns all. Since this is a language that was not thought out but lived out, it actually applied to people. Thus, the cycle of history and speech not only encircles each individual, but sets milestones in its course for the historical development of our understanding of language, history and mankind, even for the determination of the nature of man, history and speech. We contemplated not only phases of European anthropology, but also basic characteristics of potential human behaviour: the glorification of the creator by his creation, the pride of the creature man in his power to recreate, insight into the fragility of all that is earthly and human; the submission under all-powerful physical nature, the hope for an improved social existence, the acceptance of contemporary society. Similarly, the views of history examined here form a chain through time and circumscribe the problem: the course of history is revealed as the delivering grace of God, as a re-enactment of the heart of our humanity, as the corruption of the world, as a social experiment, as an attempt at a better future, as tedious labour. Similarly, thoughts on language are not merely stages in a process, but partial aspects of a larger issue: language can be understood as the voice of God or the revelation of truth, as expression of the soul and proclamation of beauty, as metaphor for a corrupt world and an avowal of faith, as the effects of nature and inquiry into the human soul, as means of communication and product of a group, as power to transform life and lead men.

Each of the six examples is conclusive within itself, but they are incompatible with each other, they cannot be summarized into a final composite, into the truth about mankind, history or speech. And little would change in that respect if we were to examine several thousand witnesses instead of six. Not that the result would be thousands of wholly different truths: as immensely diverse as historical situations and various inspirations are, the basic forms of potential human behaviour in regard to the problem of speech and history are not unlimited in number. A few of them, if not all, are reflected by our chief witnesses, and it would be easy to abstract them into prototypes. However, they would then be incapable of setting norms, either for our thinking or for our actions. They can only be effective within their historical personifications, which cannot be generalized. Isidore's system and Stalin's situation are exemplary, but not transferable. We cannot trade one for the other, we cannot apply them to ourselves generally. How do they help us, then, in our search for the essential? Does not the ancient wisdom of Heraclitus still apply when he says everything is constantly flowing, that no one can step into the same river twice?

But that is not all. A complete and clear system is most likely impossible, since history is not self-contained, as language is not, as mankind is not. Man is fragmentary, and for that reason he needs speech and history, for that reason he communicates, approaches others and recalls distant objects and past events; for that reason he is dependent on traditions and permanent surroundings. It is not his intention to hide behind the achievements of others, but to be able to determine his own self clearly and decisively. He listens to many voices that accost him from all directions; he must answer them, he must take responsibility for that which is his own. This selective self-determination is his right and his duty. Role models and patterns of events do not force him to imitate arbitrarily, but to choose and to stick to his own decision. This is precisely what thinking historically teaches: dialogue with the past. As comfortless as the chaos of knowing might be, all the more comforting is the opportunity of telling. History is not finished; the modern alienation of man from his speech and past does not have to be the final word. Language and history might change more tomorrow than ever before; but they could also return to that which we are now. What language is and what will become of our language depends on our relationship with our words.

Part II
Interpreting Government

3

The Invention and Fission
of the Public Persona

I

If you want to find out what a *persona publica* once was, the Roman statesman and philosopher Boethius is the wrong man to consult, though he examined the word *persona* around 520. He gave it at least five definitions. The basic meaning was too superficial for him: 'The word *persona* apparently has its origins elsewhere, namely, in the masks that once depicted important characters in comedies and tragedies (*eos quorum interest homines repraesentabant*).' Boethius thought it unbecoming that the word should owe its origins to stage comedians; he stressed that the stage, besides portraying the antics of such unworthy figures as Simo and Chremes, also depicted the fates of such important ones as Hecuba and Medea. Because Greek and Roman actors played individuals (*individuos homines*) using masks, they began referring to people off the stage as πρόσωπα or *personae*, as they were recognizable by outward appearances (*ceteros quoque homines, quorum certa pro sui forma esset agnitio*).

By ὑπόστασις, the Greeks meant something far more subtle and significant: the spiritual being; but because the Latins had no similar word, they adapted the same one, *persona*, to the inner image of man. Boethius followed this tradition: '*Persona* means the indivisible substance of a rational natural entity (*naturae rationabilis individua substantia*).' Thus, *persona* became a term to unite the dual sides of man, physical form and mental individuality, a word of exceeding dignity. Its greatest respectability, however, could be found in theological discourse, especially when regarding the divine and human duality of Jesus Christ. Some ascribe to him a double, a *duplex persona*, others a twin-like, *gemina persona*. In actuality, Christ incorporates both of those natures in a single *persona* (*gemina substantia, sed una persona*). If *persona* were meant in this case to unite independent elements in a way far beyond human capacity, it also indicated, when Boethius spoke of the three *personae* forming the unity of the Christian God, the exclusion of that which is supreme and without body.

One might think the word would have been used in the political arena to designate the holder of multiple offices, or when several dignitaries combined tasks. But Boethius did not apply *persona* to this, and *publicus* was used only when royal dignitaries took advantage of multiple offices to cheat the public, driven by barbaric greed to private larceny and open taxation. Boethius despised the servants of the Ostrogothic king Theodoric, who had thrown the philosopher into prison in 523 for his connection with the Byzantine emperor. In those years, two sides confronted each other full of antagonism: the Roman government and Catholic universality on the one hand, and Germanic rulership and the Arian state-church on the other; the violent acts of the powerful compelled people like Boethius to withdraw into the spiritual substance of the individual. Yet, his choice of words was not rooted in his situation alone, but in Latin and Christian tradition.

A few years later, in Constantinople, from 529 onwards, Emperor Justinian ordered the compilation of Roman law in the *corpus iuris civilis*. The word *persona* occurs often in that collection; it refers to the individual, anyone who could take on duties and rights within the limits of his class. In the book of law, of course, it refers especially to those in need of protection: slaves and the newly free, minors and others not legally independent, widows and orphans, 'pitiful persons (*miserabiles personae*)'. Individual *personae* in their private legal status were separated from larger parties; the individual as opposed to the community, *singularis persona* versus *populus vel curia vel collegium vel corpus*. In the early Roman imperial period, non-jurists, such as Frontinus, had called similar groups *publicae personae*; now, such a use of the expression had become as impossible as the antithesis *privatae personae* had become unnecessary.

Day-to-day legal transactions brought civilians in touch with legal officers. *Personae publicae* appears several times in this sense: when protecting a ward of the community, the *personae publicae, id est magistratus* of a community could intervene; in the process of adoption, a *persona publica, hoc est tabularius* had to assist. These dignitaries, too, were individuals, and did not represent the state. The emperor, however, who governed all, no longer considered himself, as Cicero would have said, 'the foremost *persona* in a community of people (*persona principis in republica*)'. He dressed himself in exclusive titles, and his property was not considered public, but his own. Roman law, therefore, offered no means of understanding the word *persona* as meaning an exceptional personage.

The language of the Latin Bible is still another story. In his translation of the Greek Bible in 383, Jerome uses *facies* wherever the appearance of πρόσωπον seems to imply 'face'; for the face of the Creator as well as in the features of mortals. *Persona*, however, refers only to men and women. The Jewish and Christian God detests 'respect of persons (*acceptio personarum*)'; nor does he favour princes (*personae principum*) who abuse the poor (Job 34:19), or Jews who bicker with the Greeks (Romans 2:11). Men, however, especially in the Old Testament, have other ways. Early judges should not have allowed, as God does not, *distantia personarum* between great and small, rich and poor (Deuteronomy 1:17); but the powerful were easily bribed, and kings were unpredictable. The pious King Solomon himself lamented that a poor man in search of gifts had to court the powerful, the *persona potentis* (Proverbs 19:6). A free man was smart to avoid crossing the paths of *persona potentis* (Ecclesiasticus 21:25). Worldly rulers fancied themselves godlike, distributing favours and punishments as they deemed fit, disdaining legal process. A despotic king cynically reminded his Jewish enemies of the favours he had given them publicly and privately (2 Maccabees 9:26).

Harmonious society had no chance to develop under Oriental tyranny, but it did among the Jewish People of God. Envoys of the judge Jephthah of Gilead negotiated with the Ammonite king *ex persona sua*, on behalf of their beloved Lord (Judges 11:12). Such proxy representation was recommended by the New Testament as well, for Christ led the new People of God as king, though not like the kings of this world, but with love. Paul forgave the enemies of the Corinthians, not in his own name, *propter vos in persona Christi*, but for the sake of the community and on behalf of their Lord (2 Corinthians 2:10). In the same letter (1:11), the apostle bade the Corinthians pray to God so that their thanks for the favours given him by so many (*ex multorum personis*) could be made public. No Christian lived for himself, was a *persona*; every man and woman was considered part of a community which, in turn, did not live for itself, was also no *persona*. The diverse parts formed a body, the head of which was Christ, the Son of God (1 Corinthians 12:14–30).

Even when the gathering prayed openly, the adjective *publicus* did not apply. The Latin Bible never used it for people, only for governing institutions and objects like coins and weights, store-houses and prisons. Numerous were the kinds of men, it taught, who lived disgracefully in the public eye, and not only the leaders of this world. Tax collectors (*publicani*) and prostitutes deserved more pity than respect; these were nothing more than sinners, never achieving the high rank of *persona*. The categorization and evaluation of public and private behaviour in the Vulgate was different from that in the *corpus iuris*, but both founding texts of European society life agreed on that one point, which for Boethius was a central one. The world of oriental tyrants, Germanic kings, impoverished Jews and orphaned Romans was filled with viciousness; to escape it, one Latin-educated Christian withdrew as far as he could into introspection.

II

Seventy years later the world had changed. The concepts of Roman government and Byzantine empire lost their influence in Italy; the last Latin power, the Roman papacy, found itself facing the Germanic empires in the North and West: the Langobards, Visigoths, Franks and Anglo-Saxons. The former municipal prefect of Rome, Pope Gregory I, was still enough of an ecclesiastical politician not to follow Boethius into the cell. In his commentary on Job, composed between 580 and 595, Gregory's interpretation of Job 34:19 conforms at first to Boethius' ideas. The noblest part of a man, it teaches, is his *natura rationalis*. 'Yet, because we turn away from the secret and the intangible, and delight in the visible, we judge man not by what he is, but what he is surrounded with. Since we see not what he actually is, but merely what he can do *in acceptione personarum*, we let ourselves be guided not by *personae*, but by the accompanying trappings.' God, on the other hand, it continues, sees the moral deserts, not the material condition. Gregory's paradoxical formulation gains its vitality from the duality of the term *persona*: applied to man, it refers to the inner character as well as to the exterior façade. In mentioning *acceptio personarum*, Job had been referring to the political–judicial struggle of governments with the poor; Gregory on the other hand interpreted 'governments' as being proud of heart, and 'the poor' as 'the humble'.

It was far from his mind to damn the powerful. According to Job 36:5, God does not hate *potentes*, since He Himself holds power. 'Power (*potentia*) is good in its own place, but it requires rulers to live cautiously...' if temporal government is to be a form of worship (*ministerium*) as the Epistle to the Romans (13:4) insists. Rulers guide the activity of their *corpora*, that is, wholes made up of many parts, by taming their own lusts and subjecting their thoughts to virtue. Princes who govern an earthly community (*terrena respublica*) should follow the examples of church rulers (*potestas ecclesiastica*) most especially that of the prince of apostles Peter, who thought of himself as just another man when among the faithful, but who, when judging sinners, became a greater prince than any other. Furthermore, the distant kings of the ancient People of God are examples; not Saul, who at the height of his power was puffed up with pride, but David, who, as a ruler, governed himself first, humbly inspecting his own soul. The image of the king was meant to be defined by the image of the priest.

The kind of priest Gregory had in mind, of course, displayed more the governing characteristics of a bishop than the ministering traits of a monk. The Pope admired the monastic patriarchs of the West but did not subscribe to their terminology, which made *persona* the embodiment of worldliness in a biblical sense. Two early examples, with both of which the Pope was familiar, demonstrate how impossible it was for the concept of the public *persona* to thrive in the tradition of Latin monasticism. Around 400, Sulpicius Severus explained why some bishops had complained when, in 371, the church-going common folk elected a certain Gallic monastery founder named Martin as bishop of Tours. He was, protested the bishops, a 'contemptible *persona* (*contemptibilis persona*)', unworthy of the responsibilities of a bishop, a man of drab appearance, dirty clothes and ungroomed hair. And if one ever approached the saintly Martin in royal robes and glowing pomp, or in the *persona* of pagan gods, one was the devil 'in person'. No wonder Sulpicius Severus never referred to his saint as *persona*; even when Martin, as bishop, had public responsibilities, he was not described as performing those duties personally, but as Christ acting through him.

The judgement of the Italian founder Benedict of Nursia was even more severe. In his monastic rule of around 540, he restricted all public life to the confines of the abbey and limited the social *corpus* to the assembly of monks. Their king was to be Christ and no one else; not even the prophet David could be referred to as lord or prince. Abbey superiors were not public *personae*, even though instruction from other sources was objected to as 'private orders (*privata imperia*)'. An abbot degenerated to *persona* if a corrupt convent elected a similarly degenerate superior; in that case, the Christian 'public' was to intervene in cloister life and put an end to the wicked activities within. The conscientious abbot was urgently warned against *acceptio personarum*, which favoured individual monks and disturbed the harmony in the monastic body. *Persona*, therefore, referred to figures of the world and their superficial pomp and arbitrary behaviour, rulers not bound by morality or community. Pope Gregory, however, displayed an ideal closer to the world: priestly as well as princely rulers were supposed to earn the respect of the Christian public by leading an exemplary life.

The fact that reality did not conform to the ideal was condemned by the Pope with carefully-chosen words. In 593, he ordered the Bishop of Cagliari to take up the cause of the nuns of Sardinia; instead of consecrating themselves principally to God, they were forced to waste their time on worldly concerns, as tribute and other services were required from them *per publicas personas*. He rebuked others as well: the local despots and high-handed *ecclesiasticae personae* in Dalmatia in 593, and the *saeculares personae* in the Frankish kingdom in 602. *Persona* referred to a new group now, dignitaries of state and church who abused their offices like Old Testament tyrants, despite the moral expectations of the New Testament. They, too, were two-faced, and the curse of God was upon them if they did not mend their ways.

Personae in the Germanic kingdoms, especially bishops and counts, did not consider themselves servants of a pope or king, but as lords in their own right. Among the Franks more than anywhere else, the meaning of *persona* was shifting in that direction, supported by qualifying adjectives. In the council of Paris in October 614, following a series of infringements by the throne, the assembled bishops and nobles forced the Merovingian king Clothair II to make weighty concessions. Some examples: according to Clothair's *Edictum*, a clergyman was no longer permitted to appeal directly to the king or to any other ruler when in the district of his own bishop, *ad principem aut ad potentioris [!] quasque personas*. A mixed clerical–noble court was to be established to handle civil suits between the nobility and the bishop's unfree retainers (*inter personam publicam et hominibus[!] ecclesiae*). Pigs belonging to the king's estate could not be fed in the forests of bishops or nobles (*in silvas ecclesiarum aut privatorum*); that referred to the same group of people as *episcopi vel potentes* did. Since a ruler had to govern his personal estate in addition to public offices, he could be referred to as both private and public *persona*. The effort to differentiate precisely between his various aspects, put into practice, could cause a great deal of difficulty, if not one's own life.

Nevertheless, the Franks learned Gregory's lesson. A Frankish bishop should be worthy (a *persona condigna*) and his merits (*meri-*

tum personae et doctrinae) should distinguish himself above others. Worldly rulers could not ignore this moral standard; non-Christians deserved neither earthly nor heavenly rewards. King Clothair II, at least, conformed: in 626–7, at the synod of Clichy, he became the first king to be compared to the priest-king David with his reverence for God. Of course, not even that pious Merovingian could be expected to improve the legal status of lowly *servi et vilis[!] personae*.

In Visigothic Spain, King Rekkeswind reaped less emphatic praise at the eighth council of Toledo in 652–3, when he made a statement in the style of Gregory the Great: 'The business of the limbs that are to be guided is the head's well-being.' The bishops instructed the king on the correct interpretation of Paul's metaphor. The head of the body, by which the church is meant, is Christ; the activities of the limbs are guided by the eyes, that is, by the bishops. The king cannot simply compare himself with Christ, who is God and man *in unione personae*.

> All lower members of the entire people look up with due reverence to the princely head. They expect aid in their need and render him tribute, partly of their own will and partly as is required. The royal class (*ordo*) may lay claim to all that is produced, because he consciously guides all, and the profits resulting thereof are rightly incumbent upon no one else but him. Yet they are doubtlessly due *non personae, sed potentiae suae*. Law (*iura*) makes the king, but not the *persona*, for he maintains his position not on strength of his own commonality (*mediocritas*), but by the dignity of his office.

The occasion of this chastising sermon was the legal transgressions of Visigothic kings, kings who were elected to royal offices and therefore could not pass them on to their children, yet could bequeath royal property within the family. Many of the middle and upper classes (*ex gentis nostrae mediocribus maioribusque personis*) had to starve, the bishops believed, because the princely stomach devoured too much; of the other classes, the *mediocres* were not provided with the subsistence necessary and the *maiores* were not accorded the dignity due them. Legally, the elected king stood no higher than many of his fellow men. The council, inspired by Roman law, separated his *persona* from his authority of office, especially when it concerned the dispensing of property. But that was not all: the position of the king in society depended on his moral behaviour, as Rekkeswind himself formulated: according to whether he satisfied his personal desires (*privata voluntas*) like private individuals, or the common law (the *communis lex*) of all. No matter whether the king was head or stomach, he never was and never would become a *persona publica*. He would have had to combine, as Christ did, the divine and human in one *persona*: at the least, a faultless life and limitless governing power. The bishops made it clear that Rekkeswind was not living like a saint; the nobility stopped him from living violently. There was still no public personage living in the Germanic seventh century capable of combining in himself Gregory's dual Christian–Roman concept.

III

The Carolingian kings, who had risen to power as part of the aristocratic opposition of the Merovingian crown, did not share the scruples of their predecessors. The basis for their new self-confidence is revealed in the first description of the Carolingian rulers' ethos, a *Fürstenspiegel* or book of advice for young princes, which was composed in the last years of Charlemagne's life, probably between 811 and 814, by the Benedictine abbot Smaragdus of Saint-Mihiel, and meant for Charlemagne's successor, Louis I the Pious. The first line of the dedication states:

> Almighty God has nobly created you, most celebrated king, when and where He pleased of royal and noble heritage, and He has mercifully led you to the waters to be born again. Your head He has anointed with the consecrated oil of chrism and He has graciously adopted you as son. He has appointed you king over the people of the earth and designated you as the heir of His own Son, who is in heaven. Made rich by these sacred gifts, you justly wear the royal crown.

The succession to the throne was thus already consecrated by royal blood and Christian baptism. The sacramental charisma surrounding the Carolingian royal anointment, first performed in 752, linked the king with David, the anointed of the Lord (*christus Domini*), and made him like Christ, here on earth temporarily and later in heaven.

Of course, a king was expected to devote himself to the Christian lifestyle, to imitate the humility of the priest and King David and to overcome the pride of Saul. A 'head' equal to God he was not: 'Most mild king, may you be consumed by a becoming fervour for the house of God, in which you are also a member in Christ; for the members must follow the head.' Yet the regal office, like ecclesiastical offices, was equally valid whether administered by worthy *personae* or not. The king's responsibility was to educate his people in spiritual virtues, to take up the battle against the seven deadly sins.

> If you see a man puffed up in pride, furious in anger, intoxicated by violence, pale from fraternal envy, aflame with lusts, voracious with greed, burning with cruelty: suppress all, threaten all, tame all in the strictest manner. Do what you can for the role you represent, for the royal ministry which you sustain (*pro persona quam gestas, pro ministerio regali quod portas*), for the name of Christ which you bear, for the agency of Christ which you administer.

The 'name' of the baptized Christian and *persona* of the most high-born lord are bound together, just as are the humble ministry for God and the powerful agency for Christ. I cannot draw the line between individual and office, cannot be more precise about which *persona* Louis represented; at any rate, it was not a theatrical 'role'. Smaragdus borrowed much from Gregory the Great, but the hypothesization of the royal *persona* was new. When he became emperor, Louis the Pious made that *persona* his own. In 825, his capitulars stressed that it had 'pleased divine providence to appoint our commonality (*mediocritas*) to provide for his holy church and this empire'. This was more than just empty phrases about humility. Human commonality no longer brought a reduction of public esteem, as it had in the Visigothic seventh century, because the quintessence of ministration for church and kingdom rested in Louis's *persona*, no matter how he behaved (*summa huius ministerii in nostra persona consistere videatur*). The emperor still impressed upon the other classes what was expected of them, their *ministeria*, but he no longer spoke of their *persona* as Clothair II had.

The sacral fusion of the office and *persona* of a ruler was reiterated by the bishops of the Carolingian empire. In 828, Louis the Pious had directed them to investigate whether he, in '*persona*' as in 'ministration', could be corrected; '*quicquid in vobis, id est in persona et ministerio vestro, corrigendum inveniretur*', as it was phrased in their reply in 829. The bishops reassured the king saying that his personal and official piety made their work easy. More important was the observation that the church of God was a single body with Christ as its only head: the body, however, was divided into 'two main *personae*, the ecclesiastical and the regal (*in duas eximias personas, in sacerdotalem videlicet et regalem*)'. The bishops quoted famous statements from Pope Gelasius I: back in 494, however, Gelasius had not spoken of two main *personae* in the church, but of two main powers in the world, *auctoritas sacrata pontificum* and *regalis potestas*. Instead of *auctoritas*, personal esteem, and *potestas*, official power, one could now speak of *eximia persona*; the duality of the highest *personae* within the single body of the church had been postulated.

The interlocking of office and *persona* could not but affect the nobility, insofar as they were loyal to the king; their loyalty made them unimpeachable too. In 858, in Quiercy, a group of West Frankish bishops and counts swore an oath to Charles the Bald that they would faithfully support the regal power of the throne given him by God *secundum meum ministerium et secundum meam personam*. The king, in return, swore to honour and protect each of them *secundum suum ordinem et personam*. With that, they had become *personae publicae*, but in a different sense: no longer as lords in their own right, but as participants in the personification of a commonwealth, as servants of state. In a charter for an Italian abbey in 833, Emperor Lothair I, hoping to eliminate encroachments by third parties (counts, for example), referred to '*cuiuslibet aministrationis aut privata persona*'; a member of the first group, an office-bearer, was referred to in documents meant for Italian recipients during the late Carolingian Empire simply as *persona publica*. The ruler himself could not be mentioned in the same way, as he was dependent on none but God.

In protest against such exaggerated appraisals of individuals, Archbishop Hincmar of Reims, in a *Fürstenspiegel* of 873, instructed Charles the Bald in the need for personal virtue more than anything else. To attain it, Charles needed only ponder on the exemplary images of kings developed by the fathers of the church. As an example, he quoted Gregory the Great on cautious living and on the humility of David. Furthermore, he reiterated the teachings of Augustine: a king served God in a variety of ways: first, because he was a man, and secondly, because he was also a king. As a man, he was expected to live according to his faith, and as a king he was expected to decree just laws and enforce them. Yet even Hincmar did not dare separate *persona regis* from *regium ministerium*; he dealt with them together, 'for the sake of common interests (*reipublicae causa*)'. The king stood far above all other men, above the *speciales personae* whom he was called to judge. As the heart of the social body, and being properly anointed, he was *persona* itself.

IV

It was not until the eleventh century that the Carolingian equation of royal *persona* and throne was shaken, on one hand by religious reform movements in the Romance countries, which demanded saint-like lifestyles from bearers of sacramental offices, and on the other by political reform movements of Norman origin, which aimed less at the authority of the ruler than at the rationale of the administration. The division of the duality of royal autocracy began in France. At first, what Bishop Gerard of Cambrai taught in the reform synod of Compiègne in 1023 sounded like a repetition of Carolingian concepts. The holy church was to be led by 'twin *personae (geminis personis)*' namely by regal and ecclesiastical *personae*; to the one was allocated the task of war, to the other the task of prayer. Gerard stressed the union of soul and body, the twin natures of Christ. He named the preservation of common peace as the foremost duty of bishops and kings, especially as a service to the third partner in this new, earthly trinity: the peasants, whose task was to provide the other two classes with subsistence, which they could do only in time of peace. Following this interpretation, the various dignitaries responsible for the physical security and salvation of the soul could no longer be juxtaposed or merged; their contrasting duties were clearly differentiated from one another.

Once the absolute anointment and unrestricted jurisdiction of the crown was curtailed, it was not long before the common dignity of the throne and the offices of the various lords went separate ways. As early as the reign of the Salic emperors, restlessness invaded the German Empire; the imperial chaplain Wipo was infected by it when he recorded the deeds of the Salic emperor Conrad II in the manner of a *Fürstenspiegel* for Conrad's son and successor Henry III in 1046. Describing Conrad's anointment as king in 1024, Wipo put an almost Carolingian sermon into the mouth of the consecrating bishop. A worthy king had to be free of the seven deadly sins, as far as a man could be; only in this way could he take Christ's place and guide his people by example. Here, the purpose of the royal consecration was to lend Conrad the sacramental strength necessary to do this; in the manner of 1 Kings 10:6, it was meant to make another man out of him. And behold, 'just as we read of Saul, he walked about as though he were a head taller than all others, as though transformed, with a bearing that had not been observed in him before.' The royal anointing even changed a man's appearance; Wipo extolled the Emperor as '*gloriosus in persona, pulcher sua sub corona*'. The glory and beauty of a man originated in his crown.

Yet office and *persona* did not completely coincide. It was not by chance that Wipo alluded not only to David, but also to his predecessor Saul, and his uncontained anger. Conrad's personal politics, too, were measured by Christian standards, and criticized. Even the emperor was mortal, and Conrad II himself appeared aware of this. In 1024, following the death of Emperor Henry II, the burghers of Pavia destroyed the neighbouring imperial castle, then defended their actions in Constance in 1025 by arguing that the king had abandoned the building in death. According to Wipo's report, Conrad replied:

> I know you did not destroy the house of your king, for at that time you had none. But you cannot deny that you destroyed a royal house. When a king dies, the kingdom (*regnum*) continues to exist, as a ship still exists whose helmsman has fallen. Those were public buildings, not private ones; they were subject to the laws of others, not your own.

Even if *publicus* here implied little more than 'royal', it refers neither to the individual ruler nor to the whole he represents, but, after the biblical pattern, to objects or rights, a building or a ship. Since the ruler did not quite meet the high expectations of his Christian office, his *persona* did not quite coincide with the continuation of his legal position.

It was not however until emperor and pope fought a personal struggle over the proper world order that the duality of the highest-ranking *personae* in the body of Christianity was divided. In 1081, Pope Gregory VII explained to a German bishop how the holiness of the popes had to be separated from the kings' lust for power, and had to be set above it. With a thundering voice of rebuke, he named several lords (*personae principum*) whose behaviour he condemned. Though history knows nearly a hundred saintly popes, he said, it knows hardly more than seven saintly lords. Immediately after Gregory's death, in 1085, his followers in the curia (the papal court), in order to prove his holiness, retrospectively put words into the dying man's mouth, expounding on the worthlessness and injustice of many *principales personae*; among them, the so-called German king Henry IV. It goes without saying that the circle of supporters surrounding Gregory VII never applied the far too human word *persona* to the Pope.

Emperor Henry IV, on the other hand, still considered it a lofty honour. He warned the German faithful in 1089: because there was no higher position among men than that of kings or emperors (*regum vel imperatorum persona*), it would be a great danger to humanity if they were deposed. The singular sounded as if all kings possessed the same *persona*; even here, the differentiation between self and office crept in. The unknown follower of the Emperor who described the life of Henry after his death in 1106 was also familiar with this distinction. Between two sections describing Henry's personal Christian virtues and his public appearances as emperor, the author inserted a statement explaining that at times Henry had borne the *persona* of the emperor, and at other times that of a knight, thereby proving both his honour (*dignitas*) and his humility (*humilitas*). The change of costumes in no way implied a division of the *persona*, which remained imperial by reason of its humility. But in earlier periods, the tension between those opposing poles would not have been formulated so antithetically.

In 1100, the tension was deepened to a rift by the so-called 'Norman Anonymus'. This clergyman in Rouen, who may have been the local Archbishop William, wrote a series of theoretical treatises defending royalty in favour of the Anglo-Norman king and his state church against the claims of the papal reform. This exegete insisted on the Biblical equation of bishop and king:

> The Old Testament speaks of two offices (*personae*), that of the high priest and that of the king. Both are anointed with sacred oil and consecrated by divine blessing to guide the people and, so doing, personify and exemplify the aspect (*figura*) of Christ the Lord and represent his *imago* in the sacrament. During this anointment and consecration, the spirit of the Lord, with all its power, entered into them and made them divine. By thus receiving it, they were to become the aspect and image of Christ; it was meant to make of them different men, so that each in their human selves (*in persona sua*) would be men, but in spirit and power they would be other men. Aaron, for example, was the first anointed of the Lord, as Saul was the first anointed king, and each was a man in his human self, but another man in spirit and power. For though this man was Aaron in his human self, as the other was Saul, in spirit and power he was something completely different, the anointed of the Lord (*christus Domini*). It can be seen, therefore, that there was in each of these persons a twin *persona* (*gemina persona*), one of nature, the other of grace, one in the character of man (*in hominis proprietate*), one existing in spirit and power; one in which the man in question, due to his natural qualities (*per conditionem naturae*), conforms with

other men, and one in which he towers above all others, due to the majesty of the divine (*per eminentiam deificationis*), and the power of the sacrament. In the one self he was by nature a human individual (*naturaliter individuus homo*), in the other, due to the power of grace, he was Christ; in other words, God and man at once. The initial self was always his own (*unicuique propria*), and the second was shared (*communis*).

Even the choice of words gives it away: Anonymus transferred the Christological–Trinitarian discussion of early Scholasticism, especially the thoughts of Anselm of Canterbury, to the long since politically interpreted Pauline allegory of the church as the body of Christ. He passionately fought for the unity of the church in the entire world, for the body of which Christ was the head. In this one body, however, no earthly superior could take the place of Christ and rule over other parts; even the highest dignitaries remained fragile mortals, not only the King of England and the Archbishop of Rouen, but emperor and pope as well. What did Christ mean with his statement about the tribute penny? ' "Render unto Caesar the things which are Caesar's", but not unto Tiberius himself that which belongs to him personally. Render unto the office (*potestas*) not unto the person. For the person is nothing, but the position is just. Tiberius is unjust, but the emperor is good.' In the same way, the pope had more than one self, for example, in case he should become a murderer or debaucher. 'In the *persona* of the pope, he stands over all men; in the *persona* of a man, among men; in the *persona* of the sinner, below men.'

For Anonymus of Rouen, Gregorian church reform and Norman government clashed with particular severity; but by the late eleventh century, the clerical and temporal communities had elsewhere too separated from each other and redefined themselves. Ecclesiastical and governmental groups still needed human representatives (*personae communes*) but that was more to be able to personify the intangible, to bring home the timeless, than to organize practical reality. In sober practice, even the highest dignitary was an individual with the same peculiarities other men had. The principle the Carolingians wanted cast in bronze once again appeared in public undisguised. The fission of the *persona publica* became visible about 1100.

V

The twelfth century began questioning whether a man could equate his private character with his public office, whether he could be equated with the society he rules, and whether the common denominator *persona* could be used to label this equation. More than from anywhere else, doubts arose from the new communes, social cooperatives whose norms demanded more of their members personally, and which assembled loosely at first, in the Romance countries, but quickly spread to an international level and organized themselves into fellowships. Monastic orders, lay brotherhoods, heretical sects, orders of knights, merchant and craft guilds and universities needed no monarchial representatives. Their most radical speaker, the French philosopher Peter Abelard, denied the unity of what had been known until then as *persona* and began re-evaluating the entire scope of the term.

Around 1133, Abelard turned his empirical eye on his fellow man in *Historia calamitatum*. In it, in the spirit of ecclesiastical reform, he criticized as power-hungry personalities France's clerical dignitaries, who were sitting in judgement over him in court. In 1121, he wrote, enemies had brought an accusation against him 'before bishops, archbishops, abbots and all possible *religiosi nominis personae*'. These were men who carried honorable titles (*religionis nomen*), and respected benefices (*sedis dignitas*), but were neither the most learned nor the most pious. What Abelard said of the Abbot of Saint-Denis applied to others as well: 'The higher he rose above others in prelate rank, the more notorious a life he led.' With the exception of the king, Abelard called secular lords tyrants, but reserved the word *persona* for clerical *potestates*: *ecclesiasticae personae*. The only significance of these men rested in the power of their office. This custom was adopted by the French tongue, which used *personae* to refer to clerical dignitaries.

In his theoretical analyses, however, Abelard adhered to wholly different definitions, for example in his *Theologia Christiana* of 1134–5. It dealt with the doctrinal controversy of equating, in the Trinity, 'the divine being (*identitas divinae substantiae*)' with the 'diversity of the divine personages (*diversitas personarum*)'. *Persona* here referred to the characteristics (*proprietates*) and mutual relationships (*relationes*) within the Trinity, not to be confused with its common substance. Abelard made use of linguistic examples to define more clearly his theological interpretations. When talking, a single man can appear as three different selves simultaneously: first, as the speaker; next, as the one being spoken to; thirdly, as the one being spoken about. Abelard sharply disassociated this rhetorical personalism of human existence from the theological–philological personalism of relationships. As an aside, he mentioned the *personae* of jurists and their separation of transaction and object, then went on to the philosophical definition of Boethius, where *persona* was thought of as the indivisible substance of a rational natural being. Abelard did not actually reject this, but in his opinion it did not apply to the divine personages, which would otherwise have to be comprehended as three substances.

Once on the subject, Abelard mentioned Boethius' statement to the effect that the word *persona* had originated in the theatre, and he summarily interpreted: 'We also refer to people active in the theatre as *personae*, namely the men themselves, who, with their voices and gestures, communicate to us something that has happened or was said.' In his analysis, the more distinguished tragedies which featured important historical figures were absent: only the antics remained. The example of the masks was superfluous, for no one could 'wear another *persona*', except as a pun. His summary was devastating: 'There are, then, three or four or perhaps more ways in which this word *persona* is used.' Of these, only one had real importance, the theological definition, for the three divine personages embody all power, wisdom and mercy that aids in the perfection of grace. Men could hardly achieve this ethical norm; even David, 'the greatest among prophets and kings', a man after God's heart, became an adulterer and murderer in the twinkling of an eye. A man whose life was even more exemplary than that of kings was the philosopher Socrates, for whom moral living was a basis of philosophy. But could any single man fully become a 'personage'?

To close the gap between divine perfection and man's sins in the church's sense, Abelard's commentary of 1135–7 on the Epistle to the Romans adopted Pauline characteristics. According to Romans 12:5, the community of Christians constituted a single body under the head of Christ, encompassing many parts separate from one another (*secundum diversitatem personarum*). This meant that every believer had to render to his neighbour that service (*officium*) which he commanded better than others. Personalism was a relationship to others, service to the whole, the antithesis of the self-righteous pompousness (*dignitas vel excellentia*) of prominent *personae*, who, according to Romans 2:11, did not count before God. Communities of the faithful were like single personages, despite the constant diversity of individuals within them, but they could and had to help the individual behave morally. Abelard was speaking allegorically: he was not hypothesizing collectivity when he mentioned the *generalis persona* of the Jewish people, of the Christian community, of all the children of Adam. In theological allegories such as these, the community of many appeared as *persona* for the first time, though vaguely. That was only possible because Abelard no longer saw *persona* as the self-dependent whole of the individual, but as an aspect of dynamic relationships, in the divine Trinity and in human society.

This political–theological model ignored the political realities of collective institutional states. In 1159, the clerical secretary of the Archbishop of Canterbury, John of Salisbury, who had studied in Paris and then isolated himself from his academic friends, tried to make allowance for those states. The Englishman dedicated his *Fürstenspiegel*, *Policraticus*, to the English king's chancellor, Thomas Becket. John, like Abelard, did not trust a uniform definition of *persona*, but preferred to analyse functions as opposed to definitions, to make the extent of the word comprehensible. He examined the various ways an individual in society could achieve esteem (*reverentia*): *a natura*, via kindred and ancestry; *ab officio*, via the fulfilment of duties; *a moribus*, by letting a spiritual attitude guide one's actions; *a conditione*, via legal status and material estate; *a fortuna*, by chance, which was not defined.

Officium referred to the correct performance of everything required by superiors or morality of individuals [*personae singulae*], whether publicly, meaning in co-operation with others, or privately, meaning alone. The significance of public duties was measured against the standard of the 'eminence of the various offices (*eminentia cuiusque magistratus*)'; this was judged according to the degree of worthy administration. Whether and how much an office was respected or disdained depended on the esteem or disgrace of the subjects. For this reason, the public proclamations of rulers tended to speak in the name of many people, 'so that the basis of accord will appear not so much as that of one *persona*, but of all (*non tam personae quam universitatis*)'. This is the only place in John's catalogue of *personae* where the prince appeared; the esteem enjoyed by the prince was due neither to his distinguished ancestry nor to his private lifestyle, not to his legal status nor to chance, but to his discharge of duties. His foremost example was not the often bloodthirsty David, but Melchizedek, the first priest-king, who supposedly had neither mother nor father and was thus free of personal ties.

However, he wrote, more often than not a prince was deluded not by his relatives, but by the flattery of the court; that was what corrupted the community and deserved no respect. Courtiers of that kind relinquished their 'inborn human dignity (*naturae vel personae dignitas*)' to imitate the shameful antics of an actor who wears the face of another. Unfortunately, John wrote, public officials today make little effort to perform historical duties (*res gesta*), making no more than an uncommitted attempt (*temptatio*): it resembles a comedy in which 'everyone forgets his own *persona* and speaks as someone else (*quisque sui oblitus personam exprimit alienam*)'. Most of the world is so absorbed in play-acting that they could not return to their true selves even if they had to. The loss of identity via the assumption of roles! Only the old exemplary figures, the classics from Themistocles to Titus, and the biblical ones from Abel to John the Baptist, have managed to retain their natural dignity, and from their position in heaven at the side of the Creator they observe this ridiculous game of chance in the theatre of the world (*theatrum mundi*).

The situation did not have to go on forever, however: the princes could improve it, for the *res publica* was one body with the prince as its head. Though the prince was not the whole, he directed it by performing his duties. 'He faithfully performs his task (*ministerium*) when he, aware of his position, remembers that he represents the *persona* of the totality of his subjects (*universitatis subiectorum se personam gerere*).' John adapted the old theatre expression here, then makes it positive, though *persona* remains ambiguous: as with Abelard, a comparison with the whole was intended, but just as intentional was the role played by the leader of the society. John repeated himself: by serving the common good of the *res publica*, instead of his 'own will (*privata voluntas*)', the prince acts as a personification of the public (*personam publicam gerit*). Neither prince nor the whole of the community could become *public personae* by strength of their beings, they become them only via co-operation. With that, John rejected not only the oriental despots but the Late Roman monarchy as well, and defined the limits of modern communes, of the opportunism of court officials, and of the dogmatism of academic intelligence. Could this balance between reality and terminology hold its own in European monarchies, could it even, perhaps, become institutionalized?

VI

In the twelfth century, Hohenstaufen Germany opened itself to religious and political reform movements from the west and south without letting its conventional state and ecclesiastical constitution be undermined. In the wake of the first Hohenstaufen emperor, the attempt was made to reconcile the old with the new, to regain the unity of the differentiated term *persona* by making it more dynamic and lending it political significance. Since as early as the end of the Investiture Conflict and the establishment of Roman law, the advisers of German kings had accepted this juristic specification: *persona* indicated the current leader of an ecclesiastical or state institution, as opposed to its permanent organization. The document of 1152 in which Frederick Barbarossa notified the Pope of his election as king promised general royal protection 'for Holy Mother Church and all her office-bearers (*sacrosanctae matri nostrae Romanae ecclesiae et omnibus ecclesiasticis personis*) and especially for the Pope, promising additionally the fulfilment of the king's official duties (*tam ad vestram personam omnino specialem quam ad... ecclesiae...defensionem*)'. The Pope was a special persona not only individually, but as the intimate friend of the king. To imply for himself and his empire an equal rank to that of pope and the church, Frederick, after his coronation as emperor in 1155, praised the Count of Dauphiné for his loyalty to the Empire and to the *persona* of his imperial majesty (*circa imperium et nostrae maiestatis personam*). The intentional connection of those two terms, until then unusual for royal German documents, was doubtless aimed at the transpersonal exaltation of the office of emperor; this was also expressed as a contrast to his German aides: the bishops and high aristocrats were classified by Frederick as simple officials (*publicae potestatis personae*), in 1154.

Barbarossa's uncle, Bishop Otto of Freising, used a similar approach at first to describe the deeds of Emperor Frederick in 1157. In the prologue, the bishop explained to his nephew that his sole intention was to tell of the emperor's *persona* (*de tua persona*); only in order to elevate the glory of Frederick's deeds would he include details of the Emperor's ancestors. The Emperor was not seen here as one member of a distinguished family, but as an outstanding and isolated case. In the next sentence, Otto excused himself for the necessity of relating the deeds of this or that *ecclesiastica saecularisve persona* of other kingdoms, but the actions of these men applied to the Holy Roman Empire. He was referring to officials, prelates and princes not included in Hohenstaufen government, and therefore below it. The bishop accepted the modern differentiation between *persona* and institution even when writing of his fellow ecclesiastical dignitaries. During the Italian march of 1154, Frederick picked out various bishops who had failed to participate without excusing themselves and divested them of their regalia. Otto wrote that the punishment applied to the individuals only: the regalian rights 'had been endowed by the prince not to the *personae*, but to the churches, for all time'.

Below the surface, however, archaic and liturgical associations were growing, as when king and bishop approached the altar together during the royal coronation of Frederick in Aachen in 1152, Bishop Frederick of Münster receiving his episcopal anointment simultaneously. 'One and the same day saw, in one and the same church, the consecrations of the two sole *personae* who are sacramentally anointed in the manner established by the Old and New Testaments and are rightly named *christi Domini*.' Even more significant was the analogy with Christ in Otto's description of that coronation of 1152. The German princes had congregated 'as a single body' and unanimously elected 'that *persona*' Frederick of Swabia as head of the empire. Because his ancestry included both Guelphs and Hohenstaufen, he was capable of overcoming the long conflict of those two families, which had sprung from personal jealousy, and thus better serve the *res publica*. *Persona* was the reunion of what had been divided, the personification of common interests; these 'public interests', that is, the empire, were compared to the Pauline body of Christ. The superhuman efforts that these expectations demanded of the Hohenstaufen have been overlooked by historians in the past; they have failed to notice the connection of Otto's ideas and another long exposition in another part of the book. This digression had nothing to do with the emperor, but did inform the reader what Otto really meant by *persona*.

Otto of Freising, who had studied in Paris, explored in his philosophical excursus the opinions of his teacher Gilbert de la Porrée about the divine Trinity. Earlier, Otto had rejected Abelard's teachings about the non-substantial relationship between the divine *personae*; now he, like Gilbert, subscribed to Boethius' teachings of substantiation.

> Of natural beings (*naturae*), the essential characteristic (*proprietas substantialis*) is in one sense common (*universalis*) and in another unique, indivisible, individual. The indivisible (*individualis*) is in some cases a kind of *persona* (*personalis*), while in others it is not. I speak of *persona* in a figurative sense, derived from *personalitas*, not, as in the Greek, from the holding of a mask, and not, as in the Latin, from the penetrating sound of a tone; I mean what Boethius, disputing with Eutyches and Nestorius in his book on *persona* and natural beings, called *persona*, letting himself be guided not by etymology but by the idea behind the matter: a term that corresponds to the Greek hypostasis. Thus, he defines *persona* as meaning the indivisible essence of a reasoning (*rationalis*) natural being. I call it common not because it is the identical among the various – which is impossible – but because it unifies the

various in their similarities, and because it is called *universalis*
– due to the unity of all that becomes similar – namely, that
which turns all to one. We call such a similarity of the various
corporeality in the broadest sense, animation in the narrower
sense, and humanity (*humanitas*) in the narrowest and last
sense.

Then Otto stressed that, in the sphere of physical inseparability,
neither body nor soul can attain that state of *persona*; the next best
thing, as an initial step in the right direction, is the union of both
within the constitution of a single individual, *ad constituendum
hunc hominem*. The individuality of *persona* is founded in its characteristics (*personalis proprietas*), but also in the substance, so that
one could agree with Gilbert (and later Roman philologists), that
persona is *per se una*. Gilbert had transferred a part of these definitions, originally meant for the natural sciences, to theology. If the
Bishop of Freising had been interested solely in the doctrine of the
Trinity, he, like Abelard, would not have dwelt on anthropology. In
his initial philosophic excursus, he had detached man, as a creation
that had become natural and acted within history, from the simplic-
ity, primacy and uniqueness of the Creator, and had used the fragility of man to explain the inconstancy of his history. In this second
excursus, he spoke of the dignity of man, who, in the misery of his
feebleness, can still prove himself rational, whole and meaningful.
He may fail to do so, like the holy and wise King David, deceived by
his slave. But we all have time before the final night falls.
The clearly recognizable nature of the human *persona* did not
imply constancy and identity: at the most, it merely implied the
process of the dissimilar becoming similar; within the course of
history, one and the same whole could not be formed out of the
many. As early as his chronicle of 1146, Otto had noted that only
the Creator could exist eternally and unchangeably *in identitate sua*;
not until the end of time could the community of the faithful be
freed from change and mortality. Nevertheless, history knows
change towards permanence; Otto stressed that, also in 1157, when
he presented his work to the emperor. Everyone in this world
(*persona mundialis*) is subject to earthly laws, except for kings, who
are answerable directly to God; it is easier for them to sin than for
others. But God exalts them with a magnanimous heart and opens
their eyes to the knowledge of the Creator. Otto describes the
Hohenstaufen quickly uniting his empire into a uniform confeder-
acy: the prince of peace gives to the world, after a rainy and dark
night, the morning's serenity of peace. Immediately, his empire's

standing is strengthened, his *persona* is further exalted. If God, who has blessed us with this good start, will grant us perseverance as well, the emperor will be able to realize 'through many courses of time' the ideal of the public *persona*, a harmony between God and the world. Otto of Freising must have realized the weakness of his scheme. He had expounded a didactic prototype in the form of a political reality. It depended not only upon goodwill, but on the unlimited power of the ruler, and that century could no longer rely on either of those conditions.

VII

Of the many attempts made in the twelfth century to redefine the scope of the word *persona*, the thirteenth century acknowledged only the tendency to differentiate, not the tendency to comprehend it in its totality. The public *persona* was not to be revived. The interpretation concentrated on a fragmental area, on the aspect of the individual. The individual appeared, as before, as part of a public community and as a member in a complex of relationships, but he was now viewed more and more from the perspective of his individual features; more often than ever before, he was referred to as *persona*. This was finally to be confirmed by an Italian theologian and jurist, Innocent III, the most important pope of that century, in formulations that were then adopted by Catholic ecclesiastical law and which deeply influenced medieval societies.

In 1204, Pope Innocent described the Catholic church, in the tradition of Paul, as the body of Christ. The high priest stood closer to the head of the church than did the secular prince, which is why the former was anointed on his head, the latter only on the shoulders or arms; the Carolingian duality of the anointed had dissolved. It was only the high priest who, Innocent said, 'represented, in the office of priest, the *persona* of the head (*personam capitis in pontificali officio repraesentat*)'. That sounded like John of Salisbury, who had perceived office as a role; only this time the role described was not that of the whole, but of its head, Christ. In bold imagery, the head stood for the body because Christ was a *persona* of the Trinity. As Innocent disapprovingly quoted at the Lateran Council of 1215, the idea that their unity was merely collective and ostensible, 'as we might call many men a nation or many faithful a church', did not apply to divine *personae*. A group of mortals certainly does not form one and the same thing, the same for each member; their unity comes from common faith or mutual love. Like the doctrine of the

Trinity, the doctrine of transubstantiation, formulated at the same council, insisted on a strict differentiation between the *una persona* Christ and the *mysterium unitatis* of his church, between the true and the mystical body (*corpus verum* and *corpus mysticum*), as Innocent taught. Thus, all attempts to personalize common interests in the manner of John of Salisbury were stopped.

In the same way, the Pope called a halt to all hypothesizing on the individual the way Otto of Freising had. Quoting a passage of Gelasius in 1201, Innocent practically used the image of *persona* as a foundation for his words when he compared the royal *potestas* with the body, and the papal *auctoritas* with the spirit of the church; he ignored the Carolingian interpretation and spoke of offices (*dignitates*), not of *personae*. In 1202, the pope named the elected German king *persona*, but meant in this case the individual whose moral life was to be scrutinized. Since transferring the empire in the year 800 to the shoulders of Charlemagne (*in personam magnifici Caroli*), it was the papacy's duty to determine whether the regal candidate was personally qualified, whether he was a *persona indigna* or *idonea*. The same separation between office and self applied to clerical office-bearers. At this point, the council of 1215 even established a new word derivation, excluding the misunderstandings inherent in Abelard's style, and defined public office as an abstract: *dignitates aut personatus*. The same decretal which forbade the transfer of multiple offices to one *persona* allowed exceptions for *sublimes et literatae personae*, men personally qualified by character and education.

There was no room for the expression *persona publica* in the early medieval sense; when it did appear, it was promptly employed for other purposes. In the twelfth century, initially in Italy and as a result of the reception of Roman law, the job of notary had been so expanded into the public sphere that it was compared with the *tabularius* of the *Corpus iuris* and was given the same name. Notaries were referred to when the Lateran Council decided that legally binding protocols were to be made of all trials, either by two qualified men 'or if possible by an office-bearer (*aut publicam, si potest habere, personam*)'. Innocent III did all he could to stop the development of the word *persona* from the sixth century on.

In the Late Middle Ages, it was used in the way church law had defined it. Even when some theologians and jurists in the thirteenth century described a transpersonal community as *persona mystica*, or a king as *persona idealis*, the adjectives made plain the ineffectuality of such expressions. When the public *persona* was subdivided into community and individual, the *persona* of man appeared, not in the dignity of its substance, but in the tension of its relations. The difference between the shell and the core, between social duties and individual morality could not be defined. Not until the sixteenth century did the individual begin to liberate himself from the norms of his society and assert his own subjectivity. But even then, it was the intellectuals whose pride in subjectivity gradually led them to aim at personal identity. To average mortals, this theoretical discussion was hardly accessible, and even now we are still participating in it by using terms loaned from the language of medieval theologians, philosophers and jurists.

The contents of medieval discussions about public *personae* became rich in consequences for European history. For though the common people hardly took part in this discussion, the kings could not ignore it. Mankind today would be able to establish its own identity more simply if the scholars of the early modern period had identified themselves voluntarily with their own societies. That would have been possible if the societies of the High Middle Ages had identified themselves with their human leaders as unquestioning as had been the case in the Early Middle Ages. And if public life had personified itself permanently in the figure of its ruler, political life today would take place largely in the study, where Boethius found it.

Part III
Interpreting History

4

Universal Histories in the Middle Ages?

I

It is almost a truism that the historiography of the Christian Middle Ages consolidated the history of salvation and the history of the world into a single panorama, in which every era from the Creation to the end of the world corresponds to the hub of Christ, and where every country from Thule to India corresponds to the hub of Jerusalem. Latin titles of books by modern historians, such as *Chronica mundi* or *Historia mundi*, support this preconception. But such titles mislead: as incredible as it may sound, not a single medieval historian of any real status ever named his work *Chronica mundi* or *Historia mundi*. Actually, we should not speak of medieval world histories or world chronicles at all, nor of universal histories; I will shortly illustrate how late in the Middle Ages titles such as *Historia universalis* first appeared. Of course, we can speak of medieval universal historiography, but only under the stipulation that Karl Heinrich Krüger provided in 1976 with his study, *Die Universalchroniken*: that we should realize we are applying modern descriptive terms to a literary genre that referred to itself as *Historia* or *Chronicon*. As such titles show, history was written in the singular; but whose history it was and what time-frame it chose has yet to be ascertained. Modern alternative terminology does not help much: the subject of such historiography is not man, either as an individual or as a species; its spectrum is neither natural nor denaturalized time. Let us examine three examples of that history.

II

Bede's *Historia ecclesiastica gentis Anglorum* reaches its climax in chapter V:23:

Such is the current condition of all of Britain in about the 285th year after the arrival of the Angles in Britain, or in the year 731 of the incarnation of the Lord. May the earth rejoice in His continuing rule and, since Britain likewise exults in His faith, may all the diversity of islands rejoice in the memory of His holiness.

It was Bede who established the year-numbering system we use today, by counting the years since the birth of Christ; naturally, he based his chronological computations on the astronomical courses of sun and moon, and on weather cycles like seasons and days, yet in doing so he was still measuring time, not evaluating it. He moulded his conception of time to fit the two societies he was describing, the nation of the Angles and the Catholic Church. The time that had passed since the beginnings of those societies did not constitute an era suitable for historical orientation, for it had been far shorter than the ages of the world, certainly much longer than the stages of a human life. The time-frames of those groups were differentiated within themselves, were not homogeneous even for Bede's era: in 729, the appearance of two comets foretold disaster, and the Saracen threat to the Church of God was thrust upon the empire of the Franks; at the same time, peace seemed to reign in the British Isles, *serenitas temporum*: this means 'good weather' or 'restful times' – both translations are possible. Nevertheless, this condition was unnatural; it appeared to have been brought about, said Bede, for the time being by Catholic proselytizing. That is what tamed the hatred between the Picts, Scots, Britons and Angles, and what bridged the various dialects with the common Latin language of the church. For now, the sun is shining, but 'how this thing will end is up to a later time to discover'. Bede resisted any kind of eschatological mood. The lasting unity of the entire earth under Christ the King appeared a pipe-dream for the time being. Christ had already caused the small kingdoms of the British Isles to keep peace; it was in order to teach the peoples how to make that peace permanent that Bede described how it had come about. But whether *ecclesia* and *gens* would continue to co-operate in the future was for a future time to say. What Bede wrote here is the history of salvation; it is not yet world history.

III

In *Chronica sive Historica de duabus civitatibus*, Otto of Freising ends his summary of the ages and kingdoms of the earth with chapter VII:34:

Now I have reviewed the order of inconstant things as well as I could, from Adam unto the current year. It is the 1,146th year since the incarnation of our Lord, the 1,918th year since the founding of the city of Rome, the ninth year of Conrad, who is the ninety-third emperor since Augustus, and the second year of Pope Eugene III. I have permitted myself to deal with the diverse miseries of humankind, but now it would hardly be fitting to ignore the diverse orders of monks, the holiness of which, as I have said, makes the wickedness of the world endurable before the judgement seat of God. Thus, let us answer the confusion of the great evils of this world with the excellent restricting and reversing achievements performed by clear-thinking men.

The co-operation between the Holy Roman Empire and the Catholic Church, practised for centuries, shattered within two generations during the Gregorian Reform. Otto may date his present by referring to the two founders of those societies, Christ and Augustus, but they are not the ones he depicts as holding the order of the world together. During the confusion of the present, Otto sees time as little more than natural inconstancy, the ups and downs of day and night; history progressed in *revolutiones*, similar to the movements of a man sick with fever who twists and turns in his bed and can find no peace. This might be world history, but it is no longer the history of salvation. That history progresses in the small communes of the devout and learned, in orders and schools. Here are men who live day in and day out together and provide an example of the right way to live for their fellow human beings; that is how they keep the world intact. These include the Benedictines, whose order has existed for six centuries, as well as the Carthusians, whose community was founded not two generations before. For them, time is undiluted present; their work, until the night breaks in, is restriction and reversal.

All day and all night they occupy themselves so tirelessly and circumspectly with praying, reading and working, that they believe it blasphemous to lose even a fraction of an hour without devout exertion, except for the moment in which they grant their tired bones a rest upon a bare straw cot or coarse blanket.

This is time applied to reality, it does not wait for an eschatological after-life; these communities cover the face 'of all the earth', but do not comprise any of humanity. What will come of this, only tomorrow will tell; the future of the world depends on the works of these devout communes.

IV

Giovanni Villani opens his unfinished *Cronica* with chapter I:1:

> Now this is the state of things: among the old Florentines, there exist but few and disordered memories of the past days of our city of Florence. The fault lies either in their own negligence or in the loss of writings from the time when Totila, the Scourge of God, destroyed the city. When I, Giovanni, citizen of Florence, watch the nobility and lords of our city in the present day, I realize that one must retell and commit to memory the origins and beginnings of such a famous city, both her favourable and unfavourable transformations. Not that I should think myself capable of such a great work, I merely wish to offer those who come after us the raw material, so that they will not neglect the memory of noteworthy events that will happen among us in the course of time, and so that they can offer future generations examples of those transformations, of things past, their causes and reasons. In this way, the generations of tomorrow can learn to apply virtue, spurn vice and bravely endure adversities for the good of our society.

It was Villani's intention to write the history of Florence, not of the Catholic Church: he wanted to explain the upheavals in recent decades, not the array of the ages since the Creation. But a famous city like Florence had reached historical importance long before the eleventh century; the ups and downs of its development could not be explained using current issues alone. Thus, Villani began his narration with the creation of the world, and ended it with the year of the plague in 1348, when he died. His claim that Florence, founded by Caesar, was destroyed by the Gothic King Totila does not mark a division of ages between the antique and the Middle Ages, but the danger of sudden disaster for any history: the one we experience ourselves as well as the one we tell. Doubtless, Villani believed that, in the beginning of his fourteenth century, 'Our city Florence, daughter and creation of Rome, is at a stage of growth in which she is ready to pursue great things, while Rome is in the midst of deteriorating'; but the asymmetry of things coexisting is complemented by the transience of all things present. What Villani actually tells of the changes in his home town during his lifetime constitutes a succession of blows of fate and natural disasters, more a history of doom than of salvation. Only he who can soberly think beyond the present moment can bravely endure such adversities, and by doing so he assures less the salvation of his personal soul than the survival of the community. And whether or not future events can be made truly useful for the nobility and lords of Florence, only those who come after can know.

V

At the end of their historical works, where their chronicles end, Bede, Otto and Villani name a universal historical reference for their narratives: the years that have passed from the incarnation of the Lord until the time of their writing. By doing so, Bede created a continuous time span that was to become indispensable for the development of world histories, for had one been limited to the regionally scattered chronologies of earlier historians, a long-range continuity of historical processes would have been hardly recognizable. These are some alternatives that Otto only hinted at: the Greek Olympiads, enumeration *ab urbe condita*, or according to the reigns of individual rulers. Even when the length of a year was still being measured by the orbit of the sun, according to a natural and cyclical phenomenon, the succession of years following Christ formed into a straight line; one might even call it an arrow, for, starting with the birth of the Saviour, the centuries following aimed straight at his second coming in the Last Judgement, and the end of the world.

Bede finished the chronological summary that ended his *De temporum ratione* with such a conclusion; Otto of Freising did the same in the last book of his chronicle, and even Villani, in his final sentence before falling silent, quoted the conviction of his contemporaries that the newest series of disasters had foretold the end of the world. Thus the time-frame for world histories was defined, especially as Bede had calculated the precise time from the Creation to the birth of Christ; Otto and Villani used his conclusion. We should not ignore such prerequisites for world historical observations, just because we take the standardized time-frame of the calendar year for granted; rather, we should ask ourselves why medieval historians applied their own achievements differently from the way we do, why they did not attempt to fill the gaps in their time-line. Even medieval readers began noticing this: they started suggesting a more exact differentiation between historiography and chrono-

graphy. But these questions of definition bothered the most important authors the least; they made clear what was on their minds
simply by stressing their main points.

Bede, Otto and Villani wrote history in the singular, a history of
clearly arranged human societies striving to redeem life here and
now. It was not the history of the individual, nor of all humanity.
For these societies, time was the time of social co-operation, measur-
able neither by the natural orbital rhythm of stars nor by the lives of
men, nor by the denaturalized time of clocks and calendars. This
history of salvation concerned itself neither with the time continuum
nor with the unity of the human species, because it did not confuse
the goal of the after-life with the ways of this life. The history of
salvation could not become 'world history' until both world and
history came to an end, until the Church of God was identical with
humanity; in other words, not in the near future.

VI

How and when it came to a transition from that kind of story of
salvation to universal history has yet to be investigated. I would
guess that three strains of development contributed, each of which
began around 1300. As an example for the first, an obscure Thuringian priest named Siegfried of Ballhausen will serve. In 1304, he
wrote a history of the People of God from the Creation to the
present and took the risk of using, as far as I can see, for the first
time, the title *Historia universalis*. He quickly became aware that the
universality referred more to his own scholarship than to reality; in
1306, he gave the new edition the more fitting title of *Compendium
historiarum*. Since the fall of the Hohenstaufen empire and the
papacy of Avignon, a *Historia* of the People of God was even less
conceivable than in Otto's time. Since then, titles of universal–
historical works have been heaped upon each other: *Flores historiarum*, *Breviarium historiarum*, *Memoriale historiarum*, *Epitome
historiarum*, *Summa historiarum* and *Mare historiarum*. All these
works were completed under the impression of a discontinuity of
times and societies; they described histories in the plural, mostly
limited by the lifetime of the author, often bordering on the genre of
national histories, on a path leading to more and more distinct
detail.

The second strain of development can be seen in the very middle
of Villani's chronicle. He was prompted to compose the history
while staying in Rome during the jubilee year of 1300, viewing the

antique ruins there and reading the Latin histories. At least twenty years passed before he actually put pen to paper, but the caesura of 1300 left as deep an impression on Villani as it did on his fellow citizen Dante Alighieri. Why? At that time, Pope Boniface VIII was celebrating the initiation of the church into another hundred years, 'in honour of the birth of Christ', yet visibly in the tradition of Augustus' Roman secular celebrations. In so doing, he invented a new kind of time-frame, the 'century', without which historians today could hardly work. At first, the century was not meant to be a time measurement, but a unique celebration that would take the living closer to the distant promise of salvation and the eternal cycles of the heavens. Nevertheless, the date was set by man alone and was suitable for 'secularizing jubilees', which soon became more and more common. One other thing that condensed time in a similar way was the invention of the mechanical clock, also around 1300. In Dante's *Divina Commedia* we read that the makers and users of the early clockworks and carillons had in mind not so much the hectic cycle of earthly duties, but the joy of heavenly roundelays. Again, the clock was the work of man; it transferred the Aristotelian definition of time as measurement of movement to a machine, and granted urban citizens, merchants and craftsmen less time than any astronomical or liturgical rhythm. Time became verifiable and could be estimated in advance; it had to be earned and sought after. This artificial, subdividable, practical time challenged historians to fill the gaps in their time-lines more completely, though in such a chaos of facts one could hardly read more than a diversity of paths, as opposed to a visible goal. By adding dates, Villani made his chronicle of Florence into an early-fourteenth-century history of the world. As he approached the jubilee year of 1300, he began supplementing his wording of chapter I:1: he still intended to pursue the deeds of the Florentines in detail, but would now 'briefly' add 'other noteworthy events in the entire world (*altre notabili cose dell'universo in brieve*)'.

The third strain of development originated in the same situation following 1300, in the impotence of universal institutions and the growing strength of individual states and cities. Dante Alighieri put it into words when he spoke of the *humana civilitas* in *De Monarchia*, and of the longed-for community of the races of man under a single global emperor, a society which would no longer look after the souls of men, but provide for their earthly happiness; there was no other way for men to live together in peace on this crowded 'threshing-floor' of mortality. Dante could not base his concept on the continuities of history, but solely on the model of a global

Roman empire. Because this model would not fit into the established time-line, the humanists never wrote a true world history, but finally did postulate one. From the middle of the fifteenth century, more and more books began appearing in such circles, bearing titles such as *Historia mundi* and *Chronicon universale*: they were indicators of a new historiography that, in the tension between individual and species, strove towards a more and more abstract basis of thought. This tendency could be traced back to two events that completely shattered the global concept of the People of God: the victory of the Turks in 1453 and the discovery of America. It was not until Europeans were forced into a corner that they were able to trace their development back to the Mosaic tablet of peoples and forwards into the world's future. It was not until then that a 'universal history as aggregate' could arise.

VII

It would appear that there is only one thing modern historiography has in common with its medieval counterpart, and perhaps with its antique counterpart as well: that the concept of history is usually expanded following historical situations in which familiar continuities and trusted societies are shattered, and questions about the scope of time and about the subject of history have to be reconsidered. In this sense, world histories are retrospective projections, an attempt to derive one whole History from a collection of many historic parts.

The difference between medieval historiography and its modern counterpart, but not from its antique counterpart, is far more basic than Bernard Guenée supposed it to be in his brilliant book of 1980, *Histoire et culture historique dans L'Occident médiéval*. As scholarly as numerous historians were in the Middle Ages in their research of sources, they were hardly the peers of modern historians in this regard. Historiography was not practised as a profession, as little by the monk Bede as by the bishop Otto or the merchant Villani. They carelessly merged memories that could be verified retrospectively with assumptions that never can be. They understood history in relation to the viewpoint of their age and society, they wrote 'current history' and looked at it as we look at our unfinished lifetime, referring to sporadic events and assuming universal foundations. It is only we moderns who believe we have reached the summit of our science; up there, if the view is clear and the weather good, anyone willing to make the effort should be able to ascertain the low points left behind and work out the best way to the next peak. The first to reach the summit will be able to see the entire path behind us, and interpret it.

Medieval historians, on the other hand – and that is the difference between them and classical writers – saw themselves as travellers through a primal forest that was so dense they could not make out anything behind or ahead. Then and again, they would rest to gather the group together, let the stragglers catch up and their leaders take counsel with each other. They had carefully avoided swamps and cliffs and would do so in the future, but were less concerned about the course and direction of their path. They took their time. Of course, they could catch sight of their goal of salvation at any point along the way and at any time, simply by looking up, but none of them would be able to reach it in their lifetimes; along the way, they had to be careful to retain their character and cohesiveness so that no one would be left by the wayside. It would have been no surprise to them that we do not look upon them as an example: they would have agreed that we make progress much faster than they. They might have been jealous of our view from the peak, but most likely they would simply have asked how much room there was up there, and how long we would be able to keep our places. It is a good question: why do we gather so much information about the world's past when our knowledge of the subject of our history, of the scope of our time and of the things concerning our salvation is so shallow?

5

Historical Time in the Writings of Abelard

I

Historians have seldom participated in the discussion of the problem of time, which has largely been dominated by physicists and psychologists, for they investigate not time itself, but processes within it. They have always seemed content to borrow physical theories, starting with Aristotle, or psychological ones, starting with Augustine, to establish their reference to time. If time is 'countable spatial movement', as Aristotle described it, then it consists of divisible particles and constitutes a continuum. This natural concept of time provides historians with a framework for their chronology, for the discussion of historic process within a time-frame. If time, as Augustine put it, is the 'broadening of the soul', since the past can be remembered and the future anticipated, then it constitutes discontinuous singularities, which at the same time constitute points of culmination. This experienced time provides historians with a framework for interpretation, for the correlation between the memory and anticipation of mankind implicated in the historical process.

Actual historical time, it would seem, lies somewhere in the intersection of natural and experienced time as represented by the 'historical incident', which can be accurately chronologically dated, but which at the same time includes the experiences and intentions of those who noticed it. Like Leopold Ranke, historians have certainly never viewed the historical incident as isolated points, but as the culmination of long-term, interrelated influences; yet, the 'gradual and continual interlinking of the great world powers' studied by Jacob Burckhardt never became apparent until the incident emerged as phenomenon, never became history until there was a historical incident. That is why Johann Gustav Droysen limited himself, in expounding on the concept of time, to two observations: that a historical process arises first in an already existent situation (we could say in a historical structure), and that the process is additionally affected by outside, simultaneous processes with their own development ('incidental' development, so to say). The main interest of historians was focused on historical processes themselves, their diachrony more than their synchrony.

Not until recent decades has the question of time become acute for historians, not because of the interdisciplinary impulses of biology, physics or philosophy, but as a problem inherent to history, arising when social–scientific methods were first introduced to the study of history. Fernand Braudel's essay of 1958 with the title *Histoire et sciences sociales: la longue durée*, became famous. Its central statement was: 'The traditional science of history, which concentrates on the short period, the individual, the event (*événement*), has got us used to its hasty, dramatic, short-breathed style of narration. The new economic and social study of history shifts cyclical fluctuations to the focus of its research methods, and expects it to last.' Braudel assumed several levels of historical time; against the background of the slowly flowing curves of economic structures, he envisioned the history of political and literary events like blips on a radar screen.

The challenge of the French school of *Annales* that centred on Braudel was unanimously rejected by German historians at the Bremen Convention of Historians in 1953. True to their traditions, German historians renewed their covenant with philosophical hermeneutics, for which no typical course of historical process existed. For many, like Hans-Georg Gadamer, time meant more than anything else the distance between source and interpreter, and this distance could only be bridged by overlapping both worlds. The importance of experienced time led to a reconciliation between the sciences of history and literature, and also to the simultaneous renunciation by historians of the systematic social sciences. According to Max Weber, general theories of social behaviour ignored historical dimensions and even today are only indirectly conscious of them. The results of such suppression became obvious at the 1970 Convention of Historians in Cologne, when Reinhart Koselleck found it necessary to defend our discipline against the systematic social sciences with his lecture 'Why history?' More than anything else, Koselleck encouraged the theory of historical times; only that, if anything, could differentiate the study of history from the other social sciences, and provide it with a framework for its own aims.

In 1968, Koselleck began developing the beginnings of such a theory himself; they were collected in his book of 1979, *Future Past: On the Semantics of Historical Time* (English version, 1985). Koselleck stayed true to the German tradition by dealing mainly with the hermeneutic sciences, linguistics and literary theory, fitting their structural models to his historical one. Koselleck's theory of historical time is basically a history of the discovery of historical time. By writing it, Koselleck intended to correct the old scenario of progress, which said that time in the antique world was understood as the cyclical return of the never-changing; since the dawn of the Jewish-Christian era, time has supposedly been a linear, goal-oriented road toward eschatological fulfilment, and this linear concept of time was to have dominated, in a secular form, the modern philosophy of history founded by Voltaire around 1750. Koselleck, however, drew a deep caesura right around this period, in 1770, which he called a 'straddle-period (*Sattelzeit*)'.

According to Koselleck, it was around 1770 that the word 'history' appeared in German in the singular with its modern meaning, which refers both to the environment of a phenomenon as well as to its portrayal, that is, history as a setting for process and for the awareness of process. Before 1770, there had been a more strict separation of 'history' as process, the result of performed or suffered actions, and of 'history' as research, the retelling of the process. While scholars had always been able to write history in the singular before, as a single, enveloping concept, people always experienced histories in the plural, as a collection of individual stories with specific subjects, for instance the history of Charlemagne, of France, of the church. Not until the modern period did 'history in and of itself' become its own object, a unit. Thus, the conditions of time must have changed radically: after 1770, time was open to the future, it was performable, could be manipulated, planned, and of course it was also unique, could be neither anticipated nor repeated. That time had many levels became painfully obvious in the non-coincidence of the simultaneous. Confronting constancy, this new idea of time was reoriented toward expressions of movement: acceleration or delay, regress or progress. Time was, thanks to the technical invention of the 'straddle-period', abstract and denaturalized. Koselleck calls the turning-point of 1770 'the discovery of a specific historical time', the actual beginning of the modern age.

Koselleck's thesis was put through immediate and eager discussion, though mainly as a proposal for a period, as though the issue at hand were a re-evaluation of the eighteenth century of Europe; with the slogan 'straddle-period' Koselleck had called the misunderstanding down upon himself. But had he wanted to present a theory of historical time, he would have had to demonstrate that it applied to all periods, and with this in mind he collected a series of classical sources, for example, the Greek succession of government models. Koselleck's general impression was that until about 1770 it was more or less the Aristotelian, physical concept of time that dominated. Natural chronology constituted a substratum of potential histories; all individual histories 'were left in the natural, predestined condition in which they were found', for instance, in the courses of the stars, in a family's succession of generations. In the face of the great number of isolated histories, the non-coincidence of the simultaneous was hardly visible. Koselleck noticed that even the modern 'history for itself' has predecessors, and recalls Augustine, who tracked *historia* in the singular back to God, discovering along the way the most beautiful *ordo temporum*, the parallels between the six days of the Creation, the six ages of man and the six periods of the world. This *ordo temporum* is immovably fixed, despite the fluctuations of all phenomena, and it includes them all.

Thus, a simple connection between structure and incident is formed. Structures, according to Koselleck, are situations whose temporal constancies reach beyond the chronologically recognizable scope of experience of the participants in any one phenomenon. Before 1770, thanks to peasant living conditions, structures were so stable that for centuries there had hardly been any changes at all. In the framework of structures like these, historical phenomena had their fixed place. Koselleck refers to phenomena as units of awareness with sharply defined temporal limits, with a minimum of before or after. As long as structures remain stable, phenomena can be repeated; we can learn from history, and profit without loss: *Historia magistra vitae*. But with the French and Industrial Revolutions, structures began changing so quickly that phenomena could not be repeated; we can no longer learn from history. As structures and phenomena converge under the sign of permanent change, modern history, says Koselleck, becomes a process.

II

A millennium and a third came and went between Augustine and Voltaire. Not only Koselleck's thesis claims that time stood still during that period, especially during the thousand years of the Middle Ages. Some of the most important German representatives of medieval historical scholarship support him, Otto Brunner for example, who in 1958 described the interior structure of the West from the sixth to the eighteenth century as highly static. And in 1957, Herbert Grundmann characterized the concept of time in medieval historical writings by saying, 'They look for the *ratio temporum* in history, that order of time fixed by God, an order which, within this framework, is typical...and representative, timelessly valid and exemplary.' When not only historians of the Middle Ages like Brunner and Grundmann, but also modern historians like Braudel and Koselleck make a special effort to track down a system of historical process, that is, long-term chronological structures, one suspects that we modern historians have not tried hard enough to penetrate our abstract modern concept of time; that we, our view restricted by time's mountains, cannot imagine the landscape on the other side, except in reverse, the static flatness of a mirror image replacing the dynamic variety of its peaks and valleys.

This complaint was applied to historians in general, though none were specifically named, by the sociologist Norbert Elias in 1984 with his book on time, *Über die Zeit*. He claimed that, 'by subdividing the human past into individual periods, each appearing to have a life of its own', the short-range perspective of historians hinders 'the investigation of continual processes of longer duration, which do not stop at the borders of periods'. Elias' long-range perspective, based on developmental sociology, initiated a dynamic historical study of time: it starts out extremely fragmentary, then ends with highly complex time syntheses; it dissolves the link with nature and leads to a world of symbols created by man. Galileo was the first actually to confront the previously valid 'social' time, which was specific to mankind, and sift out an impersonal 'physical' time, which was simultaneously an antithesis to the older 'natural' time. There is only one epoch which Elias considered to have been static, the Middle Ages. He sees it as a long period of suspension between two calendar reforms, Caesar's classical reform and the modern Renaissance reform. The medieval Roman church had done much to impart antique knowledge to the period, but it was unwilling to break with traditions. At the same time, it created the two most important requirements for a modern concept of time: the calendar with an uninterrupted year count based on the birth of Christ, and the standard division of the day into twenty-four hours via the mechanical clock. Elias voluntarily narrows his perspective when, like other historians, he reduces time to the relationship between continuous dynamic chains of phenomena. Yet it is possible that time was not always a connection between natural or social processes, but one between various highly individual persons who saw themselves as neither part of society nor as part of nature, yet needed a chronological standard for their mutual activities. Such a theory can be verified by selecting one representative of the times which preceded the 'straddle-period' and posing to him questions about history, natural or experienced time and structure and event.

I have chosen Peter Abelard for two reasons. First, all modern scholars agree that Abelard had a sense of general principles but not of tangible history; if there was such a thing as a medieval theoretician, it was he. Though the two most important historians of the twelfth century studied in Abelard's Paris, the German Otto of Freising and the Englishman John of Salisbury, the historian Johannes Spörl stated decisively in 1935 that 'there exists no connection between the Scholastic theologians and the historians'. In 1960, the theologian Marie-Dominique Chenu drew the line at the same point: what philosophers like Abelard wanted was 'complete relinquishment of the historical system, the reduction of all facts and phenomena of the divine process of salvation to 'scientific' categories that could be systematized under the aspect of general terminology and synthetic principles... As one can see, this system excludes every single trace of historical process.' But if we can stop seeing time as a process for a little while, we might discover important clues to an alternative interpretation of time in Abelard's writings.

Secondly, Abelard's general ideas about time seem to fit Koselleck's model: as philosopher, Abelard adhered to Aristotle's philosophy; as theologian, he adhered to Augustine's theology. Yet both vital authorities propagated multi-faceted views on time. In his *Politics*, Aristotle took a different view of time from that in his *Categories*: not as spatial movement, but as a dialogue between the people of the *polis*. In his most important work, *The City of God*, Augustine saw time not as he did in the *Confessions*, as psychological memory and anticipation, but as the progress of the pilgrims, of the Christian community. If either of these men had separated historical time as a social framework for action from 'physical' and 'psychological' time, there would be evidence of this in Abelard's writings, as he knew his Aristotle and his Augustine well.

III

Let us begin with the theory of time itself. In his central philosophical work, *Dialectica*, written shortly before his death in 1142, Abelard describes time as a quantity, using quotations from Aristotle: the continuing sequence of time is subject to the laws of nature, as opposed to the action (*operatio*) of man. Only when we humans employ words to depict our deeds or afflictions do we measure them against this concept of time, using subjective aspects based on our experienced present. That explains our constantly putting verbs, which are actually words of doing and enduring, into active or passive, and our connecting them to a time-reference within our experienced chronology: the present, future, past. Thus, we set accents and create relationships. The natural flow of time itself knows no such differentiations; it consists of a series of equal moments (*instantia*). These shortest units of time are natural, not historical. In the life of man, they take on the character of a bolt of lightning that strikes 'instantly'. This is especially true of death, which overcomes man in an instant, in a single point in time (*puncto temporis*). Abelard knows what he is talking about: the 'point' (*punctum*) is the smallest measurement of distance, as indivisible as the shortest measurement of time, the moment. The thought of nearing death preoccupies Abelard constantly, but he expects it to come not as a consequence of historical process, but from the hand of the Creator.

Since one can never know what will happen in the future, surprises are possible at every moment. In a long excursus of *Dialectica*, Abelard deals with the common argument that everything that happens occurs as it must, for God's providence or *fatum* requires that everything is predetermined. Not so, says Abelard: since everything past and future is pure present for God, he can predict not only all that actually takes place, with all its consequences, but also all that is possible but which does not actually happen, with its possible consequences. This means, however, that human history in its specific aspects is not subject to unalterable decrees, but that it has room for options, even if those options are always determined by chance.

Human history does not consist of a chain of rapidly changing moments, but neither does it consist of a series of long-range, predetermined periods. It is true of that longest of all time epochs, *aetates*, however, that they are not actually historical, since they belong to God's timeless plan of salvation. In his hymns for Héloïse's nuns, the theologian Abelard constructed a strictly Augustine outline of the history of salvation, that is, the six periods of the world and the six ages of man. That the history of salvation was subdivided on an analogy with the ages of man had something natural about it: the macrocosm paralleled the microcosm. Since the birth of Christ, we have been living in the sixth and last *aetas*, which, in the life of a man, corresponds to the period of his death; with it comes the transition to paradisiacal perfection in the eternity of God. This is meant to be understood literally, not as an allegory prefaced with 'like' or 'as it were'. The biblical exegete Abelard finds the simple meaning of the word most interesting: 'First, we shall determine the truth of the phenomenon, as it were the historical root,' he writes at the beginning of his interpretation of the divine six-day Creation. Both the historical and the contemporary have their roots in God, rather than in man; Abelard refers to Genesis as the history of divine work (*divinae operationis historia*). Since the origin is divine, so is the course of *aetates temporum* or *aetatum series*. In his hymns, Abelard praises God with the words: 'Thou hast created for us space and time, the night to rest in, the day to work in.' In this, we discover what human and historical time is: not a framework, like the moment, for natural *operatio*, and not a framework, like the epoch, for divine *operatio*. Historical time is the span *between* moments and world history, the framework for human *operatio*, our actions and afflictions (*actiones vel passiones*). The representative unit of measurement for historical time is neither the moment nor the century, but the rhythm of day and night, the periods of work and rest. At this point, let us note that this historical time has the dimensions of action and affliction, but not that of knowing and thinking, like 'physical' or 'psychological' time. In Abelard's concept, historical time is not related to theory but to reality, because Abelard does not confuse the day-and-night rhythms of historical time with the macro-cycles of natural and creation-time.

He is consistent even in his passionate efforts to formulate lasting truths about God. In his central theological work, *Theologia Scholarium* of 1140, he asks the question: 'What good have all our Holy Fathers' discourses on faith done if doubts remain today that cannot be satisfactorily clarified? Heed the poet [Horace]: "If the goal is unattainable, it is enough to go as far as one can." They were satisfied to analyse the questions they heard, to explain the doubts of their time and to provide their successors with an example of how similar problems must be approached when they appear.' It is not the eternal God who asks questions of theologians, but their own time. No matter how convinced Abelard is that he is bringing his time closer to the truth of God, he knows it will not satisfy later times. To this day, the historicization of theology has seldom been taken further.

IV

Yet these are hardly more than marginal notes in other contexts. Abelard himself never dealt directly with historical time, neither in his philosophical nor in his theological discourses. He laid no foundations in those theoretical books that might have led to the writing of history, because Abelard knew what we modern historians often overlook in our search for significance: that different themes demand different methods of portrayal and different literary genres. Abelard's opinions about time and history are most densely obvious in his record of personal experiences, which at the same time holds numerous expectations for his personal future. In the following, I will concentrate on the *Historia calamitatum mearum*, written about 1133, to investigate Abelard's practical use of historical time, initially using the largely terminological–historical method of the philologists. In so doing, I must assume that the book is not a forgery, and I must leave the question unanswered as to whether it is a consolatory or autobiographical work. It is, in the strictest sense of the word, a singular book; therefore I will discuss at the outset two terms that are decisive to its singularity.

In its second sentence, Abelard states that he wants to write about *calamitatum mearum experimenta*. In the final paragraph, he returns to the beginning and names the book *calamitatum mearum hystoria*. He is not necessarily equating here the terms *experimenta* and *hystoria*, 'attempts' or 'experiments', and 'history', but he does associate them. What does that signify? If we go over the other text passages in which the word *experiri* appears, we find that Abelard does not use the term 'experience' (*experientia*) at all. The philosopher is not referring back to a life rich in experience, he is not observing the acts and affliction of man from a distance. Abelard says himself that the true philosopher is characterized less by knowledge (*scientia*) than by life (*vita*). Life, however, consists of experiments with unpredictable results, *incepta atque conatus*, which the inexperienced must risk from anew. Past experiments can serve as examples to others, but only as an example of the attitude necessary to endure new trials, not as recipes that guarantee specific desired results. Each new situation demands a new *experimentum*, the success (*gloria*) or failure (*calamitas*) of which cannot be predicted.

In the Benedictine Rule and in monastic writings, the term *experimentum* had a meaning that the Benedictine abbot Abelard knew well: in a monastery, experiment and attempt serve as a method of realizing mental principles through action, of proving convictions through deeds. Unlike the modern experiment, which can be equated with *historia*, in the writings of Francis Bacon, for example, the medieval *experimentum* belongs less to the field of science than to practical life. Abelard calls the recording of these kind of experiments *hystoria*.

Most of his contemporaries see *historia* differently, as *ars* or *scientia*. Historians, as Otto of Freising said, see the past as a doctor sees the sickness, against the background of art (*per artis noticiam*) or in the light of wisdom (*per sapientiae gloriam*), not as the patient sees it, *per experientiae miseriam*, in the misery of experience. Abelard is familiar with this traditional sense of *historia* too. He prefaces the story of his love for Heloise by stating his intention to depict the *historia* of his pride and fall, *verius ex ipsa re quam ex auditu*, and *ordine quidem quo (res) processerunt*. That means the *historia* is factually true, it can be separated from fiction and rumour, should be portrayed by eye-witnesses and is bound to chronological order, *ordo temporum*, both as event and as narration. We see that 'story' and 'history', the context and the portrayal, have always been bound to one another, even earlier, when they were not connected by the conformity of awareness, but by the veracity of facts and the truthfulness of witnesses. Besides this, Abelard's literary narration closely follows the chronology. This chronology, however, is not the subject he chooses to deal with. He never names the date of a year, nor does he construct what John of Salisbury called a time sequence (*series temporum*). Abelard could easily have adopted Augustine's terminology, which labels the history of mankind a *series calamitatum*. But the history of mankind for Abelard is located on a time plane wholly different from that of his own life; what he portrays is *historia*, not as *series*, but as *experimentum*.

V

If one were to read Abelard's *Historia calamitatum* as an autobiography, one would probably assume that the most important time plane in the book is the experienced time of the episodes described, a time that would necessarily be defined by the various situations, and be discontinuously and emotionally influenced. Yet, in such a case, the experienced time of writing would also become visible; the author would retrospectively justify his earlier actions and identify his current self with the peaks of his earlier life. Abelard, however, describes his experiences almost exclusively in the time continuum of the past situation, the situation of the acting Abelard, not that of the one writing. His reflections on the future, too, reflect only the aims and expectations of the past Abelard, and what actually came about later was usually wholly different from those expectations. Time is experienced subjectively: for example, he shortens one span of about five years by saying '*in proximo*', but stretches out another by saying '*aliquibus annis*'. The main theme of the book, however, is not the moods of the author, but his interactions with contemporaries.

These descriptions take on eventful characteristics: Abelard, born to a chivalric family, refers to such interactions as war (*conflictus*). For him, social acts, like military actions throughout the twelfth century, have short life-spans; he usually relates them in the Latin historic perfect of episodic incidents, hardly ever in the dramatic or even general present tense. *Tempus* refers to a few moments, two days, several months, at most five years; in his sermon, Abelard inserts a *revolutio temporum* into the events of the thirty years of Christ's life. The reason for this is that every action of one party must be followed by the reaction of another party. Individual deeds bear no significance and are more or less coincidentally caused by Fortune; they are not 'historical events'. The word *eventus* appears only once, referring to the victories that Fortune gave Abelard in his wars, but which did not last long. That is the definition the French word *événement* retained until Voltaire; it means the absolutely unpredictable end of the things that man begins. Therefore, if it is desirable at all to project the term 'event' back into the past, one must not attach to it such epithets as 'teachable', 'repeatable' or 'significant'. Events are not predictable and do not carry significance within themselves. For the sake of caution, it should be emphasized that, for Abelard, the moment is not an epiphany in which divine providence is uncovered in a flash; such a manifestation of the eternal in the moment can be found in the autobiography of the Benedictine abbot Guibert of Nogent around 1115, but not in Abelard's writings.

Human acts and afflictions are influenced by patterns, if not by events: at least Abelard's suffering is, for he is afflicted by the *consuetudo antiqua* in Benedictine monasteries and by the *longevus usus* at cathedral-schools. Yet Abelard does not reject all customs. In schools, for example, it is expedient when peers (*contemporanei*) agree on a common terminology, as opposed to everyone inventing his own vocabulary, which could only provoke conflict and misunderstanding. In monastic life, it comforts Abelard to be received kindly by old acquaintances in monasteries where he had previously resided. But these customs regulate communication with contemporaries, not with generations of past fathers.

Abelard also respects traditions that jump the boundaries between generations, but not all are worth retaining: he would have emphatically rejected the statement of the French Minister of Culture, Maurice Druon, who said that tradition in and of itself is a kind of progress. On the contrary, *usus* and *consuetudo* must constantly justify themselves before the judgement seat of *ratio* and *ingenium*, for it is not long-range patterns that are the acceptable status quo of institutions, as in our modern understanding, but the deeds and inclinations of man, determined by intellectual convictions. These are the causes for short-range behaviour. Abelard usually recalls such acts in the imperfect tense, the tense of habitual or repeated attempts to realize stubborn intentions.

VI

Now I must stop my historical analysis of terminology and relate two of Abelard's experiments, for only they can illustrate accomplishment amid risk, and what it is that combines deed and conviction, action and state, perfect and imperfect tenses, and what constitutes historical time. To reveal the results in advance: time appears here as a background for the behaviour of one or more human communities. For one example, these communities can adhere more to *consuetudo*, or, for another, to *ratio*; the unresolved tension between the two extremes lends Abelard's historical time its multiplicity.

First example: Abelard has become a monk in the Royal Abbey of St Denis; his first theological book has just been burned at the Synod of Soissons in 1121. That makes him suspect to his fellow monks at St Denis. 'After only a few months had passed, coincidence provided an opportunity.' They had had to wait, but if you have conviction, you can wait. 'By chance one day', probably toward the end of 1121, Abelard comes across a passage in Bede's writings in the abbey library, in which Bede claimed that the monastic founder St Dionysius was not the bishop of Athens, but the bishop of Corinth; in that case, he would not be identical with the philosopher Dionysius the Areopagite in Athens, student of the apostle Paul. 'For fun', Abelard shows the passage, which would diminish the apostolic fame of the convent, to a couple of monks standing around. One of the monks asks Abelard if he believes Bede the fraud more than the abbot Hilduin of St Denis, who himself travelled to Greece 300 years earlier and investigated the factual truth of this same question. Abelard answers that he admires Bede's reputation in the Latin church as a whole more than that of the local patriot Hilduin. Now the fellow monks begin screaming that Abelard has always been an enemy of their abbey, and now he is going so far as to insult the French crown. They 'immediately' run to the abbot, who is happy to hear of the 'incident' and 'hurriedly' reports it to the

King. Abelard defends himself by saying that it is not Dionysius' ancestry that is important, but the life he led; however, this does not help him. He is forced to flee the monastery at night, into the Champagne district to Count Theobald IV of Blois, whom he knows from earlier times and who now provides protection for Abelard.

One can see that events quickly change from words to action, then, with increasing momentum, from action to reaction; in the end, the initial coincidence has grown to a *calamitas*. But behind this whirlwind of actions, patterns take shape, basic opposites that have long prospered but which now take on distinct motivation. They are the answer to an ethical question: what takes priority in a convent, traditional claim to glory or current endeavours? This question destroys Abelard's membership in an institution that has existed for centuries. Abelard's fellow monks speak of the object, of the *monasterium nostrum*; Abelard speaks merely of his fellow men, *nos*. The other monks swear by a tradition that can be traced back uninterrupted to the time of the apostles; Abelard refers to the 'communal life of the apostles' that must be imitated 'in our midst'. At the heart of the matter is not what actually happened once, but what should be done now.

Second example: after his dismissal from the Abbey of St Denis, probably in the autumn of 1122, Abelard builds a prayer chapel in isolation near Nogent, and settles in. When his former pupils hear of it, they begin streaming together, erecting tents, subsisting on herbs and brown bread, sleeping on heaps of straw and providing Abelard with his vital needs so that he can teach. These hopes never mature; Abelard describes the acts of the students with his favourite verb, *ceperunt*: they were making a beginning. How it would turn out, Abelard does not say; we do not even know when and why he left the location, perhaps in 1126, perhaps in 1128. This experiment, however, does not end in *calamitas*. It becomes more than a beginning, it becomes a tie to the past, for his students 'truly' imitate the old philosophers that once lived ascetically together; Abelard expressly recalls Plato and his academy and the Pythagoreans. In the middle of his *calamitates*, this decision in favour of such a state of existence is a great comfort for Abelard's life, a *consolatio*. Since the consoling spirit is present among these men, Abelard consecrates his prayer chapel to the Paraclete. This decision, made more than ten years before describing it in his text, is the only one Abelard the author defends in the 'general' present tense; the house that Héloïse's nuns turned into their home around 1129 still bears that name as Abelard writes, as a reminder (*memoria*) of his consolation, and that is 'not contrary to reason, if unfamiliar to habit'. At the location of his earlier consolation, a community flourishes still; for this community of nuns Abelard writes, if not his *Historia* as Durant Robertson supposed in 1972, then at least numerous letters, tracts and hymns. This is where the presence of God governs despite all the whirlwinds of time; God, as Abelard joyfully writes, has done more good for the nuns in one year than Abelard could have brought about in a hundred. For it is at this place near Nogent that people strive not for preservation of tradition, but for intensity of life.

VII

The two communities Abelard describes have two characteristically different concepts of time: for lack of anything better, we can designate them using the pair of opposites that Jacques Le Goff in 1960 termed 'the time of the church' and 'the time of the merchant'. In the Benedictine monastery, the long-winded, liturgical, enduring time dictated by the ringing of the bells was still the rule: time considered to be a gift of God, which coincided so well with the agricultural conditions of life of the early medieval peasants and aristocracy. The practice of resorting to arbitrary traditions of the past flourishes, traditions that are assimilated in a simple merging of perspectives. At the prayer chapel of the Paraclete, which has nearly become the early core of a university, one can already feel something of the nervous hurriedness of the city dweller, who thinks of clock-time as his possession, and sells it for money, 'out of greed for gold and fame', as Abelard admits of himself. The only resort is the subsumption of selected and occasional traditions of the past, which are critically examined before being adopted. I do not want to make this difference in time planes into a new 'straddle-time' around 1130, but only to verify my supposition that historical time was being given a specific shape by the conflict between different ideas of time, and more specifically in the form of intentional confrontation and synchronization, a non-coincidence of the simultaneous. These various fluctuations are largely the general behaviour and opinions of the communities, and the ostensible individualist Abelard is no exception.

His story shows that several different concepts of time clashed in his thinking. Abelard was not at home in any contemporary form of living, neither in the chivalric home of his family nor in the lecture-rooms of his scholarly period nor in the monasteries of his early teaching occupation. In his old age, Abelard did not even have a permanent dwelling; the *Historia* was written on the road somewhere, and the final version of the *Dialectica* was created in the sanctuary which was finally granted him by the Cluny abbey. Abelard did not understand 'time' as a point of intersection of various social institutions, because none of these had become a self-evident constant in his life, and he was not the only one who had to join forcefully in his mind what he had experienced disjointedly in reality.

If this is true, then historical forms of time cannot be forced into schemes, charts, diagrams or time-lines as if they had histories of their own. What standard of measurement is there to distinguish acceleration from prolongation, what charts are there on which to construct curves of progress and retrogression? The standard by which historical communities judge themselves, at least in the Middle Ages, was not the ticking of a natural metronome, but other historical communities. For Abelard, there were two: for the monk, the early Christian community of the apostles and the early monks up to Origen, Jerome and Augustine; for the philosopher, the Athenian community of thinkers in the footsteps of Socrates, Plato and Aristotle. For Abelard, as well as for many other scholars of his time, both model communities merged to become a model era revolving around the birth of Christ and the Mediterranean. Thus, Abelard emphasizes in his *Theologia Christiana* that the great philosopher Dionysius the Areopagite met the apostle Paul in the 'city of Athens, famous for its studies': this is where intellectual and religious movements have their common, simultaneous focal point. The present is isolated from this model era by decay and tradition; it is the job of the present to get out of the rut of chronology and to revitalize the communities of that model time.

Then it was called a reform, later it was to be called Renaissance: changing the present state of affairs to regain that which is always valid. The selection of such model eras and model communities, which, since Joachim of Floris around 1200, could also be predicted in the world's future, is important to the behaviour of man in the present; it, too, represents a tension between the various time-planes, a tension that can liberate conscious historical activities, synchronizations. It, too, is non-coincidence in the simultaneous, and classical man can use their fathers, as modern man can use their forefathers, to justify themselves. Unlike natural and experienced time, historical time cannot be inserted into the chronological scheme when investigating its self-evidence. This self-evidence cannot be separated from its social structure.

Since Abelard's two model eras and communities correspond to his personal experiences and historical situation, the *Historia*, where

they are portrayed, could not have been, at least in its core, composed much later, that is, falsified. The latest defenders of the
falsification theory, the American John F. Benton in 1972 and the
Belgian Hubert Silvestre in 1985, are right in saying that the *Historia* depicts many details of contemporary history inaccurately or
inconsistently; but this would argue against Abelard's authorship
only if he were a modern, specialized historian or philologist who is
also well-versed technically. On examining his general interpretation
of historical time, the interpretation presented in the *Historia* coin-
cides with that in his principal philosophical writings, obviously
because both originate from the same writer, Abelard.

The genuine-or-fake debate has yet more to offer in our investigation of historical time. Silvestre claims the *Historia* was forged
by the author of the *Roman de la Rose*, Jean de Meun, in the late
thirteenth century. True, the *Roman de la Rose* quotes the love-story
of Abelard and Heloise extensively and uses its place in the *Historia*
as an argument for Jean's concept of love and marriage. However,
one must carefully examine the connection in which Jean referred to
Abelard's words: namely, while glorifying the Golden Age of the
dreams of Ovid and Boethius, when neither government nor property were necessary, and thus neither was marriage.

The model age of paradisiacal origin was often used in the late
thirteenth century to awaken a deteriorating society trapped in
the rut of its own institutions, as well as to contradict Joachim's
hope for the future. At this time, the model ages no longer lay in
the middle of history, as they had for Abelard, giving encouraging
examples for contemporary life in human societies. Instead, the
examples were shifted to the extremes of the historical process, to
the beginning or to the end. In other words, Abelard's definition of
historical time was not valid for the rest of the Middle Ages; even
his disciples had to redefine it, a century and a half later. There
could not have been any theory of historical time in the Middle Ages
independent of the historical experiences of those living at the time.

This specific case should show sufficiently that time is not always
a relationship between chronological sequences, but could be understood as the meeting of contemporaries. If this demonstration was
valid, current theories of time should not be discarded as wrong, but
should be considered lop-sided, and it will be necessary to comprehend the various joys and distresses of the men living in various eras
before coming to generally valid conclusions about the process of
their history. This may appear as an escape from the present, but it
is nothing more than a warning against abstraction. In 1887, the
medieval historian Ottokar Lorenz wrote, 'Mommsen knows

Roman history better than Livy did.' This statement refers to the transition of history from *experimentum* to *scientia*. I am tempted to say that whoever studies Abelard will learn more of historical time than Elias did. This statement is based on the regaining of history's experimental side. It also answers Koselleck's question: Why history? Because history can stop us from abstracting our constantly changing condition and making our limited aims appear absolute; it can lift us out of our 'straddling' conceptions about time and put us back on the ground again, in the broad field of human potential.

Part IV
Religious Movements

6

Heretics and Hysteria

I

The mentality of the heretic is so idiosyncratic, so headstrong and at times ludicrous that one would hardly consider him capable of mass appeal, and certainly not in the Christian Middle Ages, which seemed wholly dominated by the Catholic church, and persecuted all heretics. Yet heretical movements during the Western Middle Ages were of almost epidemic proportions, though most of these were short-lived. Others found few followers, but those were especially loyal. In what follows, I will attempt to answer the question as to why the attraction of medieval heresies varied so widely. The reason cannot be found in the fact of the heresy itself, nor in any especially attractive doctrine or lifestyle, for we observe that in some medieval periods, multiple mass heresies appear simultaneously, and at other times there are none. Therefore, heretical mass movements must have required historical conditions. As our sources are quite sparse, and because those available are often inimical to heretic groups, it is a difficult subject to investigate. Only a critical review of the sources can reveal how much medieval heretical movements were seismograph-like indications of the spirit of the various periods; additionally, we will approach the question of what way such movements can be called psychic epidemics. Historians do not feel comfortable thinking of mass movements of the past as epidemics or diseases, and become even more sceptical when contemporary opponents of these movements use such terms. The unprejudiced observer will rely on the statement of Carl Gustav Jung, that understanding is difficult, but condemnation is easy.

II

Around the year AD 1000, the widely nurtured feeling in the West was not a fear of the end of the world, but the desire to compete with the monks of Cluny in overcoming exterior, ritualistic devotion. The devotion of Cluny rejected the world-hating, exaggerated features of early medieval asceticism, especially that of Irish monasticism, and returned to the Benedictine *discretio*, the moderate and balanced life of the devout living in a true brotherhood. It appeared that only contemplative clerics, monks and possibly also hermits could successfully prevail over the world, but hardly the active layman. That is when the case of Leuthard arose, a peasant from the village of Vertus in the Champagne, who was attacked by a swarm of bees while working in the fields; he ran home as if out of his wits, chased out his wife and destroyed the effigy of Christ and the crucifix in the village church. His neighbours thought he was mad, but Leuthard claimed that the bees had enlightened him: all his acts had been performed according to divine instruction. Immediately, numerous followers gathered about him, for they had been waiting for this, the opportunity to follow Christ in the spirit of the Gospel. Of course, the excitement quickly dissipated when Leuthard was called before the diocesan bishop and was unable to defend himself. The public quickly abandoned him as a fool and, humiliated, he jumped into a well in 1004, becoming one of the Middle Ages' few suicides. This brief eruption of Western cultism, the first of its kind known, features a lightning-quick enlightenment that immediately led to radical action and which required no rationale; it excited simple temperaments who were hoping for a living example to follow. This kind of enthusiasm dwindles as soon as a persuasive alternate example, even one with rational arguments, is propagated.

Beside heresies of this kind there had been since about 1017 heresies of another mentality, represented mainly by clerics or nobles in France and Italy. They banded together to live in small communes and adhered to their ideals privately, were organized and proselytized cautiously; they had a dogmatic rationale for their ascetic, world-rejecting way of life. These exclusive communities would sometimes gather undisturbed in secret meetings over decades, and when they were discovered, they remained true to their opinions and were willing, as in 1022 in Orléans, or 1028 in Montfort, to die for them. Unlike heretics of Leuthard's kind, these communes of intellectuals were not geared toward quick diffusion; they required rationality and perseverance.

Since esoteric groups of this type did not force themselves upon the public, they appeared especially dangerous to Catholics of the day. The first reason was that the heresy appeared based not so much on frenzied revolt as on stubborn deliberation; the other was that few precise details were known about those secretive groups, and the worst was feared. Since 1022 a distorted Catholic image had been attached to these insulated, anti-social heretical groups, and it soon inspired a kind of mass hysteria. The presumption was that anyone who could join such groups of unbelievers and meet secretly in cellars and caves was capable of performing the most vile of acts. The devil was said to appear among them, in the shape of a black cat or a giant Negro; his perverse followers bowed to him and kissed him, they put out the lights and in the darkness lost themselves in shameless promiscuity. Children conceived in such orgies were burned, their ashes used in magic potions to ensnare proselytes. Heresy was said to spread secretly, creeping like snakes and crabs; its poison came over you slowly, the virus of heresy. Members would never betray their cruel and disgusting cult, for fear of being revealed; that is why they claimed that all they wanted was to live according to the Gospel. They were deceivers, wolves in sheep's clothing; all heretics performed the same acts, and they all followed the same Manichaean doctrines that had been disproved by the Church fathers long ago. They were like foxes with separate faces, perhaps, but tied together at the tail. Yet, arrogant as Lucifer, they persevered in their stubborn, misleading teachings and decadent, Satanic lifestyles. This Catholic image of heretics, which in many ways persists today, interpreted the heretics' withdrawn isolation as hypocrisy, their determined loyalty as arrogance; it ignored all historical differences between various heretical groups, as well as the commonality of their aim, which conformed to those of the best Christians of the time: for the heretic, too, it was the active realization of the Christian Gospel and spiritual triumph over an imperfect world.

III

In the late eleventh century, the Gregorian church reform made monastic ideals of this kind unnecessary; in the age of the crusades, the central idea was to make the entire world safe for the followers of Christ. During the crusading movement, the masses actually did desire to possess the Holy Land of Christ and the apostles, and they undertook pilgrimages there amid tears and songs of joy, accompanied by ecstatic visions and the massacres of Jews. Not long afterwards, in 1105, other groups, in the budding cities of France and Italy, similarly had the desire to experience the existence of Christ and the commune of the apostles in a tangible way. Petty bourgeois and craftsmen, mostly, let themselves be swayed by wandering preachers to join a new church in the spirit of apostolic poverty. Again, it came to vehement acts of violence against the satiated church of priests, and participating in such violent activities seemed almost to ensure salvation. In 1105 in southern France, the followers of the heretical priest Peter of Bruis destroyed churches, smashed altars, burned crucifixes and beat priests. The friends of the Breton nobleman Eon of Stella broke into churches, burned hermitages and even killed hermits. With fanatical enthusiasm, these heretics adhered to every word from their leader's mouth, they honoured him 'like an angel from heaven', preceded him carrying golden crosses and dressed him in gold brocade. As in the crusades, a certain distance from home was an important element in the new heretical life-style. Women especially followed the wandering preachers in flocks; it is said that in their ecstatic devotion they even drank the bath-water of the Flemish heretic Tanchelm. This account was probably based on a misunderstanding or slander; from it, the indignant clerics drew conclusions as to obscene heretic customs, certainly without justification.

Far more dangerous than an occasional excess, might have been the common idolization of the pure Virgin, who made not only the priesthood, but divinity itself accessible to every layman. Tanchelm went through a public ceremony of marriage to Mary, the mother of God; Eon of Stella not only claimed that his followers were as apostles, he named them so; he considered himself the final judge over life and death. For contemporaries, this liberation from all natural or social chains was the most fascinating thing about the wave of heresy. And the reaction was as irrational as the movement's initial effects: the heretic Peter of Bruis was burned in 1126 by a furious mob, and the heretic Tanchelm was beaten to death in 1115 by a Catholic priest. When, around 1114, two heretics were discovered near Soissons who had supposedly celebrated diabolical orgies and killed children, the clergy were still discussing what action should be taken when the mob dragged the heretics out and burned them, 'with immense joy'. Their leaders dead, these heretical movements collapsed in 1155 at the latest, since they lacked both organization and doctrine.

Once again in the twelfth century, as had happened in the eleventh, quiet and more responsible groups of heretics formed parallel to such brashly violent ones, most importantly the Cathars,

the first real Western sect, the groups gained a footing all over
Europe from about 1143. The Cathars were not dreamers, they had
organized communities with their own hierarchy and formulated
dogmas. Most importantly, they differentiated between the good
spirit of heaven and the satanic god of this world, that is, they
championed a dualism that subordinated Satan to God, and thus
could not be called Manichaean. Beyond all doubt, the Cathars
promoted the good to be found in heaven, and practised radical
abstinence from the world. At first, however, it was not the dogmatic reasoning that attracted such a large number of followers, but the
unprecedented asceticism of these new heretics. Their proselytizing
was accomplished not in the excesses of mass psychology, but secretly, as their opponents claimed, through example and individual
instruction. The conviction of their members enabled the sect to
retain its following over decades, and to draw growing numbers of
converts from families that were already convinced; they converted
whole villages and areas, especially in southern France. The Cathars
did not avoid publicity, but were wary of violence; they talked, at
first with Catholic bishops, later with Dominic and his helpers. They
found followers in clerical and aristocratic circles, people looking for
logical arguments. They abstained from ecstatic mass processions
and provocation, like the Waldensians, a similarly well-organized
sect of strongly convinced followers from around 1173 on.

The Waldensians' answer to the dualistic dogma of the Cathars,
which was swiftly becoming too rigid, was the Christian deed in the
spirit of the Gospel. This, too, was devoid of emotional excess. In
the second half of the twelfth century, following the rise of the early
Scholastics and the dissipation of the Crusade movement, eruptions
of emotion were no longer in favour anyway. Thus the Catholic
reaction was correspondingly moderate; the leading men of the time
held discussions with the heretics, intending not to destroy them, but
to convert them, maybe even to learn something from them. The old
prejudice continued to grow, however, underground and among the
people; but under Pope Innocent III, at the beginning of the thirteenth century, the dialogue between church leadership and the sects
seemed to function well; the Dominicans were learning from the
Catharist apologetics, the Franciscans were doing the same with
Waldensian ethics, and the pope reclaimed parts of the heretical
poverty movement for the church.

IV

During that period, the time of Innocent III, however, the dialogue
was broken off at its peak. The results were disastrous; the religious

conflict degenerated to mass hysteria on both sides. Both sides were
to blame: the mentalities of the over-juridic, centralized church and
of the eschatology-oriented heretics had changed. This basic shift in
the intellectual climate was caused by motives initially banal, local
and political. Cathars surrounding the Count of Toulouse had become politically active and opposed Catholic church politics on its
own ground. In 1208, the result was the killing of a papal legate by
men closely associated with the Count and the Cathars. The murder
sparked off the Albigensian crusade, which released immense hatred
on both sides. One example should demonstrate the opponents'
obdurate attitude: during the assault on Minervae in 1210, the papal
legate offered to free any prisoners who would deny the Catharist
faith. His fanatic Catholic aides, however, were extremely worried
about such excessive generosity. The legate assured them, however:
'There is no reason to fear, not many will convert!' He was right:
140 Cathars went voluntarily to the stake.

Following the Albigensian war, however, the Cathars' public
attraction sank considerably, not only because they were being
persecuted, but also because other heresies better fulfilled the expectations of the time. The heretics of the Later Middle Ages
adopted two scholars as their ideological founders, both of whom
had previously died at peace with the church, in 1206 and 1202: the
Parisian philosopher Amalric of Bène and the southern Italian abbot
Joachim of Floris. Both had insulated themselves from the responsibilities of practical reality and were fascinated by the future and
the approaching end of the world. Both believed that the physical
church of the flesh would end in a few years or decades, and an Age
of the Holy Spirit would begin. Once again, these doctrines resulted
in ecstatic spiritual fanaticism, both among Joachim's Franciscan
heirs, the Spirituals, who derived enough courage from poverty in
the holy spirit to suffer anything, and even more so among Amalric's
pantheistic heirs, for whom the spirit could even justify evil – in fact,
it carried everything, including evil, within itself. The self-idolization
of a man who has denied himself for God was no longer based on
fanatical deeds, as in the twelfth century, but on esoteric knowledge.
Thus, pantheism spread slowly, in small circles, but it was difficult
to stamp out once it took root, and take root it did: all over
Germany and in the Netherlands, among the Beguines and the
Beghards, among the Brethren and Sisters of the Free Spirit and
other loosely organized groups. The personal experience of God led
no longer to mass movements, but to the heretical mysticism of the
individual.

Again, it was the nearly invisible tendencies of the heretics that
especially disturbed their Catholic opponents. And again, the

rumours of frightening secret rites arose; in 1233 they were officially denounced in a bull by Pope Gregory IX, the same Pope who instituted the papal inquisition of mendicant orders. To him, the dark, anti-social elements that prospered secretly in heresy and iniquity were like a deadly plague that had to be exterminated. As late as 1250, one German inquisitor was still unwilling to participate in the slander of his rivals; he refused to believe that heretics kissed cats and frogs and performed lewd acts. But two generations later, Bernard Gui, a southern French inquisitor, openly expressed his belief that heretics habitually practised diabolical promiscuity under cover of night. It is soon thereafter that we find, in inquisitory files, the first confessions of satanic orgies, forced out of captives under torture. That inquisitors believed heretics capable of every possible perversion was explained by the fact that neither side was talking with the other. Some of these inquisitors may really have seen themselves as 'saviours of the soul'; but their saving art – like all medicine of the time – consisted almost wholly of burning and cutting. The inquisitors' fanaticism is illustrated by a certain Dominican from Pavia, who, though tormented by advanced rheumatism, still travelled on horseback to forty-six towns and cities in one year; yet in twelve years of office, he found only five heretics he could burn at the stake.

For their part, the heretics went underground. In one night of 1242, Cathars murdered ten southern French inquisitors; one of the killers later said he had never experienced so much joy in his entire life. But before the tribunal, they lied and broke their oaths as much as they possibly could, thus confirming the suspicions of hypocrisy and perversion; by now, they really did meet at night in caves and forests, to avoid being discovered. There, in secret meetings, they turned the old Catholic notion of heretics around and claimed it was the prelates who were the true heretics, all of them hungry wolves and enemies of God, Pharisees filled with arrogance and hypocrisy, not practising what they preached. In truth, the early-fourteenth-century church, with its fiscal bureaucracy, was no longer an example of good Christianity. The heretics, too, however, were becoming less and less concerned with Christian deeds than with their dogmas and the excesses of emotion. Both sides lost what they had to give to each other.

V

What could the church have learned, for example, from the flagellants? This was a group that had no plans at all for the present world, and therefore had no clearly defined doctrine, no hierarchy and hardly any liturgy; they were awaiting the end of the world, and their way of living certainly suggested something far beyond day-to-day life. In the year 1260, which Joachim of Floris had predicted would be the year of destruction for the church of the flesh, a hermit appeared in Perugia claiming to have heard voices from heaven; everyone was to repent if they did not want to be destroyed. Thousands followed the visionary and left their homes. The flagellants made long marches to Bohemia and Alsace, each lasting thirty-three and a half days, and along the way they beat themselves bloody several times daily. It was mainly petty bourgeois and craftsmen, weavers, cobblers and smiths that marched through the landscape holding flags and lighted candles, singing fervent hymns and with exalted demeanour, attracting many to join them. The end of the world seemed near, perhaps the Messiah was too, and whoever flagellated himself needed no other kind of repentance. The asceticism of the masses, exaggerated to the point of self-salvation, collapsed as early as 1262, though later it was to flame up during the Great Plague of 1348 and several times again during the fifteenth century, accompanied by Jewish pogroms. But one can hardly suppose an organized sect of flagellants continued through those periods.

The old concept of apostolic living, too, was ecstatically reinterpreted in the thirteenth century, especially by the Italian group of Apostolici. Again, in 1260, the epochal year of the Spirituals, they began leading a life of poverty and begging; the founder of the sect sold his house, gave the proceeds to some children playing nearby and began wandering. As the century neared its end, the Apostolici believed that they had done enough, and that the time for the church of the spirit had come. Their new leader Dolcino, the son of a priest, claiming he was sent from God to be prince of the Apostolici, gathered thousands of followers and began plundering churches, this time using organized storm-troop detachments. The church of the flesh was to be destroyed, the chains of the body to be cast off forever. Dolcino considered himself wholly pure, though he participated in intimate relations with some of his beautiful female followers: this, he even taught, was greater than the resurrection of a dead man, and thus greater than the greatest of Christ's miracles. The unrestrained self-idolization of the Apostolici in their poverty, who followed their leader's example with all the strength at their command, transported Dolcino's followers into blind rapture; it was finally necessary to burn or otherwise destroy them in a crusade organized especially for that purpose in 1307. None of them, facing the stake, converted, but on the other hand, no one tried seriously to convert them. For by then they were burning the Franciscan Spirituals too, who wanted nothing more than to embrace the poverty of the Christian church: they were burned at the stake by order of a pope who was more financier than cleric. This same atmosphere of mutual suspicion and reproach, of inflexible legal sentences on the one hand, indescribable yearning on the other, would soon become a feature of the witch craze.

VI

The number of examples could easily be expanded, but I think we can make general conclusions based on these. The heretical movements of the Middle Ages were not especially predisposed towards psychic epidemics, as long as (and because) they fitted into the framework of church and general religious history of the time. They formed and spread because the Catholic church would listen to new religious demands only hesitantly, or within the community of clerics. Under these conditions, heresies became the active, radically progressive wing of a religious movement that would usually enter into the church at some later point anyway. The Church and heretical movements participated in religious competition and debate, correcting and goading each other. Within the church community, those same extreme heretical impulses were weaker, but fruitful none the less.

Heresies evolved into mass movements only when society was accordingly predisposed, in times of religious agitation and upwardly striving social classes: in the early twelfth century, at the peak of the enthusiasm for Crusades, and in the later thirteenth century, when the bourgeois of the cities were becoming self-dependent. In times like these, mass hysteria could erupt when, with no rational arguments, wandering preachers stirred up crowds with a call to action, tearing them loose from their homes by giving them a living example to follow. Irrational characteristics swam to the surface then: violent acts against those who thought differently, and, correspondingly, the elevation of one's self-image to self-idolization. The rules governing Christian faith and human society were quickly discarded when deemed necessary in the service of a higher ideology. As quickly as such heretical movements spread over wide areas, so were their effects short-lived: they usually ended with the death of their leader. Soon after, the initiatives of the heretics were reconsidered by the church, sometimes, happily, even practically adopted;

in other cases, heretical movements were replaced by newer, stricter sects. In the long run structured communities were far superior to formless masses, as was their historical significance, as long as they valued coherent religion and intellectual receptiveness.

A second form of mass hysteria, one that, to me, seems far worse, is when dialogue between church and heretics is neglected. That is what happened with the common people at the beginning of the heretical movements, in the early eleventh century, and with their leaders two centuries later. Both parties made the respective enemy into a bogey-man and believed themselves largely free of any responsibility for humanity and understanding. The church inquisition and the esoteric ecstasy of the heretics motivated each other respectively; they both radically damaged the religious life of the later Middle Ages, and afterwards mutual reconsideration was impossible. It was the rigid antithesis of friend-foe that made the mass hysteria so destructive; on both sides, the transgression of norms found in the Christian Gospel and a disdain for a behaviour most suitable to reasonable and social persons were the consequences when Christian and humane attitudes were reduced to self-justification and slander of one's opponent.

VII

The cry for leniency in faith and humane openness sounds very modern and appears to have little place in an age of unconditional belief like the Middle Ages. Certainly, many late medieval authors teach that true belief is a stranger to tolerance. But when, around 1040, when Western cultism was first on the rise, Bishop Wazo of Liège was asked what should be done with the heretics, this shepherd of souls answered that God had patience with sinners; therefore, he would let the tares grow together in the field with the wheat until the last day. Man, he said, born of dust as he is, should not anticipate the judgement of the Creator with the sword; for what is ripped out today as tares might have become grain as early as tomorrow. Because man in his limitation cannot tell the difference between wheat and tares, Wazo asked his brethren in office to show, especially to the heretics, the kind of patience that characterizes the doctor and the true saviour of souls. In Wazo's words, his office was 'not to bring death, but to give life'.

7

The Origins of the Witch-craze in the Alps

I

In the face of bleak prospects for Europe's future, there are many who comfort themselves by proudly looking back on Europe's past. Among the main preconceptions of our view of history is the supposition that 500 years ago, on the heels of a Middle Ages filled with oppression and barbarism, the spirit of modern Europe established the dominion of reason. Humanism, princely states, early capitalism, voyages of discovery and the Reformation are thought to be the great breakthroughs that created our world. One example of this presumption can be found in the first volume of the German historical encyclopaedia *Propyläen Geschichte Europas*, edited by Hellmut Diwald, which appeared in 1975 with the daring title *Anspruch auf Mündigkeit, um 1400–1555* ('The Right to Emancipation, circa 1400–1555'). This book claims that Europe emancipated the world in the fifteenth century. A brilliant but one-sided work, it discusses princes, generals, scholars, bankers, merchants and reformers in detail, but hardly considers normal burghers and peasants at all. Taking a look at the index under 'witchcraft', for example, all we learn is that around 1430, Joan of Arc, the Maid of Orleans, 'was revered by half France as a saint and hated by half England as a witch', but was neither one nor the other. Was this saint/witch pattern nothing more than a brief regression into the Dark Ages? Were there, after Joan of Arc, no further witch-burnings? Did Europe really become emancipated in 1500?

Of course, Anna Spülerin from Ringingen, a scullery maid, as her last name indicates, was not as famous as the Maid of Orleans and does not appear in Diwald's book; her story was that of an average citizen, not twenty miles north of Biberach. In 1507, her mother was burned at the stake in Blaubeuren as a witch; in impotent fury, her daughter swore to her neighbours in Ringingen that they would soon regret having murdered her mother. It was not long before twenty-three neighbours banded together, seized Anna and dragged her as a witch to the prison in Blaubeuren. Judges from Ulm and Tübingen soon arrived, interrogated and tortured her, but could prove nothing and finally had to set her free. The woman's health was ruined, so she dragged her Ringingen neighbours to court and sued for damages, claiming that they had known that she would come to harm and intended her to do so. The case went from the court in Ulm to the Imperial Cameral Court in Frankfurt, and from there to new trials at the court of the imperial city of Biberach; by 1518, the case was still unresolved. We do not know if or how it was ever concluded. How does the 'Right to Emancipation' apply to this case? The Ringingen burghers were no fools from the back woods, they constituted a free community with a long-standing legal tradition, and had good contacts with the University of Tübingen via their pastor. The judges from Ulm, Tübingen, Frankfurt and Biberach were even more emancipated and modern in Diwald's sense. Nevertheless, they all believed in witchcraft and were overcome with panicky fear for their life and safety; it was to appease this fear that they destroyed the life of one of their fellow creatures. How was this possible?

A convincing answer on the whole was provided by the English historian Hugh Trevor-Roper (later Lord Dacre) in 1967. His thesis is that intellectual progress in the sixteenth and seventeenth centuries was narrowly intertwined with social relapses; indeed, that the pride of the modern age, the scientific method, was the cause of the disgrace of Europe, of the collective witch-crazes (originally in his book of 1967, *Religion, the Reformation and Social Change*). 'In those seemingly rational years,' Trevor-Roper writes, 'the light was retreating before the darkness.' His thesis, which has a suffocating effect on our current awareness of history, is obviously correct as long as Trevor-Roper's definition of witch-craze is acceptable, and it is. He is not referring to oppressive superstition, which is present everywhere and at all times: magic, conjuring up of bad weather, communicating with spirits and magic healing. He is referring to thought-structures, limited both in period and location, that make a system of demonology out of a superstition. It was not Anna's naive mother in Ringingen, who might have been picking healing herbs at full moon and murmuring magic formulas, who was responsible for the witch-craze, but the subtle theologian from Tübingen, who wrote in a Latin tract that the woman was acting in the service of hell and to the harm of all Christianity; just as responsible was the learned jurist from Ulm who ordered her tortured and executed. This is evident for the sixteenth century and for the case of Anna Spülerin; it was hardly significant what the poor woman actually did or believed, but what the scholars got her to say under torture.

For the origins of the witch-crazes in the early fifteenth century, however, this thesis is insufficient. Somehow, the intellectuals must have known actual witches from somewhere; they could not have simply thought them up. Trevor-Roper has an explanation for that too, but it is unsatisfactory. He claims that the origin of European superstition lies in the Pyrenees and especially in the Alps, a final retreat for the archaic image of the world, a borderline for modern progress. Even Christianity, he says, could not penetrate those isolated mountain valleys, pagan superstition was never fully expelled. The imagination of the Alpine inhabitants was especially prone to hallucinations and pathological nervous conditions; imposing natural phenomena such as storms, avalanches and roaring glaciers easily led them to believe in the workings of demons. This religious mentality was encouraged by their social organization. The individualistic grazing economy of the mountain farmers in the Middle Ages never adopted feudalism, with its property ownership and distribution of the work force, while in the plains, feudalism laid the basic pattern for modern European society. In this way, the Alps remained a kind of European ghetto, a breeding ground for religious and social backwardness. Conversely, the disappointed population of the flatland had given up their initial missionary attempts in the mountain regions, making the mountain inhabitants into scapegoats for disruptions of the progress of modern ideas and social structure, and began a kind of crusade against the Alpine peoples. The European witch-crazes were nothing more than the ideology of this crusade from the plains, the proof of a conflict between two incompatible cultures, a pagan–farmer–Alpine culture and a Christian–feudal–bourgeois one.

What is most irritating about this thesis, for the historian, is that it is so logical. It makes social history confirm what cultural history has always claimed, that the Alps are a hotbed of superstition, in direct antithesis to the urban centres of rationality. That is what the Dominican John Nider of Basle taught as early as 1437, just as the anti-clerical American Henry Charles Lea did in about 1900. Trevor-Roper added a nuance to this antithesis only by trying to make self-conscious urban intellectuals feel guilty, which is their favourite pose anyway. The self-reflection of men of letters now eagerly precludes any consideration of the other side, that of the

Alpine inhabitants. Is that not a prejudice, an ideology similar to that of the witch-hunts?

In his book of 1972, *Witchcraft in the Middle Ages*, Jeffrey Russell protested, and rightly so, against Trevor-Roper's opinion that witchcraft is most widespread in remote regions. He emphasized that its roots had always been deeper in the most densely populated, thoroughly industrialized and intellectually most progressive areas of Europe. Russell was unwilling to include the Alpine region in this category. 'The earliest forms of witchcraft did appear in the Alps, when witches and heretics escaped persecution by retreating into the protective mountain regions.' Witches and heretics? Russell really believed that witchcraft, which he viewed not as a mania but as a practised conviction, had issued from heresy; thus he looked for witches where heretics gathered most densely, in the cities of the flatland. Here again, the historian must object. Belief in witchcraft certainly did appear in the Alps earlier than anywhere else in Europe, that is, in regions that as yet held no refuge for heretics, and in forms that displayed no sign of heresy. If that is true, one must examine more closely what both Trevor-Roper and Russell agree on, that the Alpine region is a forever backward area. Is Alpine life really largely isolated from the history of the rest of Europe? Are not remoteness and backwardness phenomena restricted to locality and period, like witch-hunting itself? And were the Alps, at the beginning of the witch-craze around 1400, really backward? Was not the Swiss Confederation at the time as modern as the urban communities in Northern Italy and Upper Rhine, as the monarchies of the Valois and Hapsburgs?

Yet, if the Alps in the early fifteenth century were not a kind of ghetto, why did the first witch-burnings take place there, between Lower Valais and Valle Leventina? And why did the German word for witchcraft, *Hexerei*, which is still used today, first appear in the Swiss Alps, in Lucerne, in 1419? To answer these questions, we have to do what Trevor-Roper and Russell both neglected to do, that is, attend to the dirty details of the first witchcraft trials and put them into the historical context of their specific locations, instead of spending time on religious and social history at large. To do this, we must ignore the intelligent book of 1977 about the origins of witchcraft, *Aus der Zeit der Verzweiflung, Zur Genese und Aktualität des Hexenbildes*, in which Gabriele Becker and others portrayed the social situation of women; for the main participants in the earliest cases are men, not women. The otherwise attractive book of 1985 about the theology behind witch-hunting, *Der Teufel in der Wissenschaft*, in which Gerhard Prause unfurled a panorama of church doctrinal opinion, offers as little help; for at the pivotal points in the persecutions we find laymen, not clerics. Finally, we must ignore the lustfully lachrymose witch cult of our day and its hallucinations of the Middle Ages, since we will be concerned with the persecution of peasants who had no time for self-indulgent fancies. What did the hunters and the hunted want, then, if they cared neither for a theory of God's creation nor for improvements in human society? That is the central question. I can answer it here only rudimentarily, by investigating the oldest and most interesting Alpine case. Reports of it have been circulating for nearly the past 500 years and can be found discussed in almost any book about witches; nevertheless, it contains an abundance of surprising clues which have so far been overlooked.

II

The scene of the first Alpine witch trials around 1400 was the Upper Simme Valley in the Bernese Oberland. The source of the Simme River is in the south of the valley at Wildstrubel, and some thirty miles north it flows into the lake of Thun. Along this short stretch, the settlements have a variation in altitude of about 3,000 ft; the middle of the valley around Boltigen and Zweisimmen is some 2,800–3,000 ft high; most of the surrounding mountains surpass the 6,500 ft level. The Simme Valley is steep, narrow, shadowy, has an abundance of forest and snow, many waterfalls and much flooding. A number of other valleys and passes continue on to the west and south, but beyond Jaun Pass, Col du Pillon and Rawil Pass is the French-speaking region: Gruyères, Vaud and Upper Valais. The Simme Valley lies on the language border and was settled in the ninth century by Alemannics who had come up through the region around the lake of Thun and was still biased toward the German-speaking north. Traffic passing through to the south was sparse; the Middle Ages came to main passes, the Great St Bernard and St Gotthard, via other roads. Practically the only thing known about the Simme Valley today is its main product, Simme Valley spotted cattle. Cattle breeding and Alpine meat and milk products have dominated the Simme Valley economy since as early as 1400. But in those days they were relatively new.

It was during the late fourteenth century that the Simme Valley farmers went over like everyone else on the rainy Alpine north face, to grazing and cattle-breeding, gradually abandoning their tradition-al activities, grain-farming and sheep-breeding. In so doing, the inhabitants of the Simme Valley isolated themselves economically, for their neighbours to the south in Upper Valais remained self-sufficient as of old. The conversion of high-altitude grain fields to hay fields around 1400, that is, the formation of today's Swiss shepherding country, meant a renunciation of the local self-sufficiency that had survived until then; now the Simme Valley could export cattle, but had to import grain. It was impossible in this new Alpine grazing economy to survive as an independent community, much less as an individual; survival required intensive market ties to neighbouring regions, in this case to the three-field system of the Bernese Mittelland to the north. This market interdependability required the development of available markets in the valley itself, which, like the quickest-growing communities of Erlenbach and Zweisimmen, lived off the cattle trade. The transformation must have cost the Simme Valley farmers a great deal of restlessness and insecurity, and this is where the witchcraft had its roots. It is important to point out, however, that witchcraft was not discovered up in the isolated barnyards of poor mountain shepherds and dairy-maids, but down in the wealthy market districts, in the focal point of country communication.

These church villages had been Christianized long before by the diocese of Lausanne. From the tenth century on, most of the Simme Valley had been part of the property of an Alsatian Benedictine abbey with the responsibility of tending to the serfs' religious needs. The oldest church in the valley, in Erlenbach, had been built on a Carolingian foundation. Since the thirteenth century, the villages of the valley, about thirty in all, had been organized into six parishes: in this sense, the witches were not isolated from civilization; the home of the sorcerer Stadelin, the community of Boltigen, had an old parish church. In addition, during the High Middle Ages, the cloister of Därstetten flourished in the Lower Simme Valley; thus, an abbey was not lacking either. Nor were castles. Today, the ruins of seven strongholds can be seen in the Lower Simme Valley; in the Upper Simme Valley, near Boltigen and Zweisimmen, stood the four most powerful strongholds of the entire valley, again in close proximity to the sorcerers.

Feudalism was not only present, it practically rampaged through-out the fourteenth century, through the feuds of the local nobility, changes of government, the distribution of sovereign rights, and above all in the extravagance and indebtedness of the barons, who had to squeeze all they could out of their serfs and, in the end, were still forced to sell their castles and rights. Take the fortress Sim-menegg, just above the witch village of Boltigen, constructed in the twelfth century. At the beginning of the fourteenth century, it belonged to the barons of Weissenburg, whose family seat was further north in the Lower Simme Valley, near the castle of Wimmis. There, in the Lower Simme Valley, financial straits forced the Weissenburgs to acquiesce to a Bernese military advance in 1334, but at least they did not have to abandon their seat of power; around the same time, they sold the property of Simmenegg in the Upper Simme Valley to the barons of Brandeis, who had their home further north, in the Habsburgs' Entlebuch. But they had run out of money by 1337. They were bought up, as it were, by prosperous Berne, but were able to keep Castle Simmenegg and the village of Boltigen until 1374. Then the estates were fought for and gained by Rudolf of Aarburg, who came from even further north, from Habsburg-owned Aargau. Finally, in 1391, he sold the estate directly to the city of Berne, and there it stayed. The history of the castle Mannenburg, above Zweisimmen, was similar; only here, the dominant influence was from western Switzerland. The barons of Strättligen, whose home was the lake of Thun region, sold Mannenburg in 1336 to the counts of Gruyères, who in turn sold it to a citizen of the Habsburgs' Fribourg in 1356; he then sold it in 1378 to his home city of Fribourg, which was forced to hand over the ownership of Zweisimmen to Berne in 1389.

This characterizes the political history of the Simme Valley. In the early fourteenth century, it still belonged to the native nobility. Their impoverishment led to an invasion by foreign nobility with Habsburg connections, who originated in northern and western Switzerland. These feudal lords, on the other hand, were quickly forced out by the rich bourgeois cities in the north and west, Berne and Fribourg. The battle of Sempach in 1386, in which Fribourg helped the Habsburgs and were defeated by the Swiss Confederate Bernese, decided the fate of the Upper Simme Valley; from 1389 to 1391 it came under the direct rule of Berne. That the agitated history of the region had thereby been settled once and for all was something no inhabitant of the Simme Valley could have known, especially since the Lower Simme Valley was able to retain nominal independence of Berne until 1449. Around 1400, the new provincial government of the Upper Simme Valley was a Bernese enclave far to the south.

This brief sketch should suffice to shatter Trevor-Roper's principal supposition. The witch-infested Alpine region was, around 1400, anything but backward and isolated. Even superficially, the Simme Valley with its villages, cattle markets, parish churches, abbeys and castles gave the impression of a typical late-medieval landscape. Structurally, it was on the verge of a most decisive turn in history,

the transformation from feudal fragmentation to market interdependability, and its initiation into a multi-territorial state. Its
integration into modern economic patterns and politics could only
have plummeted the Upper Simme Valley, which until then had been
organized feudally, into a cultural and social crisis, of which witchcraft was a part; but one cannot pretend, as Trevor-Roper does, that
the roots of witchcraft were solely cultural and social.

The same political and economic prerequisites are equally as visible in the three other centres of witchcraft, for example in the Upper
Valais witch-hunts between 1428 and 1447: the valley was involved
in a tug-of-war between the Duke of Savoy and the Bishop of Sion.
The 'Seven Counties' of the Rhone valley, with their self-confident
trading traditions, used witch trials to grind down the ruling feudal
nobility and peasantry of two neighbouring valleys. In Briançon, the
market town on the road to the Mont Genèvre, pass, a witch-hunt
took place between 1428 and 1437: the city was paralysed by the
anarchy of the nobility. In the Valle Leventina, on the road to the St
Gotthard Pass, there were witch trials between 1432 and 1459: the
region was fought over by the duchy of Milan and the canton of Uri.
Here, both states established the authority of their courts by means
of witch trials in border settlements. To ignore these political back-
grounds is to misinterpret the mentality of the early witch-hunters
and to place them in the wrong social category. Nearly all early
witch-hunts were staged not by clerics or intellectuals, but by politicians and laymen, by men of action.

III

Thus it was in the Upper Simme Valley. As their first provincial
governor for the newly gained estates of Simmenegg and Zweisimmen, the city of Berne appointed a member of their city council,
Peter of Gruyères, from a line of patricians which was already
famous and still exists today. He resided not in one of the old noble
castles, Simmenegg or Mannenburg, but further up the valley in
the thinly settled land surrounding Castle Blankenburg, which he
appears to have been the one to convert from a farmhouse to a
castle. As castellan, he managed the military integration of the
Upper Simme Valley into the Bernese territory, and as provincial
governor, he organized it judicially. Politically, the governor's hands
were tied, for the farmers of the Simme Valley country were granted
generous rights of self-determination. Peace reigned following the
battle of Sempach, and so the governor's activities were limited to

jurisdiction. This, too, was largely predetermined by the valley's traditional laws; in other words, to establish Bernese jurisdiction, he needed unprecedented legal material.

The best opportunity was witch trials. What Peter of Gruyères did in this regard we have from his own records. In 1406, after fourteen years of office, he had laid down his function in the Simme Valley and returned to the city council in Berne. Some time after 1406, he met the Swabian Dominican John Nider and related his experiences to him. Nider, who in the meantime had become prior in the Dominican convent at Basle, included Gruyères' account in his Latin book *Formicarius*, which he wrote during the Basle Church Council from 1435 to 1437. The book exists today and examines witchcraft in the Upper Simme Valley; it is one-sided, but detailed, and not only about the facts, but about the background as well.

Gruyères, unlike Nider, saw witchcraft not as a specifically Alpine vice, but one rooted in primitive times; he pointed out that its history had arisen about sixty years previously; in other words, counting back from the time of the composition of the *Formicarius*, in the years from 1375 to 1377, shortly before the Bernese triumph. Separately and independently, the origin of witchcraft was located in the Dauphiné in 1375; a while later, its beginnings were estimated at around 1358 on the basis of the files of witch trials in Como. In the Alpine area, experts are in surprising agreement about the decades between the plague of 1348 and the papal schism in 1378; I will return to these European contexts later. In the governor's opinion, one man founded witchcraft in the Upper Simme Valley; he was named 'Scavius', the Scabby Man. It would be tempting to think of Scavius as leprous, but he was no outsider in the community, but a powerful and feared man who belonged to the valley's upper social stratum; otherwise, his enemies would not have had such difficulty in persecuting him, nor would they have made such a great effort.

He boasted publicly that he could escape any enemy simply by turning into a mouse. In fact, he did escape his hunters again and again, though they had many people and efficient weapons at their disposal. In the end, they caught him. He was sitting in an inn by the window, carefully keeping one eye on the door, as always; his enemies crashed unexpectedly through the window and ran him through with swords and pikes. If they had been executing a death sentence by the official court, Gruyères would have mentioned it. As it is, however, the scene fits very well into the political order of the Upper Simme Valley around 1380. The successive castle lords in Simmenegg and Mannenburg had let public control slip from their hands. In the villages, government had deteriorated to self-help and clan revenge, those bloody private wars between peasant families to which the Swiss Confederation had tried to put an end in 1291. Scavius was not the strongest in his area: his only weapon was cunning.

The more timid among his neighbours probably avoided him as the Scabby Man and decried him as a disturber of the peace; yet he had friends, at least one, a man named Hoppo. As Scavius repeatedly escaped his enemies, it became easier and easier to believe that he was a sorcerer, who, as in the tale of Puss-in-Boots, could change into a mouse. This fairy-tale association was a common European tradition, and as well known to the urban knight as to the mountain farmers, a folk belief, not a feared occult phenomenon. It was not until later that mice became witches' animals; when they did, curious spectators would gather at witch-burnings to see whether the victim would turn into a mouse and leap from the flames. In the Simme Valley, none of these features were present. The transformation into an animal was merely a way for the hunted to protect himself; it did not yet serve the purpose of bringing harm to others, as it was to do in Upper Valais in 1428, where sorcerers were said to change into raging wolves. Scavius had no such satanic element. He left Hoppo behind as his pupil; of this man, Gruyères could say nothing more than that he, in his turn, instructed the sorcerer Stadelin. Here, as almost everywhere in early Alpine witchcraft, it was men who dominated; not until the late fifteenth century did the fear of witches concentrate on women and on the suspicion of sexual orgies. In comparison, early witchcraft seemed masculinely sober and politically active.

IV

This was a feature it quickly lost: the sorcerer Stadelin became a symbol for this transformation. Gruyères knew him personally, interrogated and burned him; Stadelin, therefore, must have lived between 1392 and 1406. He lived in Boltigen under the dominion of Simmenegg, but probably not in one of the richly decorated farmers' houses for which the village is famous today. That Stadelin was not among the wealthy farmers and cattle-traders is hinted at by his name: he had a 'little stable'. He was not, however, impoverished: he owned several parcels of property and harvested not only hay, but grain; that is to say, he farmed in the old style, tilling fields and breeding cattle at the same time. Instead of political interest, he was dominated by economic ambition and by jealousy of the wealthy. He was said to make the horses of the rich go mad whenever they were mounted, and not many could afford a horse. The most important witchcraft of which Gruyères accused him, however, had nothing to do with animals, but with crops. Stadelin was supposedly capable of invisibly transporting a third of all manure, hay and grain from other fields to his own. The trial in Valle Leventina in 1432 also concerned a third of a hay crop. What really happened is easily imagined: Stadelin's fields had far better yields than those of his neighbours, and this aroused suspicion. Moreover, Stadelin seemed capable of damaging crops and houses of other farmers with hailstorms and lightning bolts. Accusations such as these are, for us, clues to a merciless war of rivalry in the village; every crop failure appeared to point to the wickedness of malicious neighbours.

A later case, which occurred in 1459 at Steinberg near the Furka Pass, makes the tendency even more obvious. There, wolves chased grazing cattle down a steep slope, killing two cows. A fox throttled the swine of two farmers; other farmers suffered rock falls and avalanches on their fields and houses. Members of the Regly family were injured suspiciously often. It was not the Alpine natural phenomena themselves, but the frequent and specific damage they caused that made farmers suspicious and encouraged them to seek the origins in jealous neighbours. This is where they found their witches: not from the richest, nor from the poorest in the village, but from those who were aspiring and self-dependent, who cared little for others in the way they worked and thought. Obviously, the complaints against Stadelin were made by his neighbours in Boltigen and founded in the economic difficulties of this transformative period of the village.

But the judge, Gruyères, had other worries. How was it possible to prove judicially that the neighbours were right, that Stadelin directed hailstorms to other farmers' fields? The provincial governor had the sorcerer interrogated; after the fourth torture session, he confessed. He admitted standing out in an open field and, murmuring certain formulas, calling upon the lord of all devils and asking him to send a lesser devil. When the lesser devil appeared, one had to sacrifice a black hen by throwing it into the air at a crossing. Then, the demon would inflict the desired damages. Whether Stadelin's statements reflected a practice that was actually performed or whether it was put into his mouth during the torture is hard to tell; at any rate, it contained elements of old folk magic meant to manipulate weather. The black hen as a sacrifice to the devil is also well known: in Upper Valais in 1428 it was replaced by a black lamb. Nevertheless, we are no longer talking about heathen black magic here. For heathen magic, it was enough to speak a magic phrase or throw stones into water, or pour a magic brew out onto a field; immediately, the storm would appear. Stadelin's statements were ignorant of this magical automatism; the sorcerer had to go through hell's hierarchy and could never be sure that the devils would really perform his wishes. And besides that, the coming hailstorm could be changed to harmless rain by a simple prayer to the crucified Christ, that is, by means of a Christian antidotal magic, information that Stadelin provided, voluntarily this time, without torture. The sorcerer himself did not consider the practices he was accused of to be simple natural magic; even in the Alps, Christianity had instituted a basic change in folk beliefs. As Aaron Gurevich proved in 1981, it was not until the arrival of Christianized magic that witch-crazes were possible at all. In the Simme Valley, the participants viewed their economic problems as rounds in the eternal battle between Christ and Lucifer.

Let us examine the social conflicts that resulted from the transformation in the Upper Simme Valley. Gruyères told of a man who had a house there on the river Simme. At some time after 1406, he travelled to the city of Fribourg, sat down with some drinking companions in a tavern and suddenly said that he 'saw' an acquaintance at home stealing the fishing rod he had meant to fish with later. The story teller was imprisoned and, after confessing that his clairvoyance was witchcraft, burned at the stake in accordance with local, that is, Bernese law. Simme Valley farmers had become mobile, they were attracted to the more pleasant urban markets; they sought and found contact with others outside their village. However, it was their mobility that ruined the social rules back home; in an intact village community, no one would have thought of stealing an unwatched fishing rod. In the Simme Valley, the man had never before been accused of witchcraft, obviously because he had always conformed to the conventions of the village. But outside the village, he lacked the protection of long, trusting acquaintanceship; an unthinking drunken remark, and his audience reported the country stranger to their urban officials. As the world of the Upper Simme Valley opened up, it encountered unaccustomed suspicion outside, and began collapsing inside; the witch-craze was an accompanying phenomenon of opening, not of isolation.

Another example illustrates this in an especially macabre manner. Gruyères had imprisoned a woman as a witch; her apparently well-respected husband was not included in the accusation. He asked a fortune-teller in the valley whether or not his wife would survive the trial. This woman affirmed emphatically that his wife would be freed, and the husband, beaming, related this the next day to Gruyères, the judge, probably to steer his judgement in the right direction. Gruyères must have made a sceptical face; at any rate, the accused woman summoned Gruyères to her cell shortly thereafter and told him that by means of witchcraft she had seen her husband go to the fortune-teller. However, she said, the fortune-teller's positive answer was wrong: she knew very well that Gruyères would sentence and burn her the next day. The judge immediately related this prophecy to the husband, probably in order to prepare him for the worst; the husband, laughing, said that he was now really curious as to which of the witches would be right. The next day his wife was burned at the stake.

Gruyères related the story as though he had not already known what sentence he would give the next day and had had nothing to do with his prisoner's prophecy against herself, which had been promptly confirmed the next day. We can see why people ran to fortune-tellers: with his witch trials, the governor subverted the traditional legal order in the valley and the farmers could not reasonably predict the outcome of his proceedings. This episode illustrates the impression of fear with which the people watched the governor's every step from behind their shuttered windows, and the excitement with which they exchanged news and rumours in the village street. In this atmosphere, how helpless and harmless a few attempts to look into the distance and into the future seem! Socially, witchcraft was the straw clutched at by a drowning man.

V

The witchcraft dealt with up to now has matched old folk beliefs: changing into the shape of animals, controlling the weather, predicting the future – all very human desires and fears. The satanic element appears in Stadelin's hail-conjuring, but that could have been remedied by Christian magic. The limits of the new witch-craze were crossed when the life and well-being of others were exposed to the will of the devil without any possible defence. A 'fool', as Stadelin referred to the man, once came to Stadelin and asked him to make a bolt of lightning strike his enemy. Stadelin does not appear to have attempted anything of the sort. On the other hand, it was said of him that he could fly invisibly through the air, and, before the very noses of their parents, push children into mountain streams. Gruyères considered yet another, apparently provable, incident far more serious: Stadelin was said to have made a peasant family childless for many years. Not only were pregnant cattle no longer able to bear living young, but the farmer's wife bore seven dead infants one after the other. Stadelin must have killed them in the womb. This case borders on economic injury, since for farmers children were always related to economic considerations. The farm needed cheap labour, and when the children grew, it needed inheritors to take over or, through marriage, to expand it. The sharp decline in country population in the late fourteenth century disturbed this continuity. A series of miscarriages and a few accidents involving children, especially on wealthy farms, could have shifted the suspicion to Stadelin, who was not only out to ruin the farmers' annual crops, but their family futures as well.

This point interested the Bernese judge as much as the weather-conjuring, for he needed proof of deeds committed without witnesses or evidence; only the power of the devil himself could be behind this. Stadelin, of course, confessed to nothing, and what was revealed in torture was hardly sufficient: Stadelin admitted burying a lizard under the farmer's doorstep. The snake-like lizard would later become an animal of Satan, a spawn of the coitus between Satan and the witch. In old folk belief, its value was ambivalent, but often enough it was said to have a sexually inhibiting effect. For Gruyères, it must have been disappointing that the devil was not involved; connecting the burial of the lizard and the barrenness of the woman was nothing more than the automatism of traditional magic.

At this point, it is possible to conclude with some certainty that Stadelin did not believe his own confessions and never buried the lizard. The judge noted that they found nothing under the doorstep when they dug it up; Gruyères' explanation, that the lizard had rotted away, sounds too inventive to trust. Stadelin might have conjured hail down upon the fields of other farmers, but he had nothing to do with the murder of children. Why the judge was much more interested in infanticide than in hail-conjuring we will shortly see. First, a comment from Trevor-Roper. He claims that the persons interrogated were largely convinced of the reality of their witchcraft even without torture. That might be valid for later periods, when witchcraft had become almost epidemic; but no generalizing damnation or defence of torture can aid the examination of the various circumstances surrounding the earliest witch trials, only the investigation of the trials themselves.

The next complaint against sorcerers in the Simme Valley concerned a factual and punishable offence, infanticide. Within a short period, in the Bernese area, which must mean within Peter of

Gruyères' jurisdiction, no fewer than thirteen children were killed, although, as the governor emphasized, 'Public jurisdiction took vigorous steps against all infanticide.' The killing of infants in the Middle Ages has hardly been investigated by scholars at all; Philippe Ariès mentioned this gap in his book, *The History of Childhood*, (1960). Ariès thinks that, up to the seventeenth century, infanticide was publicly denounced but secretly tolerated, usually disguised as an accident, as one woman in the Upper Simme Valley admitted: the children were suffocated in the bed of their parents, where they slept. I do not agree with Ariès that the Middle Ages in general accepted infanticide. Again, we must consider the historical situation and social strata. In the Upper Simme Valley, it was not only Bernese officials who took measures against this practice; it was most certainly held in contempt and forbidden in wealthy families, which looked on every miscarriage as a major misfortune and conceived as many children as possible. Most murderers of infants were probably unmarried mothers, especially dependent maids who could not provide their children with enough to eat or anything to inherit. If this is true, the frequency of infanticide in the witch-filled Alpine valleys was a further indication of economic and social tensions.

VI

On the surface, infanticide has nothing to do with witchcraft. Gruyères tried to pin the miscarriages as infanticide on the sorcerer Stadelin, but never accused him of actually murdering young children. Nevertheless, the governor made a legal and theological connection between the two offences. This is so important for the beginnings of the witch-craze that I must sketch out its historical background, even though this means taking up one of the most sordid chapters in the medieval history of ideas. Detours in time and location are necessary; we must first examine a phenomenon which was far removed from both infanticide and witchcraft, the phenomenon of heresy, that is the dissenting doctrine of Christianity that spread via organized sects.

Western heresy began in the eleventh century with the view that both God and the devout soul were banished to the after-life, that all earthly things were of the devil. The dualistic abstinence from the world, which might have been copied from the followers of the heretic Bogomil in the Balkans, was the exact opposite of magic and witchcraft, which, with the help of the devil if necessary, had the goal of gaining power over earthly things. This antithesis was respected, for the most part, in the High Middle Ages. Yet many Catholics were convinced that anyone who believed false doctrine must also live perversely, and they believed heretics capable of the most disgusting crimes. As early as the first major outbreak of ascetic heresy, under the cathedral canons of Orléans in 1022, a naive southern French monk reported that the highly educated heretics had been led astray by a peasant. This peasant was said to carry about the ashes of dead children with him, and whoever ate of these ashes was, from that hour on, irrevocably a heretic and no longer capable of rational Catholic thought.

Thereafter, for example in the heresy trial of 1275 in Toulouse, heretics' sexual orgies began to be reported; the children conceived there were said to be killed and made into a brew, the drinking of which would instantly kill the Catholic faith in anyone. The heretics referred to here, southern French Cathars, being dualists, avoided every kind of sexual act and would not hurt a fly. But they had formed a sect, a competing church, and according to the medieval concept of a church, they had to have, like the Catholic church, a mass, which in this case was perverted into an orgy; they also needed a communion, which became the heretics' drink.

This same thirteenth-century mistrust was applied to the southern French Waldenses, who did not preach dualism like the Cathars, but simply a radical Biblicism. As the Albigensian war and the Dominican inquisition began driving the sects of Cathars and Waldenses out of the cities of France, many found refuge in the villages of the French and Italian western Alps. The suspicion of perversion followed them as zealously as the inquisition. At Pinerolo, in the Savoyard Alps, which has been the central location for most Waldensian communities from the fourteenth century until today, an inquisitor in the years 1387 and 1388 spread the news that the Waldenses there celebrated wild orgies in their meetings. In these meetings, the high Waldensian priestess would pass around a drink brewed from abominable substances; whoever drank from it even once would become addicted to the Waldensian way of life. It was not a long way from the Waldensian communities in the Italian Savoy around 1400 to Savoyard Lower Valais, where witches were discovered in 1430. Briançon, in the French High Alps, was already hiding a Waldensian group when the first witch trial took place in 1428. In Fribourg in 1438, what was soon to become the rule happened for the first time: witchcraft was called *voudessie*, the heresy of the Waldenses.

In the Upper Simme Valley around 1400, the governor, at least, must have been familiar with these associations. One of the child killers confessed to him that small children were not only killed, but eaten. They were secretly retrieved from their graves and cooked in a kettle. A witch's ointment was made from the solids and a witch's brew from the liquid; whoever drank it immediately became an incorrigible witch and knew everything about the secret art. There were many similar statements at the following trials, in Upper Valais in 1428, in Andermatt in 1459 and Chamonix in 1462. I think that, in these cases, the statements of the tortured witnesses reflected the opinions of the judges alone. One can even understand them, for to eradicate infanticide, where it was tolerated among the people, it had to be made disgusting, and diabolical motives had to replace human need: the rumour of the witch's brew provided these motives. It elevated the personal crime into a super-personal context which went far beyond simple folk beliefs. Infanticide served witchcraft, but witchcraft was heresy, for it constituted a satanic, competing church. And with that, we find ourselves once again in the religious–historical centre of the witch-craze, after a detour through cultural history, and again we must take a little time so as not to allocate this form of religion to the wrong social category, as Trevor-Roper has done.

The church of the Middle Ages had allowed practices of folk belief to flourish as remnants of the heathen religion, and in part even adopted and intensified them. One example was Stadelin's prayer against hail; other examples are weather processions with the Eucharist, the cult of relics and holy water. At the heart of this was the Catholic teaching that nature can be controlled by supernatural powers, but that these can only be used by God, who created the world. An early medieval requirement of church law, *Canon episcopi*, stated expressly that the devil could deceive only the senses of the immoral, but could never perform real miracles; magic and witchcraft were nothing more than imagination. This official church doctrine did not eradicate superstition, but it did isolate it as a phantom of the mind and make it mildly punishable, too.

It is easy to show that local priests in the Alpine valleys adhered to this doctrine in the early fifteenth century. That Gruyères did not work together with the Simme Valley priests is significant: they were not in the front ranks, tracking down witchcraft. In Valle Leventina in 1432, the local pastor vigorously defended the orthodoxy of an alleged witch. The prior of Interlaken became even more specific in 1424 when officials of Lucerne imprisoned one of his parish members for witchcraft. He wrote that he felt the man was half fool, but was not aware of any other vice in him. This was to be expected: the local clerics knew everyone in their parish and judged them as individuals, not as statistics in a vague collective body. It was strangers, among them officials, who first sensed a collective plot.

VII

Gruyères got a young man, whom he had thrown into the prison tower, to tell him just how the satanic community was to be imagined. Stadelin knew nothing about cult and community; he always appeared alone and was probably proud of it. The young man, on the other hand, proved to be more in need of support. He had heard that he could gain forgiveness for his misdeeds by a public confession, and did just that, as the judge had expected. Early Sunday morning, he said, before the blessing of the holy water, intending witches would go into the church with their sorcerer. There they solemnly renounced Christ, his faith, baptism and the Catholic church, just as newly baptized Catholics renounced Satan and all his works. Then, the new witches would do homage to the devil, in Latin *homagium*, that is, a feudal oath of loyalty. Soon, witch trials everywhere were filled with admissions of these almost political ceremonies, sometimes accompanied by the kiss of loyalty and genuflection, and feudal gestures. At the end of the rite, new witches would drink from the witch's brew, kill children and automatically come to understand the important rites of the witch sect. These are the words used in the Latin text: *ritus*, *secta*; the whole process was called *ordo*, an initiation into a religious group, irrevocable for one's entire life.

This *character indelebilis* is most visible in the wife of the young man, who, despite torture, remained an impenitent witch until her death. This, by the way, was justification for torture at the same time: only torture was strong enough to break the diabolical power of the witch's brew and to save at least the soul of the witch through confession and remorse. What Gruyères saw confirmed by the confession of the repentant sinner became basic to the witch-craze and its demonology. Except for the initiation rite described, there were no hints of witches holding regular cult rituals. But the analogy with the orgies of heretical communities had already been made, and from 1435 on, starting in the Dauphiné, there was more news of weekly witch rides at night, witch's sabbaths and satanic masses with disgusting excesses. That made the system of Satan's church complete.

The decisive point in the witch-craze had already been reached in Upper Simme Valley: if you performed witchcraft, you did not do it alone. That is why panic and fear grew among the peasants and, even more, among the officials. When Gruyères and his police were on their way to arrest the sorcerer Stadelin, a beastly stink overcame them; the bailiffs' hands began to shake. Gruyères assumed that this shaking was Stadelin's witchcraft and he told the bailiffs: 'Arrest him without hesitation, for when he is in the grip of public jurisdiction, his wicked powers will be lost.' One can see how political the governor's religious feelings were: Bernese law will secure the peace of the church, it will wrestle the satanic community to the ground. Thus, as Gruyères said, witchcraft could not injure all men, especially not those who remained devoutly loyal to Christian faith, which was practically the same as obeying public jurisdiction. Witches could not take the life of citizens of the Christian community, only some of their possessions, and God often turns the hailstorms meant for them to the fields of others. In other words, anyone in the community of the Upper Simme Valley could see who was loyal to the church of God and who belonged to the church of Satan. Not only the witches, but the injured parties as well could be servants of the devil, or at least lukewarm Christians and bad Bernese. Obviously, the governor ruled in the Upper Simme Valley with an unfathomable mistrust and saw himself, as representative of the government, surrounded by many devils; they truly did constitute a church of the devil, one that wished to destroy every moral and legal order in the kingdom of Christ. The church around 1400 was not yet, as Trevor-Roper assumed it to be, just another social group among many; church meant religious and social order, and more, it meant political, legal and moral order itself. The judge, from his viewpoint, saw this order of society as principally endangered, as did the peasants from their own viewpoints, and both were right.

The governor himself was nearly destroyed by the evil enemy. To understand Gruyères, one cannot dismiss his story, as Joseph Hansen did in 1900, as 'incredibly narrow-minded'. The witches had not been able to harm him personally for fourteen years, Gruyères said, because he protected himself with piousness, and especially with the sign of the cross. Stadelin was executed, and Gruyères handed over the governorship to a relative at Blankenburg castle, and in 1406 returned home to Berne. Later he had to travel on business once more to the Simme Valley: arriving at Blankenburg at night, he crossed himself and retired. That night, he intended to wake up again, write the necessary letters and leave the uncanny mountain valley in the morning. Suddenly he woke up, everything was light and he thought he had overslept. Irritated, he jumped out of bed, forgot to make the sign of the cross and ran down the steps into the writing chamber. The door was locked and he turned back, cursing. All he said was something like 'In the name of the devil!' but immediately it was darkest night; he fell down the stairs, lay there unconscious and bleeding and was sick for three weeks. Though he suspected the witches, he had to admit, gnashing his teeth, that he was unable to find the perpetrator. Later, he learned that it was the revenge of five Simme Valley witches, four men and a woman, who had meant to kill him. It amounted to an assassination attempt by the Prince of Hell, to whom he, Peter of Gruyères, had shown a hole in his armour. This is one case where we can talk of hallucinations, but they were caused not by glaciers or avalanches, but by a historical constellation. Both for the peasants in Boltigen and for the governor from Berne, it shattered the familiar order of the world and filled them with fear, fear of the future and of one another.

VIII

Let us reiterate this point: those involved were not backwoods inhabitants or village idiots. Nider too, who retold the gruesome tale of Simme Valley, was highly educated, a university professor in Vienna. As soon as he presented the stories for open discussion at the Basle Church Council, perfectly normal people in other locations began discovering the same satanic communities of witches, not only in the Alps, but, for example, at the university of Heidelberg in 1446, then in Tübingen, then in Biberach. It is hardly possible to separate the superstitions of the mountain farmers from the demonology of the intellectuals, as Trevor-Roper has tried to do, and even less possible to explain away the beginnings of the witch-craze out of a divergent Alpine culture. It was much more a European interaction of fear; this would be made even more obvious if I could analyse the entire first wave of witch persecutions until around 1450. In all these cases, the degree of the confusion was similar to the Alpine cases, as was the confrontation of various symptoms of a general crisis. The Alpine inhabitants reacted to the threat to their previously valid principal values not by returning to old pagan traditions, but by fearing the future. They were subjected to the will of the powerful, which came from the flatland. The powerful men of Europe made a kind of tryst in the Alps, because the focal point of the continent was here, between the economic markets in northern Italy and Upper Rhine, between the power centres in Paris and Vienna. But the powerful lost the security of their systems as they entered the mountains, and they grew afraid of their fellow man.

Thus, the crisis in the Alps flourished especially early; but it was a European crisis.

Where are its origins to be found? Contemporaries probably came closest when they dated the beginning of witchcraft in the years shortly before 1378. This was the first year of the Western Schism, which destroyed the unity of the Catholic church. František Graus, in his literary commentary on the Late Middle Ages, *Das Spätmittelalter als Krisenzeit* (1969), made it clear that the most shattering crisis for the people of the period was not the duplication of the papacy and college of cardinals, but the doubtful validity of the communion, the concern about the earthly and eternal salvation of every Christian, and the loss of the community of living and dead in heaven and on earth. In this religious crisis, political saviours failed; consecrated kings were deposed, like Wenceslas in Germany, or done to death, like Richard II in England, or incapacitated, like Charles VI in France. The ruling stratum of nobility was bleeding, as in the West, or becoming impoverished, as in the East. Since the Plague of 1348, the economic balance between merchant cities and the agricultural hinterland had been disrupted on all fronts. The ties of the individual to family, community and church were loosened, even in the smallest Alpine village. New ideas, mostly of regional communities, were devised to find a solution for this manifold crisis: in the religious sector, ideas came from national churches, like those of John Wycliffe in England or John Huss in Bohemia; in the intellectual arena, from state universities like those in Vienna and Heidelberg; in the political area from territorial states like the Milanese duchy of the Visconti and the Swiss Confederation. New social and economic orders developed more slowly, less obviously all over Europe, a social pattern that revolved largely around the princely courts, and an economic federation of currency, the centres of which were the major cities. We know the long-term successes of all these experiments, but for people living around 1400, it looked much more as if such categorically or regionally subdivided groups were undermining the rest of Christian and human society.

This is the origin of the general fear that the world is full of devils. Such a claim was made in 1437 by a certain furrier in the Alpine city of Briançon, an old man who came from Regensburg and had seen much of the world. Once, in a forest, robbers had attacked him; he escaped when a large troop of armed men appeared. A typical occurrence in those days, but the furrier believed that his rescuers had been a pack of devils. He said: 'The world is full of people who call on devils, and the devils find followers because the world is full of misdeeds, war and division.' It was a vicious circle in the most diabolical sense: the furrier conjured up devils when his ordered world collapsed. But because the old foreigner had claimed that devils protected him, the people of Briançon had no choice but to assume that he was a witch; they burned him at the stake.

In the beginning there was a reasonable fear that much of familiar society would be ruined. But it intensified to an unfounded terror of the end of all human society. From that evolved the nervous panic that a diabolical parallel society was intentionally preparing for the apocalyptical destruction of the world. And in the end came the fanatical decision to destroy all servants of Satan or, as Gruyères formulated it, to wipe the beasts off the face of the earth. In the late fourteenth century, it was not only the peasants and theologians of the Alps who were overtaken by the chain reaction of fear to fanaticism, for it was a reaction to a crisis that concerned all areas of life, and all of Europe. Those who had to live in a mad world could hope for help from scientific surveys as little as they could from social solidarity. If no one could trust his neighbour, all had to help themselves by religiously calling upon the devils who seemed to be conquering the world.

By 1450, they had survived the crisis. Why the witch-craze, one of its accompanying phenomena, nevertheless continued for another two hundred years, did not in fact reach its climax until the six-teenth century, has been clearly explained by Trevor-Roper. This hysteria has still not fully died out today, though it has slipped into the disguises of other fears and aggressions. Science and society could keep an eye only on the religious, medieval form of the witch-craze, not its all too human content. The quickest way for modern demagogues to fanaticize their followers is to paint a de-vilish picture of their opponents. One could even come to the rash conclusion that it is not only belief in progress that motivates mod-ern Europe, but the fear of our fellow-humans as well, which destroys all attempts to come to peace with ourselves. Be that as it may, it is sad enough that we cannot talk about the events in the Upper Simme Valley without taking sides, either with the patrician governor or with the rebellious peasants. Can the reason why our current prospects for the future of Europe are so bleak be that we still deal with our fellows as the masters of sorcery and the judges of witches once dealt with one another?

Part V
Social Movements

8

Patron Saints in Medieval Society

I

In Prague, no one would ever think of questioning the importance of
the veneration of Christian saints for the public in the Middle Ages
and Baroque; one can see how important it was just by looking at
the statues along the Charles Bridge. Apart from the patrons of
private persons or specific churches and altars, and helpers in time
of need for certain professions or situations, Prague exhibits the
patrons of entire peoples, dynasties, countries and communities, in
other words, patrons of society itself, such as the monuments of St
Wenceslas in Wenceslas Square, on the Old Town's Bridge Tower or
in the Cathedral of St Vitus. The fact that the political function of
saints was a part of medieval life is a truism in medieval scholarship,
so much so, in fact, that the origins, history and characteristics of
such patrons has never been researched in their entire context.
František Graus, especially with his book about mentalities in
medieval writings, *Lebendige Vergangenheit, Überlieferung im Mittelalter und in den Vorstellungen vom Mittelalter* (1975), is the only
one in recent years to have stressed that the political cult of saints in
the Middle Ages was part of a larger complex, a part of medieval
thought about the continuity and representation of extra-personal
groups, and thus a part of the medieval history of social theory and
the doctrine of social bodies.

If not only the origins, but also, and more significantly, the self-
awareness of a society are reflected in such representative figures,
their cult of saints cannot be ignored as a simple tradition, as it has
been by the older scholarship. If that were so, they would reflect
certain features of the various societies, thereby meriting historical
differentiation. At the same time, it is less the lives of the saints or

the genuineness of their legends that must be researched than the history of their effect on the groups they represented: under what conditions did a saint become the representative of an entire society, with what groups did it begin, to what extent did it develop, and how is the self-understanding of the group reflected in the portrayal of their saints? In order to sharpen our perspective to ensure precise research, I will use a general European typology to show there was no statistical, traditional cult of patron saints in the Middle Ages, but that in certain periods and regions, various features of government or communities chose wholly different saints to fit their individual needs and desires. Looking at the Middle Ages, it would appear that all human groups petitioned super-human helpers in each phase, hoping to find in them optimal protection against the fluctuation of world history. Only the modern observer is in a position to see that, within the gap dividing the sinner on earth and the saint in heaven, a movement began which brought about a change in the function and structure of society, a change so basic that there was no longer need for heavenly patrons when it was complete, because it had attained stability on earth.

I will not expand on the non-European parallels and the preliminary stages in antiquity. These range from the Chinese cult of prehistoric rulers, to the Greek veneration of founding heroes, to the idolization of rulers in the late Antique Roman period. I must likewise ignore the after-effects of related traditions on the Middle Ages themselves, for example the concept of the Byzantine empire or the Islamic caliphate: those figures were thought to be earthly representatives of God, living men to whom those societies would gladly have attributed rulership over the entire earth. Not much was left of such beliefs in Europe's Early Middle Ages, however. The Christian concept of heaven limited the glorification of human power and greatness, and all political power was divided practically in a thousand different directions in the Germanic Migration of Peoples. In the following, I would like to demonstrate how heavenly, holy representatives gradually displaced human majesties in a new pattern of society, and how they contributed to the stabilization of social groups, by using five specific examples, each expanded slightly through references to related cases and generalized into a history of patron saint cults.

II

The oldest patron of a larger European community was St Martin of Tours, the patron saint of the Merovingian Frankish kings. We have a fairly detailed description of how he came to play this role, thanks largely to the research of Eugen Ewig. In the episcopal church of Tours and in the Gaulish cloisters, the cult of St Martin had already flourished among clerics for three generations before the Frankish king Clovis adopted it. Tours lay in a region that was under Visigothic influence when Clovis passed the saint's tomb in 498. Impressed by several miraculous occurrences, he promised to be baptized soon. Clovis's baptism itself took place in the heart of Frankish power, in Reims; but the king returned in 507 to Tours to liberate the surrounding area of Arian, partly heretical Visigoths, in his full developed consciousness of orthodox Catholicism. Clovis gave his army strict instructions to spare the city of the saint: he said, 'How could we hope for victory if we angered St Martin?' The king prayed for and received a sign from the saint of coming victory: as his envoys entered the Church of St Martin, a psalm of victory sounded. Shortly afterwards, Clovis defeated the Visigoths south of Tours and donated a large part of the spoils to the saint's tomb. The miraculous power of local saints had, it seemed, helped the Frankish king to triumph over the heretics, as well as gain power over the surrounding region. In the year following, 508, Clovis celebrated the triumphant self-declaration of his empire-like kingdom before the eyes of the saint in the Church of Tours. Since then, St Martin's role was to ensure the victory of the Merovingian royal family; whenever they conquered after that, in order to secure their kingdom they built not only royal strongholds, but churches to St Martin.

Nevertheless, the patronage of St Martin would have survived only with difficulty after the death of Clovis if clerics had not helped. More than anyone else, the historian and bishop Gregory of Tours actively propagated the posthumous fame of his episcopal predecessor, finding his willing listeners mainly among the women of the royal family. Clovis's widow, Clotilda, had settled in Tours, and when, in 534, a struggle threatened to break out between her sons, she hurried to St Martin's tomb; there she prayed that the saint should keep harmony in the family. In place of the dead Clovis, the miracle-working St Martin became almost the head of the family, certainly its peacemaker. When Clovis's grandchildren agreed on a partition treaty in 567, a stipulation called for various saints, among them St Martin, to punish any breaches of contract. With similar sanctions, Clovis's daughter-in-law Radegunda secured her pious endowments to the church against her covetous nephews in 587. Soon the cult of St Martin was put to more serious activities. In 578, Radegunda's step-son, King Guntram, called upon the magical help of the saint during a duel, and was able to strike down his rival with his own hands. As a Roman soldier, Martin had after all been a warlike man. In battles throughout the seventh century, the Frankish rulers carried the cloak of St Martin, the famous *cappa*, 'in order to protect themselves and overcome the enemy'. After 679, the bondsmen assigned to royal castles swore legal oaths upon this cloak, which was stored in a *capella* (this word is the origin of the word 'chapel').

In this way, St Martin supported and represented the most important duties of a king, victory over foreign nations and the preservation of domestic law and peace. It took a heavenly authority because no one man alone could ever achieve the necessary stature in those endless power struggles in France. Even St Martin's authority was constantly challenged. In 583, when a grandchild of Clovis decided to break the partition treaty of 567 and made plans to march on Paris, he protected himself against Martin's curse by having the relics of other saints carried before him; it would soon be seen which was the stronger saint. The numinous power of saints was made to serve aristocratic whim in a superstitious and cynical way; the victory-bringers were no longer peace-keepers at the same time. Some Frankish territories, in any case, preferred to swear by other patrons, such as Hilary of Poitiers, or Remigius of Reims; later they were joined by the alleged apostolic pupil, Dionysius the Areopagite, who is buried in St-Denis. War was on the horizon, in heaven as on earth.

It was then that an alternative idea spread among the Frankish people: the concept that the power of the saints should preserve the peace and grant the little man that protection which the powerful allowed neither themselves nor others. As early as the sixth century, desperate subjects of St Martin called upon the saint, as the nation's patron, finally to bring peace to the land. This second function, that of Martin as peacekeeper, became more and more common. The cult of Martin the victory-bringer faded when the centralized power of the Carolingians arose; the French monarchy of the High Middle Ages no longer needed him. Instead, he began working in the regions of the old Frankish settlements on the Lower Rhine, mainly as aid in time of need. He had not hung his cloak about the shoulders of kings, but shared it with beggars. On his feast day, 11 November, the poor were well provided for, as St Martin's geese and St Martin's pastries were eaten around St Martin's fire. From the fourteenth century on, Brotherhoods of St Martin have been practising *caritas* everywhere, and this variation of Santa Claus is still a friend to the poor. It was in this role, as friend of the people, that he became the national patron of the Swiss peasant cantons Uri and Schwyz. He had no political functions, but never ran out of social ones. This is an example that shows how much the cult of one and the same saint in one and the same society can change during the course of time, obviously since the political and social authority of a saint was still very controversial in the Early Middle Ages, and at the same time very limited.

The roles of other patrons in the Early Middle Ages appear similarly specialized. I will mention only a few names. The apostle James appeared in the ninth century to lead the Spanish *reconquista* of the Spanish kings against the Moors. The early Christian martyr Maurice watched over the battles of the Ottonian emperors against pagan slaves in the tenth century. The Archangel Michael helped the Ottonians fend off the attacks of the Hungarians. St George preceded the Byzantine emperors in battles against the Petschenegs in the eleventh century. These were usually saintly war heroes, early fighters against heathens, and their reputation began to grow in the seventh century, when Christian religion and the aggression of war became intertwined. Saints such as these served as patrons for holy wars and warlike rulers, and signified their power; they embodied individual and prominent kindreds, but not entire peoples. The aristocratic and sacral kingdoms of the Early Middle Ages trusted their own hereditary holiness enough not to need a permanent representative in Christian heaven: all they needed was occasional reinforcement.

An exception will prove the rule: the cult of St Patrick in Ireland. Patrick converted the country to Christianity, and became in the seventh century the 'patron of patrons', the 'highest saint' of the island, which was torn by battles between clans. Like Martin, Patrick was called upon by afflicted subjects to bring Christian harmony to the nation. Some dreamed that Patrick was the actual, eternal king of the island, beyond the influence of changing rulers. Even when the bishops of Armagh cited him as the highest pastor of Ireland, thus stressing their own ecclesiastical precedence, he did not become a man of war, a political representative of Ireland: he remained the religious patron of the Irish people. In all, we can say that the Early Middle Ages were able to develop only the beginnings of hagiographic national representation, since the powerful and helpless confronted each other far too closely to be able to develop a basis for government and community.

III

The history of saintly representatives actually began in the eleventh century, which, in scholarly research, is emerging more and more clearly as the grand turning-point of the Middle Ages, the beginning of differentiation and stabilization in all regions of living. It was a time when archaic desire for power was tamed by several parallel processes: the conclusion of Christian conversion in the borderlands of Europe, which enabled the independence of Christian countries in those areas; the Gregorian separation of the holy priesthood and secular government; the development of transpersonal theories of government; the first social awareness of society as an entity in larger governed groups.

I will select the earliest known case of a saint becoming the symbol of an independent, only recently Christianized country, the Bohemian Duke Wenceslas, whose case has been analysed by František Graus. Copying the Saxon Ottonians, Wenceslas had meant to Christianize all Bohemia, and for that reason was murdered in 929 or 935 by his brother Boleslav. That same brother had the martyr's bones transferred to the Cathedral of St Vitus in Prague, when the submitted to Otto the Great in 950 and was forced to continue Wenceslas' Christian and German policies. St Wenceslas, however, was not converted into the governing family's victory-bringer, as St Martin of Tours had been. True, he was a descendant of the ruling family of Přemyslids, but they were also his murderers, and the peace-loving Wenceslas was badly suited to the role of an aggressive war hero. He won over the clergy first, chiefly in Prague, where he was buried. The ecclesiastical cult at this time was older and different from the political veneration that came later.

At first, St Wenceslas was no more fortunate in the inter-Bohemian aristocratic feuds than St Martin had been. When one side called on St Wenceslas in an instance in 995, the other mocked: 'If Wenceslas is your saint, ours is Boleslav!' (his brother and murderer). The cult of St Wenceslas grew beyond the boundaries of local feuds when the Polish Duke Boleslav Chrobry tried to take over Bohemia in 1002. St Wenceslas was said to have saved the Prague stronghold from the Polish attack by a miracle, while his aristocratic relatives were divided among themselves or even allied with the invaders. St Wenceslas later helped his kindred in the Přemyslid wars of succession in 1092, not by supporting one side against the other, but by liberating prisoners and bringing about a peaceful conclusion. When he did take part in war, it was as defender of the entire country and all its inhabitants.

Just as St Martin became the representative of the people, so did St Wenceslas, and around the same time; however, St Wenceslas' people were not defined socially, but politically, even geographically. Starting with the eleventh century, St Wenceslas was referred to as 'our patron' and 'prince of the nation' in Bohemian historical sources. Around 1120, Cosmas of Prague, the dean of St Vitus' Cathedral, wrote that St Wenceslas was the patron 'of all families of the country of Bohemia'; he did not, in other words, exclusively represent the family of the duke and their estates. As patron, he even surpassed St Vitus, who, since Corvey, was tainted with Ottonian-German colours and, as cathedral patron, appeared far too clerical. St Wenceslas was less national or aristocratic than St Vitus; he also seemed much more modern, not like a saint from a distant country who had died long before, but as a friend from amid the people living in the surrounding countryside. The Bohemians of the twelfth century even eased him into the position of sovereign ruler and called themselves 'the family of St Wenceslas', as if he were their physical progenitor and living king. When they defeated the German king Lothair in 1126, many claimed to have seen St Wenceslas there, dressed in white armour and riding on a white horse, waving the 'Lance of St Wenceslas'. A few years later, his image on coins was changed from a praying Christian to a ruling lord, complete with banner. Thus, St Wenceslas adopted duties like those of the earlier St Martin, but with a characteristic shift in tone. He represented not victory and peace, but social harmony for the Czechs and political repulsion for their enemies.

St Wenceslas' royal descendants battled against foreign pretenders as if the country were still their personal possession, as if the Merovingian period were not over; constantly changing dynasties were confronted by a permanent and unified national society, personified in St Wenceslas. He was the permanent ruler, the king merely his agent at court. Thus the seal of the University of Prague portrays Emperor Charles IV kneeling to receive the founding charter from St Wenceslas. Charles had his son and successor to the throne christened with the name of Wenceslas in 1361; Charles's Bohemian symbol of rulership was called the Crown of St Wenceslas. St Wenceslas was even recognized by the Prague Hussites in 1415 as the rightful owner and inheritor of the nation, though they dealt mercilessly with all other cults of saints. The tradition of eating the St Wenceslas goose on St Wenceslas' day, 28 September, survived far into modern times. This was practically the only way in which the cult sank into the realm of folk custom; otherwise it remained beyond local tradition. Even when the Czechoslovakian republic wrested its freedom from the Habsburg monarchy in 1918, the government, despite intense anti-Catholic resentment in the country, embossed St Wenceslas' picture onto gold coins. And when the people of Prague tried to defend their freedom again in 1968, they congregated around his statue on St Wenceslas Square, where the saint sat on horseback carrying his lance, no longer a symbol of Christian devotion, but of peaceful harmony and defence against force.

Similar personifications have repeatedly appeared in Europe since the eleventh century. Again, I will mention only a few. From 1083 onwards, the first king of Hungary, St Stephen, became a symbolic guarantor of external protection and domestic coherence. Since his canonization in 1100, the murdered king of the Danes, Canute IV, liberated his country from starvation and tempests. The Norwegian king Olaf II, who in 1030 fell in battle against the Danes, preserved the unity of the country in the twelfth century while local dynasties dissipated their energy and power in continual battles for the throne. While later kings were considered merely Olaf's successors and vassals, St Olaf ruled as 'eternal king of Norway'; his tomb in Trondheim Cathedral formed the heart of a community that had no other centre. In eleventh-century Anglo-Saxon England, King Edmund of East Anglia, killed in battle by the Danes, took on a similar position as the country freed itself from the rulership of the Danes. From the twelfth century on, the sainted son of a king, David, became the symbol of Wales's independence from England, and his Christian name was handed down in the rebellious families of the country.

An exception is the last example, Finland. It had been converted to western Christianity by Swedish bishops and was politically subject to the Swedish king. At the start of the conversion process, around 1160, a Finnish peasant had killed the English-born bishop, Henry of Uppsala. His successors in office, the bishops of Åbo, religiously and politically represented the Finnish part of the Swedish empire, also taking part in the repulsion of Russian and unorthodox influences, from the late thirteenth century on. These prelates now began to style the nation's first martyr, Henry, who had been a foreigner and whose relics were venerated in the Cathedral of Åbo, the patron of all Finland. Other than this bishop-saint, most of the nation's patrons were not early Christian ascetics or foreign apostles, but historical national regents, and in most cases they were defeated rulers who had been murdered and become martyrs sitting on thrones in heaven, symbols of the crucified Saviour. Their cult did not originate in the royal families' attempts to make their bloodlines famous; these did not dare point to a blood relationship with saintly rulers. Rather, those princely patrons stood for peace, that is, for the threatened independence and vague unity of the nation, and were against force, that is, against foreign invaders and internal struggles for the throne. In this cult of national patrons, we find the first awakenings of the much-discussed medieval national awareness.

Strangely enough, it formed on the outskirts of Europe earlier than at its centre. The explanation for this lies in the fact that in France and Germany, older conceptualizations of ecclesiastical victory-bringers continued to dominate, and they superimposed themselves on the younger stages. In France, pre-national thought remained so strong that as late as 1124, during the repulsion of a German invasion, a Carolingian patron was called upon as protector of the monarchy: Dionysius the Areopagite, as opposed to, for example, the saint-like King Robert II the Pious of the house of Capet. Though it was said that he could cure scrofula, Robert did not qualify as national patron. France was so divided by feudalism that it could base its unity only on a figure from the distant past.

Germany's case was similar with its hereditary duchies. The Hohenstaufen rulers did try twice, however, to make national patrons of earlier emperors. In 1145, Conrad III supported efforts in Bamberg to canonize Henry II, and Frederick Barbarossa, with the help of his antipope, brought about the canonization of Charlemagne, which had been propagated in Aix-la-Chapelle. Yet it merely helped the Hohenstaufen underline the propinquity of their imperial crown to God, as well as the sacral character of their empire, and could not strengthen the consciousness of the Germans as a political body. Germany, the empire without a capital, did not accept the sainted emperors as its personification; just as the cult of Henry never left the borders of Bamberg and Basle, neither did the cult of Charlemagne ever leave Aix. Neither of them passed into folklore. The Hohenstaufen reform was defeated, there as in other areas, by the old concept of the empire; in the European race for nationality, Germany fell to the rear. The countries which chose imperturbably law-oriented rulers over charismatic but impetuous personalities as representatives had much better chances. It was in such characters that the awakening nations were first personified.

IV

The twelfth century is characterized by the secularization of the monarchy, which, since the Gregorian church reform, had lost much of its sacral consecration. At the same time, however, West European monarchies succeeded in intensifying and objectifying their government, in separating the person of the ruler from the institution of monarchy, and in suppressing aristocratic feuds and anarchistic violence. This is where the growing temporal self-dependence and domestic political stability of the state had its start. It was a stability supported not only by the sovereign insignia as symbols of state, the crowns, thrones and banners, but also by the inheritability of the throne. And this could be legitimized by consecrating an ancestor of the ruling dynasty as patron saint.

The earliest and most revealing example is the canonization of the English king Edward, a case which has been analysed by Bernhard Scholz. Edward the Confessor, the last Anglo-Saxon king, was killed by the Normans in the invasion of England in 1066. His cult first flourished in Westminster Abbey, which he had had rebuilt. The abbey requested his canonization in 1138, when the Anglo-Norman state was threatening to collapse amidst the battles of the heirs-apparent under King Stephen of Blois. It was just this precariousness that made Pope Innocent II reject the petition: the canonization of a king should benefit and further the honour of an entire kingdom, and must therefore be requested by the entire English church, not by Westminster Abbey alone. The Pope was obviously familiar with the uniting function of monarchial saints; but in 1140, no one had yet realized that Edward could be anything else but a patron of the nation.

King Henry II, founder of the Plantagenet dynasty, created a system of government in 1153 that was meant to bridge old differences with legal rationalism and halt new discord through monarchial continuity. In 1161, the King urged the Pope, Alexander III, to canonize Edward. We know his reasons from the petitions of the king and his counsellors. His lieutenants stressed that the disputes between the Anglo-Saxons and Normans, newly arisen under King Stephen, had to be permanently suppressed; to that end, it would be helpful if an old Anglo-Saxon ruler were advanced to the glories of sainthood by his Norman successor. The King himself went even further, claiming to be personally related to the Confessor: 'It was I, descendant of his blood, whom the Lord honoured and set upon the throne of the same kingdom.' Henry II was the first king in Europe to trace his lineage back to a saintly ruler.

The fact that the blood relationship was far removed made no difference; it established the dynasty's propinquity to God, even opposing papal encroachments and the aristocratic right of dissent. Edward, who had propagated the good old laws, secured the legitimacy of the Plantagenets' legislation. Though they had originally been foreigners, the royal family eventually took permanent residence near the tomb of the saint, an important step in consolidating their state. Henry's great-grandfather, William the Conqueror, had been crowned in Westminster Abbey, and by 1140, following the example of the French royal Abbey of St Denis, the Abbey had already begun to proclaim its ambitions, taking advantage of the aid of falsified documents. Not until the canonization of King Edward, who was buried there, did Westminster really became the 'royal seat', the coronation and burial chapel of the English monarchy that it is today. The cult of Edward, however, never departed from its dynastic framework; it left no traces among the traditions of the people.

The news soon spread that the founder of a dynasty could legitimize his successors by canonizing an ancestor. Again, I can mention the other examples only briefly. In 1169, the king of the Danes, Waldemar the Great, had his deceased father, Duke Canute Lavard, canonized on the same day that his seven-year-old son was elected king; both acts established the new dynasty. Out of identical motives, from about 1270, Waldemar of Sweden, the first king of the Folkunger house, championed the cult of his great-great-grandfather, the Swedish king Eric IX, who had died 100 years earlier. In the fourteenth century, St Eric was made national patron, and in the fifteenth century his picture adorned the Swedish imperial seal; even throughout the reformation, his tomb in the Cathedral of Uppsala remained the palladium of the monarchy. And lastly, King Philip the Fair of France, a rigorous defender of monarchial omnipotence, strove to gain his independence from St Denis and its cult of Dionysius. The idea of the old Capet king Robert the Pious as patron saint was not given a second thought, because Philip also wanted the halo to encompass his closest relatives, the Valois, whose male line was threatening to die out. This is why, in 1297, Philip persuaded the Curia to approve the canonization of his grandfather, Louis IX of France. Louis, like all these Christian kings, had not died the death of a martyr; neither his deeds nor his virtues could have made him a saint. In this regard, nearly all dynastic saints were interchangeable; they personified nothing more than supra-personal principles.

The sainted monarchs of the twelfth and thirteenth centuries were canonized, usually during critical moments in the succession to the throne, to help the dynasties descendent from them become stable governing bodies. The sainted ancestor provided the same thing that would later be supplied by the abstract concept of the king who cannot die; through all changes of individual, he maintained the institution's identity. What Percy Ernst Schramm observed in 1939 is true not only of France: a myth surrounding the monarchy could actually secure the stability of West European dynasties for centuries. Admittedly, later attempts to create similarly stable constellations in other parts of Europe failed. We find the most important exception, again, on the fringes of the continent, in Serbia, a country that could assert itself between the Byzantine–orthodox faith and the Western–Catholic form of state. Around 1216, the Serbian ruler Stephen III, whose older brother was disputing his claim to the throne, personally wrote a legend of sainthood for his deceased father, the Grand Duke Stephen Nemanja, shortly before having himself enthroned as 'First-crowned' by the grace of the Pope in 1217. The process proved to be so successful that most kings of Serbia after him could count on being canonized by their descendants shortly after their deaths. Until the Turks conquered Serbia in the late fourteenth century, the orthodox sainthood of the royal dynasty preserved the cohesion of the nation.

Everywhere else in the fourteenth century, however, the attempt to introduce sainted rulers as political patrons failed. A list of some unsuccessful attempts will suffice. In England, Richard II tried to revive the cult of Edward; a hundred years later, the first Tudor king, Henry VII, vainly championed the memory of Henry VI. In the German empire, territorial dynasts looked around for family saints and found the Thuringian landgrave Elizabeth, the Silesian duchess Hedwig, the Margrave of Baden, Bernard, and the Habsburg Margrave Leopold. None of them attained political significance until the early modern period, in the epoch of territorial absolutism. The Jagiellonian cult of Queen Jadwiga, and later the cult of Prince Casimir, had a similar fate in Poland. In Spain, too, the perfecter of the *Reconquista*, King Ferdinand III of Castile, was not canonized until 1671, 400 years after his death. When we ask why ancestors of dynasties were no longer being made representatives of new European states after the thirteenth century, we discover two new kinds of patrons which almost completely replaced the royal patron in the Late Middle Ages.

V

The Late European Middle Ages no longer believed in the religion of monarchy because, since the thirteenth century, class confederacies had become more and more self-confident in facing their dynastic rulers. When the estates of Flanders rose up against the government of Philip the Fair of France in 1302, the rebels decapitated a statue of St Louis in Thérouanne. However, it was largely the territorial diet, which did not accept monarchial leaders, that needed saintly representatives when they wanted to be assured that their community would exist as a political entity for longer than the current moment. Obviously, sainted kings were not suitable for their needs.

I will discuss a salient case, that of the patron of Poland, though the history of his impact has not been thoroughly examined by experts. Bishop Stanislaus of Cracow was killed in 1079 by the king of the Piasts, Boleslav II, for reasons unknown. Polish historians portrayed the bishop as a traitor, as he had resisted the king, and that was that as long as Poland was ruled by Piast monarchs. But at the beginning of the thirteenth century, Poland lost its centralized government. In the divided dukedoms, there were only two social groups that could keep the unity of Poland alive, the episcopate and the lines of the feudal nobility. Under their influence, Poland became a paradise of the medieval class system. In this situation, which was complicated by the invasion of the Mongols and by the eastern expansion of the Germans, the bishops of Cracow, especially Vincent Kadlubek, pursued the canonization of their ecclesiastical predecessor, Stanislaus; in the year 1253, canonization was approved by Pope Innocent IV.

The functions of the new patron were derived from the saint's legend, which was composed by a Cracow Dominican only now, around 1260. In it, Stanislaus appeared as the son of a noble warrior and had defended the honour of noble ladies against the lusts of the adulterous King Boleslav; for that reason, the king had him stabbed to death during a church service. As a martyr of monarchial whim, the aristocratic bishop's job was thus to watch over the morals and rights of the ruling classes, the episcopate and the nobility; his martyrdom made him a qualified speaker for all Poland. In the precise words of his biographer, he represented the *principum Polonie communis equitas*, the equality and community of the Polish estates. The fifteenth century venerated Stanislaus with church hymns, not only as national patron, but as 'Father of the Fatherland'. The greatest Polish historian, the canon of the Cracow Cathedral and princely tutor, Jan Dlugosz, praised the saint in his biography of Stanislaus of 1465 as the surest guarantee 'of the salvation and freedom of the Polish people', a people that was in turn represented by the ruling classes. Though the monarchy had once more gained a foothold in Poland since 1320, using Cracow as its residence, it was too late to replace the patron of the estates with a member of the royal family, making him into a similarly popular saint. The attempts to make Jadwiga and Casimir competitively popular had, as mentioned above, failed; these two Jagiellonians

had, after all, died peaceful deaths in their beds of state, not slain for
their faith and for the social order of the people, as the bishop had
been.

Parallels with Polish estate patrons can be found wherever territorial diets in the Late Middle Ages in Europe separated themselves
from the ruling dynasty. The old national patrons of eastern Europe,
who as martyrs exhibited similar traits in any case, were modelled
into estate patrons, for example in Bohemia, where in the thirteenth
century St Wenceslas took up his position for the first time between
the national classes and the Přemyslids, who had elevated themselves
to monarchs. Hungary was a similar case, where, after the Arpads
died out, and amid a constant fluctuation of foreign dynasties, St
Stephen, wearing his crown, embodied the fatherland on behalf of
its estates. True, in western Europe, where sainted kings served as
dynastic patriarchs, the territorial estates sought new – that meant
extremely old – saints. In England, after the signing of Magna Carta
of 1215, where the crown had chosen Edward the Confessor, the
barons elected as their heavenly spokesman St George, the Oriental
knight-saint whose cult Richard Coeur de Lion had imported from a
crusade. St George was named national patron at a synod in Oxford
in 1222. The monarchy, in the person of Henry III, chose, on the
other hand, once again to champion the cult of Edward the Confessor, but under Edward III, at the onset of the Hundred Years' War,
it gave way to the demands of the estates. The Order of the Garter,
founded by Edward, was an order of St George; in the battle of
Calais in 1347, the English battle cry was 'St George', and
Shakespeare wrote, 'St George for Merrie England!' The Cross of St
George is today still a part of the British flag, the Union Jack. The
Cross of St Andrew also appears in the flag: it refers to the apostle
Andrew, whom the Scottish territorial diets had made their patron.

In the Late Middle Ages, the same apostle, Andrew, was assigned
the function of patron saint for the Duchy of Burgundy. From 1411
his Cross of St Andrew was the symbol of the 'Bourguignons' in the
bloody battles of the estates with the 'Armagnacs'; the battle cry of
the Burgundians became '*Montjoie Saint Andrieu*!' As in Burgundy,
so in Aragon, the fighting classes called the tune: they chose as
national patron a knightly saint, once again St George. In Aragon, a
relic of St George, his arm, played a similar role as a symbol of
government as did the right hand of St Stephen in Hungary. Finally,
the knightly company of St George's Shield (*St Jörgenschild*) in
Swabia, their cult of St George and their politics of the estates in the
German fifteenth century should be mentioned.

What characterized all these estate patrons was that they were designed to personify the regional nobility, but were not of the same lineage as the historical nobility of the country. In this respect they were similar to those victory-bringers who had so impressed the Merovingian nobility in the Early Middle Ages. The folk traditions they inspired had a similarly expansive influence. More than any other, St George the dragon-killer was popular with all classes; he helped the peasant whose horse was diseased and later became one of the fourteen helpers in time of need. His cult spread everywhere simply because the saint had come from an exceedingly distant time and place and therefore did not become the exclusive property of any one social or regional group. This same fact reveals the weakness of the medieval system of estates; they had to choose their ideal personalities from the distant past if they wanted to agree on one patron. This illustrates what historians already know, that the system of estates as a body was conservative, functioning mainly as a counterbalance to monarchial power, but seldom as a reservoir of a nation's independent forces. Our panorama has also shown that both dynastic and estate ties worked best in the fringe countries of medieval Europe. Central Europe, especially Germany and Italy, could find neither a monarchial nor an aristocratic patron saint to represent the entire nation. Yet even in those countries, a new, completely different kind of patron eventually appeared.

VI

The lingering influence of the old universal powers, the German empire and the Roman papacy, was still so strong in the Late Middle Ages that, in Germany as in Italy, it was impossible for a modern multi-territorial state of broad scope and effective organization to form. This vacuum, however, enabled another form of society to develop which would be significant for the future: the community of the city. The central European city was characterized by the consolidated alliance of its citizens, and by the exceptional administrative oasis of urban harmony and law, which had isolated itself from the dynasty's territorial entanglements by fighting for and gaining special privileges. Preserving peace among the citizens internally and ensuring their exceptional privileges externally were the main concerns of the elected officials, who served for limited periods, and this, more than the politics of the territorial diet, demanded a permanently effective symbolic figure. Such a figure had to be one who could permanently personify the urban burghers' self-awareness and sense of community, and in addition, who would be required to play a mediating role in the growing economic and social tensions among city citizens; nothing was more suitable for the task than the intensive urban devotion of a saint. Moreover, the saint would have to be accessible to all, at all times, nearly tangible: he would have to have been a citizen of the same city.

I have chosen the example of Milan, one of the oldest examples of its kind, to illustrate the influences of this patron type: the problem has been examined by Hans Conrad Peyer. The Milanese bishop and church father Ambrose was chosen as patron of the Milanese archdiocese shortly after his death, around the fifth century, because he had defended the Catholic faith and prevented the crumbling of the archdiocese before the advance of Arian heresy, down to the details of the liturgy. Since the sixth century, the bishops of Milan had functioned as the 'representative of St Ambrose', as if Ambrose were their actual, undying superior. His cult, however, was almost exclusively a clerical practice, centering around Milan Cathedral, where he is buried. The city's laity first began to pay attention to St Ambrose after the ninth century, when he appeared capable of repelling secular invaders. It was said that in 896 he had prophesied the approaching end of the 'Little Emperor' Lampert of Spoleto, following his attack on Milan. When the German emperor Conrad II approached the city in 1037, St Ambrose was said to have confronted him threateningly in a storm. The Milanese rallied around a banner bearing an image of the saint when they rode out to defend their city's freedom against Emperor Frederick Barbarossa. As late as 1339, witnesses at a battle saw their church father, dressed in robes of white, punishing German soldiers with a whip. In the age of the *condottieri*, the bookish scholar was transformed to a powerful warrior, though always in the defensive position.

'Sant' Ambrogio' already had his hands full settling city disputes. When the archbishop's feudal hierarchy resisted the patrician's bourgeois demands for reform in the eleventh century, both parties summoned St Ambrose as their witness, as though they both thought he would aid one side and not the other. Later, he appeared after all to favour most a specific social group, one which had, until then, never had its own patron: the lower classes. As in the case of St Martin, St Wenceslas and St George, the little man kept a particularly tight hold on sympathetic patrons; one indication is the significance of St Ambrose in folklore as friend to bees and the beekeeper. Not only that, it was St Ambrose's unprecedented duty during the conflicts of the patrician class and Milanese guilds to gain political rights for his charges that they had never previously possessed. Those classes excluded from municipal government organized themselves in the middle of the thirteenth century into the 'Brother-hood of Saint Ambrose', which saw itself as the actual urban community; it practised a form of collective devotion encouraged by mendicant friars. These *Populares* celebrated the feast of St Ambrose on 7 December, a demonstrative protest against the Ghibelline city nobility. The nobility also on occasion referred to the city patron, usually when peace had to be made between bickering aristocratic factions or social groups. It was then that the common veneration of Ambrose created a harmony among the citizenry which never lasted long.

In the end, the social unrest was not settled as the saint might have liked it; the Visconti family took the situation into their own hands in 1277 as the pioneers of the patrician class. In times of emergency, when Milan was threatened from outside, the new city lords often remembered their old patron; otherwise, the Viscontis cared less and less about him, the more aggressively their dynastic hunger for power exceeded their municipal territory. The city commune's arbiter would not fit into the new mould of victory-bringer of the seigniory; as with the monarchy of territorial princes in western Europe, the municipal seigniory displaced the city patron, though in this case it was to be only temporary. Their subjects' pent-up dissatisfaction led in 1447 to the downfall of the Visconti, which was immediately followed by the proclamation of the 'Ambrosian Republic'. The patron's feast day was celebrated with forced processions and semi-official banquets; he who had protected the city's freedom against every type of tyranny was now being used practically as a tyrant who would allow no dissent from the commune. After a new seigniory, the Sforzas, took over Milan in 1450, a conspiracy of several burghers took an oath before the image of the saint before going out and stabbing Galeazzo Maria Sforza to death in the patron's name in 1476. It was a strange saint who was made to cover up a political murder; this was an important element in the destruction of his power to integrate. When the Swiss confiscated Milan's possessions in the Gotthard Pass in 1478, the city was once more edified by a vision of their patron riding upon a white stallion, swinging a whip over the heads of their enemies. But he was too late to rescue their freedom; on the heels of the Swiss came the French, the Spanish and then the Habsburgs, and the political cult of Ambrose perished along with Milan's independence.

There are numerous variations on this type of city patron, and they can be only briefly mentioned here. Not as in Milan's case, many saints became exclusive patrons of the ruling class, such as the evangelist Mark in Venice with his heraldic animal the winged lion,

or the sainted knight Renold in the German imperial city of Dort-
mund with his Hanseatic connections. In other places, such as
Zurich or Soest, city patrons symbolized the city's independence and
self-government to the outside world. The most extensive competencies were those given to the hermit Sebald in the imperial city of
Nuremberg. St Sebald was, as St Ambrose had been, literally a
fellow-citizen; he had chosen this city during his lifetime, and this
was where he chose to be buried, and venerated, after his death. Past
and present appeared to merge here, becoming tangible and
omnipresent, as in the city of St Gall, where Gall the saint had not
only founded an abbey, but championed the municipal commune;
the city carries his name today and celebrates its birthday every year
on the day of his death, 16 October. The popularity of such patrons
was most strikingly portrayed in 1876 by Gottfried Keller in a
festival play he wrote. In it, an army surgeon from Zurich recalls a
meeting with Frederick the Great. The enlightened Prussian monarch
scornfully asked about Zurich's city seal, 'With its three decapitated
personages who offer their heads on their hands like three pastries',
and received the angry reply which no Protestant renunciation of the
Catholic cult of sainthood could undermine: 'Sire, should the Lord
permit, that seal will long remain the symbol of our Republic: do
not make light of it!' And sure enough, the city seal of Zurich still
bears the images of the beheaded municipal saints, Felix, Regula and
Exuperantius.

   Unlike dynastic patrons, city patrons do not necessarily share the
historical and social experiences of their congregation; like estate
patrons, they are separated from their charges by a vast difference in
time, or at least in place. Their relics are always present within the
city walls, however; that is the most important thing. City patrons
were, in addition, neither hot-headed aristocratic warriors nor capitalistic patricians, but either strict ascetics or gentle spiritual guides
of the people. Now, discipline and liberty have become their tasks.
They use their gentleness to foster an attitude that cannot tolerate a
permanent government of living municipal citizens in the town hall;
with miraculous power, city patrons represent a system that bows to
no secular force of covetous neighbours. That is why city patrons
are depicted everywhere, on city coinage, seals, banners and altars.
The city presents itself by holding parades and annual fairs on
its saint's feast day. The names of their patrons given in baptism
identify many citizens as members of the city commune when
travelling outside the city. Only in central Europe, between central
Italy and Flanders, after the dissipation of monarchial power and in
the dissension between the estates could such a spatially restricted

and objectively extensive body as the city thrive. The city patron was the final type of society's hagiographic representative. Later, in the early modern period, the territorial prince arose, a human sovereign predestined by God's grace; since then, communities have been ruled and represented only by the living.

Nonetheless, the medieval mentality has not completely died out. Many of the symbols of modern European nations were in part, and in name, originally patron saints. Bourgeois satire has since robbed them of their haloes and made them common, comfortable, even laughable. 'Paddy', the nickname of all Irishmen in England from the sixteenth century on, is derived from St Patrick. The jack in the German deck of cards is called 'Wenzel' because German peasants in the eighteenth century often hired Czechs as farm-hands, and most of them seemed to be named after Duke Wenceslas. The country yokel wearing knee-breeches and a peaked cap who has appeared again and again in the world's satirical magazines since 1840 under the name of 'German Michel' is hardly recognizable any more as the Archangel Michael, whose banner led Otto the Great in his victory over the Hungarians in the tenth century, and on to his imperial coronation.

VII

Our panorama, which could be complemented in many points, has demonstrated how patron saints in medieval Europe were largely intended for duties that state and society in more modern times have taken over themselves, namely, to preserve harmony and peace within the community and to ensure its independence and liberty against external enemies. These functions are the only permanent ones throughout the Middle Ages. Which saints were meant to perform them and in what way was a question that underwent dynamic and stratified developments all through the superficially static medieval period. The history of these developments is revealed by an examination of the types of saints venerated at any specific time or place. In the beginning, there were wide gaps between the various types and those who venerated them in later days; later, they were recalled into contemporary life as ancestors of the living; finally, practically as fellow citizens, they drew tangibly close to their contemporaries. As their propinquity to the present evolved, their competencies expanded, from the missionary zealousness of the victory-bringer to the royal kindred, to the symbolic figure of a nation, to the patriarchs of a dynasty or representative of a class, to the protector of a city. These changes reflect various peaks in the development of medieval society and state forms, from agricultural personal groups to institutionalized multi-territorial states, from loosely organized principalities to confederate districts, from military expansion to social balance, from sacral legitimacy to bureaucratic administration. This development would have taken place with much more conflict and far less permanence if the worldly conflicts had not been tied to principles in heaven, by means of the patron saints.

Even when the saints had not lost their earthly lives in martyrdom, they were expected to smother unbridled violence and protect the achievements of peace; they sat, after all, at God's side. Though creating paradise on earth was beyond their capabilities, they at least began tearing down mutual mistrust, and to establish a certain trust in common social rules. The modern European period discarded the belief in heaven and launched a new concept, which had also originated in the Middle Ages; for the Middle Ages had always been more or less on the road to greater permanence and rationality, a road which Europe has been treading since. It was just that the medieval part of this road was never lined with a promenade of abstract theories and directional instructions, but by a gallery of human personalities in which any observer should be able to recognize his own likeness. And at this point, I come again to the Charles Bridge over the Vltava in Prague.

The statues that stand there are not divine monarchs on earth, like those that ruled over voiceless peoples in the advanced cultures of ancient times. Neither are they the functionaries of ideologies which, in contemporary world history, use men as tools. They are transfigured, empathetic helpers that allow men the space they need for multi-levelled lives and acts, who instruct them in the rules of the game that might otherwise not have been understood. For the Middle Ages, 'representation' meant visualizing timeless examples of behaviour; it had yet to gain the meaning of personal advocacy. 'Entity' meant the embodiment of social behaviour; it had yet to refer to a legal organization of mortals. Patron saints were necessary for medieval society especially because, regardless of ancestry, men could not trust their peers, and for good reasons; patron saints helped them regulate their communal life with as much liberty as possible. The Middle Ages are over; in the meantime, we have learned to create better bonds between people, and we no longer need saints. But our task now is the same as it was then: to regulate the communal life of man with as much liberty as possible.

9

Chivalric Life in the
High Middle Ages

Everything we imagine when we think of medieval knighthood is in Dürer's engraving of 1513, *The Knight, Death and the Devil*: the kind of castle that can be seen all over in western and central Europe and the kind of suit of armour on display for tourists in any large museum. It is perhaps rarer to find a horse like the knight's noble steed; even the dogs look a little different. The visible remains of knighthood are only the dead husks: the knight's living companions are gone, as are the men themselves, and, it would seem, their ideals with them. Of course, we would all like to be chivalrous, but in the modern world we no longer confront our deaths with the bravery, nor battle against our devils with the devotion, of Dürer's knight. Our society has almost nothing at all in common with men who would go riding through the lonely wilderness half a millennium ago: we are a society that lives in the cities, far distant from dragons and primal forests. Yet there is a correlation between then and now: the parallels of different forms of organized human existence. This is what I would like to discuss.

It is not something that can be perceived through Dürer's eyes, for Dürer's knight is a transfigured, ideal figure, an abstraction retrospectively derived from a way of life that, for the sixteenth century, had long ago died or become ineffective. The real knights of the ninth and tenth centuries never faced death in person, bearing a snake's head or ram's horns. Instead of finely chased plates of armour, they wore chainmail shirts; their castles were simpler than Dürer's knightly residence. The real knights were certainly brave but only hesitantly pious, and seldom alone. Examining the real life of actual medieval knights, it is simple human beings we find, more clearly so than in Dürer's picture, and more clearly, perhaps, than we would prefer: at least well into the twelfth century, the early knights were anything but ideal figures. They came closest to the common idea of medieval robber barons; but in fact they did not belong to the Late, but to the Early Middle Ages.

It is little more than external similarities that seem to equate the two: the image of armed man on horseback and the empty title 'knight' are the only things held in common by the false companion who robbed and killed his fellow-men and the righteous man who defied death and the devil in single combat. One might even go so far as to say that the first type embodied the desperate reality of the Early as well as the Late Middle Ages, while the other was simply an empty shell, *the non-existent knight*, as the writer Italo Calvino described him in his book of that title in 1959. But real history does not run such a black-and-white course. In what follows, I will attempt to outline a movement that changed the actions and thinking of the nobility during the course of the Middle Ages. It started with the real oppression of the timid and reached out for the ideal of protecting the weak; in doing so, it achieved something else, a companionable lifestyle that embodied neither of those two extremes. That compromise is the element that has something to offer us now.

II

Since the ninth century, after the fall of the Carolingian empire, and largely in France, a wild horde of daredevils had established a crude social order and rough government. Amid impassable forests and ravaged villages, they defended a tiny stretch of land against Norman or Saracen robbers. The terrified peasants constructed a wooden tower on a man-made hill for their new protectors and oppressors, surrounding it with a wide moat and wooden palisades; they gave land and food to their armed protectors; obviously these men had to use all the time they had for weapon practice. And that is what the new lords did, some of whom had the blood of counts in their veins, while others were former stable-boys. At first, they ruled by the fist, making treaties with anyone stronger and attacking anyone weaker. Consideration of others they deemed cowardice; the bolder the enemy, the more furiously he had to be cut down. In one case it is even possible to estimate that a certain early French knight killed 650 men with his own hands, not counting those slain in official battles. Besides robbery and war, their favourite activity was hunting wild game; one of their gravestones carries this epitaph: 'He was a nobleman; his dogs loved him.' But who among men might have loved him?

The spoils of robbery and hunting were spent as quickly as possible; only weaklings, men who worked themselves, were miserly. Chastity and self-discipline were considered a form of miserliness; the crowded wooden towers were filled with children, more or less legitimate, and hardly anyone was ashamed of them. Life in those towers was spent in a noisy crowd. One sat squeezed together on long benches, talking loudly and grabbing the meat from the common bowl with the hands; what was left over went to the dogs, or it fell on the straw that covered the wet, cold floor. Few knights of the early period could read or write. At best, they might have someone read aloud about strong heroes who were like they wished they were: strong enough to split their enemy in two from helm to saddle with a single blow. They were also insatiable. They used to say: 'He who eats a great deal cannot get into mischief.' What else could prevent treachery? More superstitious than devout, these early knights gave little thought to ethical norms. If one were ever overcome with morality and swore never to inflict another wound with the blade of a sword, one simply had to beat one's opponent to death with the hilt. Women were not respected, wives were often beaten until their noses bled; many knights handled horses with more respect than they did maids or nuns.

This unconstrained life that denied no desire would be more appealing to us if it had not thrived at the expense of others. How this happened in the early twelfth century can be read in *The Anglo-Saxon Chronicle*:

> Every grand lord would build a stronghold and protect it against the king, filling the whole country with such fortresses. They oppressed the unhappy people of the land by forcing them to build their castles, and when construction was finished they filled it with devils and blackguards. Day and night they searched for people who might be wealthy, both men and women; to get their gold and silver, they would lock them in dungeons and torment them with unspeakable tortures. They would hang them by their feet and choke them in smoke. They would stretch them out and nail them up by their thumbs, then hang iron weights on their feet. They would tie ropes around their heads and twist the ends until their skulls burst.

Not all of them were perhaps as cruel as that; but what none of them had was the noble humanity that we moderns call 'chivalry'.

III

All the more astonishing, then, is the change, developing in the lower nobility, that spread chivalry throughout all Europe, initially in France of the late eleventh century and proceeding through all of Germany and as far as Portugal, Sweden and Hungary. Hot-headed warriors everywhere were disciplined and organized thanks to growing large-scale principalities, to the awe of sacral monarchial anointment and to church reforms that regulated aristocratic feuds under the Peace of God. It became rare for knights to fight against plundering strangers; now they were summoned to the crusade against the heathens of the Orient. A new adventure! One knight was so excited about it he exclaimed: 'Even if I were in paradise, I would come down again to fight the Muslims!' In foreign countries, the lords learned service, largely because they had begun thinking of themselves as an international community and had learned to pay attention to the opinions of their peers. Since around 1100, they had been calling themselves by names that had similar origins in all languages: *chevaliers, Ritter, cavalieri, caballeros*, knights, and considering themselves as an order with specific initiation rites, a code of honour and the ideals of aristocratic power and cavalry service.

Just whom the new men's club was meant to serve, however, was never really clear. At least three chivalric prototypes were propagated by clerics, singers and poets in the twelfth and thirteenth centuries, but these were hardly compatible with each other, nor with real life. The first of these prototypes was the Christ-like knight, God's warrior, the strong serving the weak. His job was to help the church, priests, widows, orphans, sick, pilgrims, animals and possibly even heathens. His selfless service was meant to overcome the disorder of the world and spread justice; his ascetic discipline was meant to elevate his earthly life and guarantee an eternal one. In 1159, the English cleric John of Salisbury wrote in his *Policraticus*: 'What purpose does ordained knighthood serve? To protect the church, to battle against disloyalty, to honour the office of the priesthood, to put an end to injustice towards the poor, to bring peace to the land, to let his own blood be spilled for his brothers, and, if necessary, to give up his own life.' Part of this ideal was personified in the crusades and the orders of knighthood, but mostly it remained theory. One has only to compare John of Salisbury's catalogue of virtues with the catalogue of vices of which the French Cistercian monk, Alan of Lille, accused the nobility in his handbook of sermons from around 1200:

In our day, knights have become predators and robbers; they no longer serve in war but in plunder, and under the cloak of chivalry they practise the cruelty of highwaymen. They battle not against enemies, but rage against the poor; those whom they should defend with the shield of their protection, they persecute with the sword of their wildness.

Though this severe complaint may be exaggerated in part, it shows what the chronicles confirm: the chivalric community was not filled with monastic devotion.

The second prototype, that of the gallant knight, was more loved than that of the Christ-like one. This knight was to serve his 'gracious lady', and might go so far, at times, as to address her as such: she was usually the wife of another man. He was to court her with elegant songs and do battle to increase her glory. It was the stubborn hope for love reciprocated in secret, an unresolved tension meant to elevate the lover. Should the coveted lady refuse, discipline and manners must force the man to maintain his self-control. The reality of love became a game of the seductive moment, an 'if' suspended in the air, and the slightest glance was practically fulfilment. An example, taken from French poetry, is the Breton *Lai de l'Ombre* from around 1200. The knight stands beside a well with his beloved lady, and gives her, as a token of his love, a golden ring. She refuses it. Seeing her reflection in the water of the well, he says: 'Then I will give this ring to my beautiful mistress, whom I love most next to you.' 'Who is that?' asks the lady with growing jealousy. 'Your shadow,' says the knight, and casts the ring into the well. Such noble prodigality characterizes many nobles of the time. Most of them, however, appear closer to its opposite, the image of greed; this image is not absent from poetry either. In the Spanish *Cantar de mio Cid*, composed around 1140, the two distinguished *infantes* of Carrión solicit the hands of the Cid's two daughters only in the hope of getting hold of the Cid's rich war spoils. As soon as they have the dowry, they drag their wives into a forest, rape them, beat them half dead and leave them lying there. Since 1964, Georges Duby has repeatedly stressed that gallantry, though certainly desired, was often rejected on grounds of bare necessity. For nobles not first-born, the hunt for a rich heiress was the search for a basis of survival, and this battle for existence was not always polite. The prototype was even less effective with the older knights, who were more settled in their ways and already had wives and estates. Not every honourable family father was ready, like the knight Ulrich of Lichtenstein, to sip his beloved's bath water or chop off his own finger for love. A minnesinger was once mocked by his audience, who told him that instead of a juicy roast as payment for his entertainment, he should get what he had been in raptures about: flowers and the twittering of birds, with a little water. And Wolfram von Eschenbach said plainly that the true concern of a man was battle service, not minstrelsy. It was a simple fact of life that a community of knighthood could not be based on gallantry.

Wolfram belonged to the propagators of the third chivalric prototype, that of the courtly knight. This knight, like Dürer's, performed purposeless tasks in enchanted forests, not for his own profit, but for the good of King Arthur's chivalric round table. Splendidly surrounded by fine weapons, robes and horses, the courtly knight would further the standards of his group: love and honour. He should be neither too gallant nor too devout; he would seek the extreme situations of chance in order to gain chivalric character. God and man would drive this knight into unprecedented dangers all alone; not until he had survived them with impeccable dignity would the courtly community accept him into their circle. Again, an example from poetry, this time German, from *Iwein* of Hartmann von Aue. In the enchanted forest of Breziljan, a knight encounters a terrifying giant surrounded by wild animals. But the monster remains peaceful. The knight calls out challengingly that he seeks adventure, namely a battle with someone, at which the forest giant shakes his head and says what any of us might have said: that he has never heard of anyone who strove for hardship and did not prefer to live comfortably. He sends the knight deeper into the enchanted forest; perhaps he will find adventure there. In the French original, from which Hartmann adapted his epic poem, the *Yvain* of Chrétien de Troyes, the knight introduces himself by saying: 'I am, as you can see, a knight, who looks for what he cannot find; already I have searched long, but have found nothing.' One could not admit more clearly that this prototype followed unrealistic goals, far from the real world. The nobility of the twelfth and thirteenth century actually greeted hardship only when it appeared a means for gaining a more comfortable future at the expense of their fellow men and competitors.

All three literary prototypes were unrealistic for the knight of the twelfth and thirteenth centuries. In France, many knights had to live down in the villages, working behind the plough, letting rust slowly devour their armour. In Wolfram's Frankish castle, not even mice had enough to eat; another German poet lamented that knights never talked about Parsifal, but only about crops and milch cows. They had no time to fight dragons and sorceresses in the wilderness, and they had no chance of choosing between service to God, to the lady or to the court. Not even Walther von der Vogelweide had good advice to offer on how to place the three prototypes into one shrine, how to unite them in the hearts of men. Yet nearly everyone learned something from these ideals: they respected the church, courted the women and hurried to court. We should not underestimate the self-declarations of such chivalric prototypes; they encouraged moral and mannered behaviour. Yet, ideally, could they have been more than aesthetic norms, pretty gestures, exchangeable pretexts? This question must be tested on an actual case, on the behaviour of a knight in the face of danger, and for this we need not the poets, but the chroniclers.

IV

To see how medieval knights lived together, we will take as an example the seventh crusade in 1248, in which Louis IX led the knights of France, and an account of which was given in 1305 by a participant, Jean de Joinville, in his description of the King's life. In a chronicle like this, something becomes obvious that preachers and poets generally do not mention: that knighthood could only have developed within a sharply defined circle of persons, within a community. As steward of the Champagne, Joinville was an official of his Count, not of the King, with whom he was merely on friendly terms. A noble lord with a beautiful castle and expansive lands, Joinville had dependent vassals, lower nobles whom he called his 'knights'; he took ten of them along on the crusade. That is one meaning of the word 'knight': feudally dependent, aristocratic warriors on horseback. They have a rank of their own. In 1251, at Caesarea near Damascus, one of Louis' bondsmen laid hands on one of Joinville's knights. Joinville complained to King Louis, who tried to dismiss the affair by claiming that the bondsman had only slightly jostled the knight. Joinville threatened to withdraw his detachment if he were not given satisfaction, and if kings' bondsmen were permitted on principle to mistreat knights. At that, the King gave in. The bondsman had to enter Joinville's quarters in shirt and trousers, an unsheathed sword in hand, kneel down and hand the sword over to the knight with these words: 'Sir, I do penance for laying hands on you maliciously, and offer you my sword so that you may chop off my hand, should that be your will.' The knight forgave the bondsman, because this was what everyone expected of a knight; until such time, however, a knight could demand that his dignity be respected.

Men were not born into this rank; if you were worthy, you entered into it by means of the dubbing ceremony. Joinville did not speak of this ritual; more important to him were the expectations which, when fulfilled, resulted in it. He himself, while travelling, knighted a noble squire, Huon of Vancouleurs, following his first chivalric trial. Joinville had heard that the Turkish sultan was making knights of his particularly well-trained and brave bodyguards. It was even said that a Turkish field commander had been knighted by the German Emperor Frederick II. Among the knights of the French king, there were eight specially tested men who 'had earned a reputation on both sides of the sea for wielding weapons, and in those days, these men were called "good knights".' This is the other meaning of the word 'knight': aristocratic warriors on horseback of exceptional bravery. Of course the two meanings are connected; the feudally dependent noble receives protection from his lord, and repays it by military courage. This is, in fact, what was expected in terms of chivalric behaviour; at its most basic, it is wholly unrelated to the Lord God, the gracious lady or Arthur's Round Table.

Nonetheless, the three prototypes of the Christ-like, gallant and courtly knight can be seen in Joinville's book, though strongly filtered by the demands of reality. Joinville considered the saint-like King Louis the very incarnation of a Christ-like knight, since he – as he had in Caesarea – protected the weak from the strong. Yet Joinville disliked the king's radical asceticism. Once the king asked him what he, Joinville, would rather have: thirty deadly sins or leprosy. Joinville chose the thirty deadly sins. When the king wanted to know whether Joinville washed the feet of the poor on Maundy Thursday (something the Pope still does today), the answer was: 'Sire, no one can expect that of me; I will never wash the feet of those dirty peasants.' During the five years Joinville and the king lived in the Holy Land, Louis never once spoke of his queen. Joinville commented: 'And it was not good, it seems to me, that he became a stranger to his wife and children.'

But let us come to an actual case at the heart of the matter. Joinville disliked knights who were brave yet did not believe in God or fear sin; a knight should be both devout and brave. A man closer to his own heart was one of his priests, Jean de Voisey. When eight Saracens began to attack the Christian camp with arrows from behind a bastion, the priest did not take long to ponder: he put on a chainmail shirt and iron helmet, took a pike and approached them. The eight enemies paid no attention to a single man on foot, so he surprised and alarmed them; the camp shouted for joy when the priest chased off the Saracens. Of course, a cleric was not supposed to carry weapons, but what use was theology here? Even a Christlike knight should not be in a hurry to get to heaven. In a desperate battle situation, Joinville's detachment had to choose between death and imprisonment. A relative of Joinville's, who 'came from Doulevant', said, 'I'm all for getting killed, that is the best way for us all to get to paradise.' 'But we did not believe him,' wrote Joinville pithily; he would throw his jewels and relics into the water and march to heathen prison with less hesitation than into Christian heaven. In all the described cases, Joinville did not expect his fellow man to keep Christian principles, but to observe aristocratic convention.

The same thing went for the prototype of the gallant knight. The elderly Joinville, in any case, did not think much of younger boys' lovesick songs; in battle, things depended on action, when matters became serious. When Queen Margaret was pregnant in Damietta in 1250, she lived in constant fear that the Saracens might attack. She found comfort and protection in an eighty-year-old knight who held her hand without any romantic pretensions and promised to kill her with a knife before the heathens had a chance to lay a hand on her. No prudery there! Joinville was irritated by the queen mother, Blanche, who constantly snooped into the married life of the royal couple and disapproved of the king entering his wife's chambers even when she needed help. His judgement of a knight discovered visiting a brothel in Caesarea was just as strict. He was given a choice: either hand over his armour and horse and leave the army, or be led by his prostitute through the camp in his nightshirt, with a rope around his genitals. The knight chose material loss over public disgrace.

Joinville reacted no less angrily to knights who thought only of material gain. During the burial service for the fallen Hugh of Landricourt, six of Joinville's knights were standing around talking loudly, leaning on sacks of grain. Joinville reprimanded them, but soon they were saying with loud laughter that Sir Hugh's wife would be needing another husband soon. The death of their fellow-warrior and the pain of his widow were meaningless for them. With grim satisfaction, Joinville noted that all six fell in battle the next day, and now their wives too would be needing new husbands. Women were neither objects of sexual desire nor of material greed, nor were they an audience for boasters. At the end of a hot day of battle, the Count of Soissons cheerfully called over to Joinville: 'By God, there will be marvels to tell about this day when we get home to our wives!' Though Joinville dictated his book for Queen Joan, in it he told the ladies of no marvels, neither of himself nor of others. Aristocratic reserve was expected.

And that brings us to the prototype of the courtly knight. Joinville was familiar with the soft kind; he wrote: 'In this battle, many braggarts shamefully departed over the bridge I have already mentioned, taking flight in fear and trembling, and we could not hold them back. I could name many of them, but I would rather not, for now they are dead.' He was also familiar with the hotheads, whose names he did mention. Of Duke Hugues of Burgundy, he said sympathetically that he was a good knight with his hands, but not especially clever and wise in the head. Another, Sir Walter of Autrèche, disregarded the orders of the King that all knights were to wait in camp for the Saracen attack. Walter donned his armour in his tent, so that no one outside would notice; after mounting, shield at his throat and helmet on his head, he had the tent pulled away and spurred his horse towards the Turks, alone. He did not go far before falling; four Saracens threw themselves upon the knight, who was lying on the ground, and beat him with maces. Some French comrades managed to drag the seriously injured man out from under his attackers. Joinville tried to visit him in his tent, 'as he was a man of renown and high chivalric virtue', but he was already dead. Joinville added this rebuke: 'When this was told to the king, he answered that he would not have a thousand such hotheads, since they, like this one, never listened to orders.' Courage was chivalrous, but without obedience to one's lord it meant nothing.

What was expected of a knight was neither recklessness, gallantry nor bigotry, it was nothing extreme at all. What poets only occasionally mentioned, chroniclers took for granted: that in the real world, this chivalric ideal taken by itself would only encourage egotism, the recklessness to which every noble lord tended in the first place. What convention expected of nobles was service, but not service to God, to the lady or to the court. To whom, then? That is the question answered by Joinville's stories when they show who rewarded nobles when they obeyed convention, and who punished them when they crossed the line into undisciplined and immoderate behaviour. Certainly, it was God who let the six offenders die so soon after their crimes; certainly, the gratitude of the Queen was what pleased her old protector; certainly, it was the rebuke of the feudal lord that weighed hardest against the hothead. But basically, it was knighthood itself that ruled its members. It translated lofty ideals into social conventions, and made noblemen behave in a knightly fashion.

V

Real social behaviour must be examined at the most critical and thus most pivotal point of aristocratic life, death in battle, which is possible by comparing two statements, one historical and one fictive. For the historical narration I will again choose the story of Joinville. With ten other knights, he had been forced back into a demolished house, surrounded by a large group of Turks and wounded between the shoulders so badly that he could not wield his sword: all he was good for was holding the others' horses. Two of his knights had already fallen; two others had blood gushing out of their bodies 'like wine from an unstopped barrel'. One can imagine that men talked casually and scoffingly about their wounds, even on the battlefield. Another knight, Eberhard of Siverey, had received a sabre blow across the face 'that made his nose fall down to his lips'. In his need, Joinville called upon his patron saint, James, for help. Eberhard, Joinville's vassal, said to his lord: 'Sir, if you see no blame in it, either for me or my descendants, I will try to get help from the Count of Anjou, whom I can see out in the middle of the field.' It would have tarnished the honour of the vassal's grandchildren to leave his lord alone. Eberhard wanted to be as courageous as the others in the group, of whom Joinville later wrote that they were 'praised by all the heroes of the camp, by those who had seen their deed and by those who had only heard of it.' But now, Eberhard had the chance to help his fellow-warriors in a way that was far more effective, though less honourable and more dangerous, by breaking through the ring of enemies and getting relief. Time was short, but they talked in courteous, formal terms. Joinville answered: 'Sir Eberhard, it seems rather to me that it will do you great honour to get help for us, and save our lives, for yours, too, is in danger.' Note well: 'help for *us*', 'save *our* lives'! To show that it was more than merely a question of obedience, but also one of solidarity, Eberhard asked 'all the other knights for counsel, and they unanimously lauded what I [Joinville] too had lauded'. Not until then did Eberhard mount and force his way through to the Count of Anjou, who then cut Joinville's troop out of the trap. In the meantime, Eberhard died of his wounds; Joinville does not describe the conditions any further. It is nearly a wordless death, without loud overtones. 'God give him mercy,' writes Joinville; but Eberhard did not die for God, nor for ladies, nor for courtly fame; in fact, he did not really die for his descendants, either. Nor did he die for ideals or convention, for what he did was unexpected and unusual. He did it after consulting with his fellow warriors, and he did it for them.

It is not easy to find a poetic parallel to this historical death scene, for poets like describing the heroic death of a knight as little as they do a lady's *Liebestod*. However, around 1100, the *Chanson de Roland* described in detail the heroic death of the knight Roland near Roncesvalles. It is a grand death, accompanied by the sound of organs, so to say. Ideals are discussed, mainly those of the devout Roland. The dying knight, lying under a spruce, beats his chest and repents of his sins; then he proffers his right glove to God in heaven, for he has become God's vassal now, and angels come down from heaven to meet him. Roland thinks of the men of his kindred – not of the women, not of his bride; the ideal of the gallant knight has not become significant by 1100. Roland thinks of his lord Charlemagne and of all the countries he had conquered for that king. He lies facing hostile Spain, 'because he sincerely wanted Charlemagne and all his people to say that the noble count had died as victor'. The ideal of courtly fame has immediate influence here. Chivalric conventions, too, are present, not only in gestures like the proffering of the glove; Roland always does what is expected of him and refuses, as long as there is time, to use his horn 'Olifant' to summon Charlemagne and his army; in this regard, even Eberhard of Siverey did not meet the standards of a real knight. A knight fights and dies if he must, even against overwhelming odds. The bold Roland paid no heed to the counsel of his clever brother-in-arms and brother-in-law, Olivier, who reproached Roland: 'Prudent knighthood is not foolishness; proper moderation is better than recklessness. Because of your irresponsibility, the Franks have fallen.'

Even in dying, Roland hardly thinks at all of the deaths of the others; they have long since died and only Roland, the boldest of them all, still lives, to die a lonely death. You can feel the exaggeration rising into the monumental, and Richard Wagner's music comes to mind. But before this, there were other scenes: when the Archbishop Turpin smoothed over the dispute between Roland and Olivier; when Roland faints on seeing Olivier mortally wounded, the face of the corpse already a pale blue; when Roland takes the chainmail shirt off Archbishop Turpin and stops the bleeding with the cloth of his outer garment; when Roland seeks out his fallen comrades on the battlefield after it has grown quiet, and again falls unconscious from grief; when the Archbishop drags himself a few steps in order to fill Roland's horn with water to refresh him; how Turpin then collapses and dies. In such short, almost marginal scenes, the ideal and conventional disappear; this is where you encounter the same reality as in Joinville's tale, the solidarity of aristocratic warriors among themselves. Their life, especially when they risk it, appears a solemn game. The game was celebrated within the community and it was the critical judgement of the community that regulated it; it was, like all structured life, a life with others.

VI

The heart of chivalric life is most visible at a knight's death, but let us now turn to the principles and objects that shaped the rest of their lives, though they too had death as their centre. Biographical coincidences and structural conditions were far more noticeable in the tarnished state of daily life than in the extreme circumstances of the crusades. The European scope of knighthood nearly disappears altogether, for example, in Georges Duby's exciting biography of 1984 of the Anglo-French knight William Marshal. The collection of essays edited by Josef Fleckenstein in 1985, *Das ritterliche Turnier, Beiträge zu einer vergleichenden Form- und Verhaltensgeschichte des Rittertums*, on the other hand, provides a fine examination of the complex of forms in European tournaments, but because it ignores the risk of death, the discussion of the phenomenon of chivalric behaviour is inadequate. In the face of this dilemma, I will restrict this description of a few principles of chivalric life to generalizations, only indicating briefly the countless variations.

Without doubt, the maturing monetary system provided many knights of the twelfth and thirteenth century with a comfortable lifestyle at home. They built stone strongholds on the hilltops surrounded by sturdy walls, they no longer lived in towers, but in palaces, or at least in a roomy knight's hall, hung with tapestries and inlaid with ceramic tiles, or even marble slabs. The bath provided for cleanliness and the huge fireplace for warmth, though it often smoked so much that other countries had a saying that you could recognize a German knight by his red eyes. And though the fortress courtyard was paved with flagstones, chickens and pigs wandered around in them. But then, the basic purpose of the fortress was not to make life more enjoyable.

The children had the best of it. They grew up nearly wild, watched over by the indulgent eyes of wet-nurses and servants, often repaying their care with mischief. The earnestness of chivalric life began at seven years, but not with reading or writing, which was best suited for girls and would surely have ruined the boys. A little French, perhaps, the international language of knighthood, a little

Christian catechism, that was enough for the beginning and usually for the rest of one's life. Education revolved around riding and fencing, in the courtyard and on the hunt. Twelve-year-old boys were pushed out of the nest and sent as pages to other courts, where they were taught to serve as squires, huntsmen and messengers. In the castle, they politely waited on the lord and his guests, critically observed by the men, spoiled by the women. A certain French poet knew: 'No scholar is wise enough to teach a knight in sixty years what a lady can teach him in fourteen days.' Besides the courtly manners of noble ladies, squires learned from one another the ambition of the contest and comradeship in duty. Around twenty years of age, when, as the French saying goes, 'their feathers grow larger than the nest', they would 'earn their spurs' and were dubbed knights in a solemn ceremony.

The pomp with which the dubbing ceremony and accompanying inauguration ritual were often performed should not distract us; the novice and the body of knights took commitments upon themselves that were based neither on aristocratic heritage nor on wealth. In France, they said: 'Whoever wants to be a knight should become one.' In Germany, they said: 'Neither golden finery nor sable fur matches lance and shield as well as loyalty and generosity.' Society expected each man to aspire constantly to chivalric behaviour; in return, they gave him an honourable place in the union of men, who recognized and respected each other despite dividing borders. In this society, knights found friends, comrades-in-arms and blood brothers, and thus fresh chances of serving others. They were also eligible for enfeoffment now, and their feudal lord might give them a castle, not always the paternal one, but often one in foreign territory. The young knight had little time to fritter away dreaming in castle gardens. His marriage, too, was a public event, and included battle games and long feasts, out in the open if possible. Singers, fire-eaters, rope-walkers, animal-tamers, beggars and pilgrims flocked to the feast. When the guests had eaten and gone on, the knights answered the summons of political missions: the occupation of castles, crusades, tournaments and the duties of the legal court, matters of messengers, agriculture and weaponry. Neither could the lady of the castle afford to gaze into the distance from her balcony all day; she had work in the kitchen, cellar, spinning-room and at the sickbeds.

A knight could not, however, restrict his public life to the domestic duties of the day without paying a price. True, there were many knights described putting on 'the comfortable jerkin of the husband', and walking around at home in bare feet, whose bodies had grown heavy and whose hair had grown shaggy. Most others, however, applied the dignity of a public office to their duties, and kept their private lives, sometimes by sheer force, accessible for culture and festivity. In the long evenings, the women read their psalters; they enjoyed even more reading aloud from chivalrous romances or playing the lute, harp or flute. Every now and then, there was a knight who had to admit that the sound of a zither was more familiar than the sound of trumpets sounding to battle; but most of these lords, and, according to French opinion, especially the Germans, were not acolytes of the muses. Playing dice for high stakes was much more fun; the more mannered among them preferred what we have since called 'party games', board games such as draughts or backgammon; the more intelligent played chess, sometimes twenty games one after the other, with pieces, incidentally, so heavy that a furious loser could use them as missiles.

Still, a rough masculine atmosphere could not thrive unchecked, for women were always sitting nearby, and they, too, were bound to observe good manners. A lady – the French word 'dame' is of chivalric origin – did not let her eyes wander about, but sat straight without crossing her legs; she did not laugh out loud, but smiled; she did not talk much and kept her voice low when she did. Besides, the ladies – this, too, is our chivalric heritage – were subject to the strict laws of fashion. They wore heavy headdresses even though they could cause horrible headaches, and every day they would invest all their energy in making themselves beautiful before asking their maids the cautious question: 'Miss, is my colour good today?' Hunting, on the other hand, was less formal, which is why women too loved it so much. Hunting wild game with trained dogs or falcons, using pikes or spears, was a good way to practise weaponry, and often a dangerous one, but besides the pleasure, it filled the knights' tables with fresh meat.

VII

There were those – especially poets, those 'ideologists' of knighthood – who said mockingly that many knights would rather carry the hunting spear than the lance. And it is true that their appetites were insatiable, especially for fat and spicy meat from wild game or fowl. They followed roast and immoderately peppered pheasant or duck with heavy, old wine, this too spiced with pepper or honey. There was a saying that one cup of wine made you more masculine than twenty-four of water or beer. Yet even the richest meal always had to be balanced between inspiring the appetite and practising restraint, for it was a social event; one did not eat alone. In France, men and women usually sat interspersed at the same table; in Germany and England the men often ate alone. They still ate with their fingers, using knives and spoons only when absolutely necessary. Yet they were expected to be considerate of their neighbours; our table manners are of chivalric origin, though refined. The old knights were taught that a tablecloth was there to wipe the fat off their mouths after eating, not to blow their noses on; they were told not to eat too fast, for they might choke or burn their tongues; they were not to take the best pieces from the platter for themselves, but offer them to their neighbours.

After the main evening meal, some went straight to bed, 'because sleep is especially sweet after eating'; but on many evenings they had guests for dinner. Not all knights liked receiving guests. To show their animosity, some would whistle furiously when guests showed up; others tried explaining that their most important grain fields had just been hailed on and they had nothing to eat, even for themselves; others might mumble: 'I do not know why I do not simply throw this man out.' But most knew why they did not do so. Hospitality, towards foreigners or beggars too, was service to a much travelled and exhausted man, and it provided the host with change and excitement. 'A banquet is worthless if the host is scowling all the time,' goes the saying. As a sign of gratitude, the guest would tell what he had seen out in the world, and his audience listened gratefully; the guest provided chivalric society with information and communication.

After the meal, when the table was literally 'put away' – carried out of the knights' hall – the company would stay together for a while: the older men at their wine, until for one or the other, as the saying goes, 'the tongue began to hobble'; the younger ones played ball and danced, two activities that were so closely related to one another that we still speak of a festive dance as a 'ball'. Chivalric dance was the earliest social type; it avoided the wide, fast hop, skip and jump of peasant barn dances. With short steps, measured and sliding, you took your partner's hand and did not speak unless the dance required singing. While dancing, according to the rules, one should be able to balance a wine-glass on top of one's head without spilling a drop. This, too, was more than just entertainment, it was also ceremony, a festive game not unlike a knight's whole life, an additional life overlaying the daily one, defined by rules and stylized poses. This was a life that would culminate in festivals celebrated in the castle, which was no private home but a stronghold and banquet-hall at the same time, a stage for the conviviality of the elite. Some festive events were so expensive that they impoverished the host, but they all furthered his honour, as they served others. In such 'high times' (the literal translation of the medieval German word *hôchgezîten*), all of chivalry converged: the long hall, precious jewellery, the scent of flowers, the glow of candles, the meals with many courses, noble clothing of silk and fur, dance, games, hospitality – manners without constraint, joy without boisterousness. Those of us who know how to celebrate learned it from the medieval knights.

VIII

We have lost track in our age of that other climax of this game of self-denial: the tournament. The contest of weapons was a passion in those days, as motor-racing or football are today. In France, a tournament was held almost every two weeks, and up to 4,000 knights would participate, even though the church strictly forbade it. The prize was usually – in Germany for longer than in France – no more than a wreath or a kiss; but one fought for honour and glory in the eyes of the ladies, amid the fairground tumult of the common folk. In jousts, warriors charged at each other like 'two loosed lions'; one German knight broke fifty-five lances in two days. Then the knights would gather in two massive opposing groups, often hundreds to a faction; this was the actual tournament, the closed-rank mêlée. The scene was often described, helmets sparkling in the sunlight and coats-of-arms gleaming, the earth thundering under hoofs, an immense cloud of dust hiding the clash. All one could hear was the splintering of lances, the din of sword blows and the confusion of hoarse voices: '*Za za, hera her, spera sper, slache slac, hurta hurt, stich und stich, wicha wich, wurra wei!*' Though they usually fought with blunt weapons, many knights fell in the tournament. One seldom came away without bruises. Once, when the champion of a French tournament was to be honoured, they found him at a blacksmith's, his head lying on the anvil; the blacksmith was trying to pry his helmet loose with hammer and pliers. But the heart of the uncomfortable knight was leaping for joy.

The tournament, too, was a game, a game played for life and death, and for that very reason it was true bliss for a knight. The same went for warfare, which the knights managed to keep the way they wanted for several hundred years. Proudly, they put the glory of their suits of armour and coats of arms on display and disdained camouflage or long-range weapons. They fought armed only with lance and sword, face to face, man against man; there were no back-ups, mass armies or tactics. Within the Christian West, at least, they fought not to kill hated enemies, but in openly appointed battle between equals, that is, 'chivalrously'. Some of these chivalric rules of combat have survived to the twentieth century in the various forms of the duel. The honour they would fight for, to be sure, was often of a very material kind; but if we cannot imagine without disgust a knight hunting for the highest-paying opponents and bartering for their ransom, we forget not only that our modern star athletes follow comparable policies, but also the medieval alternative to ransom: butchering the captive. Certainly, many knights would ambush their opponents from behind and slaughter them like cattle; some medieval wars were cruelly waged and only enemy officers, class equals, could hope to be spared. But when that happened, everyone knew that it should not have happened. All in all, it was the kings and burghers of the fourteenth century with their pikes, longbows, crossbows and cannon who first put an end to the knight-ly game. (The aristocratic grudge against those spoilsports who made war serious is still visible in such expressions as the German *Spiessbürger*, which in modern use means 'bourgeois' or 'philistine', but originally referred to the lower-class 'burgher' or freeman who was sent to the front lines armed only with a cheap pike or *Spiess*).

None the less, the lords and burghers, the champions of the Later Middle Ages, loved imitating chivalric lifestyles. From about 1344, the English King Edward III had been seized by a desire to recon-struct at Windsor Castle the legendary Round Table of King Arthur; 300 years before Don Quixote, errant knights actually wandered through the forests of Spain. Through all this, it becomes clear that chivalric lifestyles were being conveyed not by literary models, but by social attitudes; those who no longer understood their roles confused the ideal with the real, they flattered themselves with fine gestures that meant nothing. Crusade vows, for example, were a part of good chivalrous manners up to the late fifteenth century; but ever since the death of Louis IX (St Louis) in 1270, no army or knightly host ever made their vows good. Christian rulers in the Later Middle Ages arranged dozens of knightly jousts among them-selves in order to resolve political conflicts; not a single one of these duels ever took place. The aims and means of combat had changed; only the label of knighthood remained.

Now, six-year-old sons of princes were being dubbed knights, as well as financiers and royal scholarly advisers. Orders of knights existed only to serve the courtly pageantry of the lords, the Burgundian Order of the Golden Fleece, for example, the English Order of the Garter, or a certain Catalan order that accepted only women as members, yet called itself the 'Order of the Axe'. These playful fraternities were no longer an essential part of life; they developed quickly into our modern orders, which are nothing more than factories turning out badges of honour. The 'chevalier' became the 'cavalier', the 'squire' became the 'page' on smooth parquet floors. Courtly festivals were moved from fortresses to palaces, from the open air into the halls, from day to night, and the common people stayed outside. The dances turned to ballets, the tournament to a masquerade ball or to a contest between professional wrestlers, where points were counted to determine the winner. The old knights, on the other hand, went to the courts as officers or officials or to the city as patricians or merchants. Those who could not join in the march of time drew closer together in their aristocracy and farther away from everything else, an exclusive birth rank with no social function but that of maintaining their own dignity. Except for a few true robber barons, they all knew precisely what behaviour was fitting; but the formal label could hardly hide the isolation of their lives. The game had lost its earnestness and its participants. Before the decisive battle with the English at Crécy in 1346, the French King Philip VI sent out a scout team of four knights to reconnoitre the English position. When they returned, impatiently anticipated and bearing the message on which the French strategy depended, they put on a show of politeness; each insisted on modestly remaining silent, no one wanted to make his report before the others. This was the same attitude for which Eberhard von Siverey had given his life 100 years earlier; only this time it no longer served common interests, but only damaged them. The duo of chivalrous service and chivalrous play, one dependent upon the other, had split up long before Dürer began portraying the purely idealistic knight.

IX

The flowering of the chivalrous lifestyle was encouraged by a short phase in social history, the time between 1100 and 1300, during the shift from aristocratic caprice to the power of the lords, from violence to manners. In those two centuries, knighthood did much for the adoption of ethical principles in everyday life and for the uniting of the Western peoples with each other. This period of the direct social influence of knighthood is over; no amount of romanticizing will ever bring it back. Nevertheless, parts of the chivalrous lifestyle have remained effective. The first and most obvious remnant is our social etiquette: table manners, festivities, sayings, forms of address, emblems, insignia. The second and deeper element is the use by numerous modern societies of behavioural standards marked by chivalrous ideals: the Italian *cortegiano* and the Spanish *hidalgo* of the sixteenth, the French *honnête homme* of the seventeenth, the English 'gentleman' of the eighteenth centuries. The third and most topical element is a human attitude we use every day. It is the tendency of man to build a social community upon the foundation of his personal freedom, who does not forget his own imperturbable generosity in service to a beloved cause. He neither sinks into the ugliest conditions nor climbs to the highest ideals, but dedicates his efforts to living with his own kind. He challenges the things that would isolate him from others, the chaos of reality and the fanaticism of power, with a uniting, regulated game.

Part VI
Intellectual Movements

10

Crisis and Reform
in the Universities of the
Late Middle Ages

I

It is almost a platitude among modern medieval scholars that in the fourteenth century Latin Christianity was in a crisis and began casting about for ways of reform. However, it will take a long time before this thesis is established in detail. For example, the question has neither been asked nor answered as to how the period's universities, vital institutions for Christianity, were affected by crisis and reform. When we discuss the crisis of the Late Middle Ages, we consider intellectual movements beside religious, social and economic ones, but universities are given attention only in passing, as in the collection of essays of 1984 edited by Ferdinand Seibt and Winfried Eberhard, *Europa 1400, Die Krise des Spätmittelalters*. On the other hand, when the universities are the central subjects of research, their history in society, state, church, law and government is treated in detail, but no intellectual crisis is mentioned, as in the collection edited by Johannes Fried, *Schulen und Studium im sozialen Wandel des hohen und späten Mittelalters* (1986). Had the university in the Late Middle Ages become so settled, structured and spoiled that there is no intellectual activity for us to find? At first sight, they seem not to have become involved in the crisis until 1350, if not as late as 1450. However, the Popes of Avignon, the main actors and defendants of the critical period, had a different outlook from that of contemporary scholars; they saw powers at work in the early-fourteenth-century universities that threatened the established values of the church, and early on they demanded a *reformatio*, a university reform as part of the church reform. Should we take this criticism of the time seriously, we must speak of a university crisis in the early fourteenth century; in other words, of a challenge to the university to meet the changes in the state of things through intellectual renewal.

Papal criticism was mild at first, as in the letter of Pope John XXII to the University of Paris of around 1317. The Pope emphasized that the university had always passed the cup of knowledge to all of Christianity, even to the most distant of peoples, enlightening them with the light of faith. Recently, however, bickering and fighting had taken root in the university; presumptuous idle talk and vain intellectual curiosity threatened to take the upper hand. The university should listen instead to the admonition of the apostle 'not to be more wise than it behoveth to be wise, but to be wise unto sobriety' (Romans 12:3).

A generation later, in 1346, the reprimand of Pope Clement VI sounded irritated and bitter, as if the university were practically already beyond hope. Clement himself had studied in Paris, but its old reputation had become greatly obscured, he wrote; the school no longer spread the truth of the sciences, but the stink of disgrace. Above all others, the Pope had three complaints to make. First, teachers and students of philosophy had become contemptuous of the texts of Aristotle and other old masters, and were instead attending to the confused suppositions and hypothetical problems proposed by foreign universities; the University of Paris, which had always been the standard, was making itself a slave to the foreigners. Secondly, it was even more distressing that Parisian theologians, consumed with curiosity, were ignoring the original text of the Bible and the interpretations of established dogmatists and exegetes, investing their energies instead in philosophical hair-splitting; 'in this miserable time', which hungers for salvation and instruction, as it did earlier, the leaders of souls were wasting their time with useless babble. Thirdly, instead of furthering the sciences by teaching and studying, the masters were spending their time in endless meetings of the entire university staff, or of faculties and nations; in those meetings, they were not consulting each other on what was most needed, but, disregarding all statutes, stubbornly bickering over titles and ranks. The mania for something new was suffocating the old truth; arrogance was growing from the *curiositas* of the scholars. In order to protect the university, even all of Christianity, from the growing threat, the Pope warned that he was ready to take rigorous action if the university did not soon return to its old ethics.

II

The Pope had not plucked his objections out of thin air, as medieval scholarship has long been aware. Since around 1320, the intellectual climate of the University of Paris had been changing, initially under the influence of English nominalism and later under that of Italian humanism. The Sorbonne could hardly have ignored these fresh impulses forever, though until 1340 it was hesitant to acknowledge either movement. None the less, the authority of the old texts, Biblical as well as Aristotelian, was questioned increasingly; the great epoch of the Parisian commentators ended with Nicholas of Lyra in 1349. Around 1330, grammarians lost faith in the power of speech to reflect reality, which until then had been the basis of classical scholastic thought. Nominalist language criticism isolated general terms from specific realities, the incomprehensible God from human experience, and made scholars seek the potential and limitation of reliable empiricism more and more inquisitively. This was when theology retreated in favour of philosophical theory and physical experiment. The saying 'Experience is the best teacher' spread through Paris, not only among adherents of secular concerns, but even among the caretakers of the Christian faith. Studies in mathematics, mechanics, economy and politics begun in Padua or Oxford continued in Paris; the motto of the rector of Paris University, John Buridan, in 1340, which might sound more arrogant than it was meant to be, is characteristic: 'I saw it.' The assurance was no longer: 'He said it.' What Avignon disliked was too much activity, not too little.

Papal critics had correctly described the symptoms of change, intellectual as well as institutional. The interior structure of the university had been loosening since around 1320, when, in addition to the nations, faculties began arising from within specific academic disciplines. Academic self-administration was made even more complicated by the growing influence of discipline-specific colleges within the university, which developed into schools within schools. Severe conflicts of competencies were the result. The relations between universities also became tense during this period; national emotions heralded the beginning of the period of the Hundred Years' War. The University of Paris had to forfeit its leadership position, largely to Oxford. The English, on the other hand, had been claiming since 1317 that Paris University had been founded during the Carolingian period by Anglo-Saxons, and was thus of later origin than English schools. On the other hand, after 1344 the English simply considered Paris out of date; a story was told about Minerva, who had once left Athens and Rome in her journeys, now, 'in our sad days', also leaving Paris and taking up residency at Oxford.

Parisian leanings towards those modern, usually English, academic achievements was what the Popes of Avignon were fighting; what they wanted was the continuation of the late-thirteenth-century scholastic university structure. In those days, the triumph of the mendicant friars over the worldly clerics and the Thomist synthesis of the gospel and Aristotle had made Paris a meeting-place for scholars so quickly that, in 1281, the German cleric Alexander of Roes could say that one capital of scholarship was enough for all of Christianity. As late as 1333, the Provençal Dominican Armandus de Belvézer said, without envy, that Paris, at least for theology, was the university of universities, the *studium studiorum*. It was in Paris that theology had become the queen of the sciences, and philosophy her handmaiden; this was where the systematic interpretation of traditional and respected texts was developed. This was where, under the supervision of the Pope, a hierarchically structured, functioning entity had been created. The Popes of Avignon wanted this old order preserved.

III

Were the criticized developments in fact symptoms of a decline, and did the restoration of scholasticism really present a solution to the crisis? Or would the Avignon Popes only hinder the university's growth with their criticism, might not their reforms cause a serious crisis, a situation of confusion and disappointment? The fact that the crisis of Paris University was in fact partially provoked by papal university reforms can be demonstrated in the behaviour of Pope John XXII. He was partly guilty of the very things he criticized, as he was the one to subvert the theological authority and the autonomous charter of the Sorbonne. John, who was not a theologian but a jurist, forced the Parisian masters to discuss his daring theses about the *visio beatifica*, the unmediated vision of God, and he casually excused applicants from examination requirements in order to shorten their length of study. The tight intellectual and legal bonds between the Sorbonne and the Popes surely contributed to the crisis of scholasticism.

But this is not generally valid; one only need think of the second model university of the thirteenth century, Bologna. The methodical interpretation of authoritative texts also flourished there, during the time of the commentators: they, too, had a strict charter; and here, too, from 1278 on, the Popes, as lords of the Pontifical State, were able to intervene directly. In Bologna as in Paris, the old impulses died around 1320. The metropolis of judicial studies was unable to reconcile old legal texts with current legal reality, and therefore could not renew itself; it suffocated in the city's limitations and patriarchal vanity. For this crisis, which indicated not growth but decline, the reformer Popes of Avignon could not be blamed; on the contrary, they tried their best to tear Bologna out of its provincial rigidity, as Petrarch gratefully acknowledged. Nor can we say that the Popes had caused a general stagnation of the universities; they simply tried, amid varying local circumstances, to preserve the unity of Christianity. It is understandable that their attempts to alter the complex structure of a university did not always have favourable results; Paris and Bologna both had enough merit to endure the crises and reforms to this day.

If we want to examine crisis and reform in the fourteenth century, however, it is best not to concentrate on the older institutions of the High Middle Ages; what the epoch attempted and where it failed is most visible in its own, newly founded universities. What constituted the crisis of the fourteenth century, how contemporaries fought it and why it thrived nevertheless is what I would like to illustrate, using the examples of the universities newly founded in the fourteenth century.

IV

In 1968, Peter Classen discovered an intimate connection between the first great reform movement in the history of European universities, that of the early thirteenth century, and the first wave of planned university foundations. Even at that time, it was obvious that institutional crises were more easily solved by creating new establishments than by changing the old ones. After that wave of new foundations, which ranged from Naples in 1224 to Seville in 1256, no new universities were founded until 1290. This meant that in the late thirteenth century, all efforts could freely be concentrated on the development of scholasticism at those universities. At a stroke, the second wave of new foundations began in 1290, and this was to become the biggest wave in the history of medieval universities. Up to the middle of the fourteenth century, twenty institutions for general study were founded, almost as many as existed in Europe already, and many more than that would be established in the late fourteenth century. Here is a list: Lisbon in 1290, Gray in 1291, Alcalá in 1293, Pamiers in 1295, Lérida in 1300, Rome in 1303, Avignon in 1303, Perugia in 1308, Coimbra in 1308, Dublin in 1312, Treviso in 1318, Cahors in 1332, Grenoble in 1339, Verona in 1339, Pisa in 1343, Prague in 1348, Florence in 1349, Perpignan in 1349, Cividale in 1353 and Huesca in 1354. Most of these universities were not set up on green fields, however, but instituted within older schools that had mainly taught church or civil law. Almost all foundation dates correspond to papal bulls which awarded those schools the character of a university, of a *studium generale*. Treviso, too, had tried to obtain a papal bull, but was not granted one, and so settled for an imperial licence. Even the autocratic kings of Aragon requested papal authorization for Lérida, and claimed later for Huesca, where they, as in the case of Perpignan, no longer asked, that a papal certificate had been received and lost. Just how valuable papal approval was can be seen from the fact that two previously valid general education institutions applied for and received theirs retrospectively, Cambridge in 1318 and Valladolid in 1346.

At first sight, it is tempting to suppose that this wave of new foundations had originated in papal initiative. Though that would be incorrect, it did have at least some relationship to attempts at church and university reform. This relationship, especially through the Synod of Vienne in 1311, was stressed in Heinrich Koller's study of 1966. Yet the reform edicts of Vienne referred not to the new universities, but to the older, famous ones in Paris, Oxford, Bologna and Salamanca. If the Popes restyled general reform plans for specific places, as we can see they did, we must take a closer look at what the coveted papal bulls required of and permitted to the new universities.

V

All newly founded universities were granted the right to institute programmes in any requested discipline, *in quavis licita facultate*, as Pope Nicholas IV had done for the first time in 1289 for the University of Montpelier, which, until then, had been exclusively a medical faculty. This same wording, changed only slightly, was adopted by secular founding documents, like that of Frederick the

Handsome for Treviso and those of the Aragonese kings for Lérida, Perpignan and Huesca, a clause that originally dated back to Emperor Frederick II's founding charter for Naples of 1224. By comparison with the scholastic universities, this was a major change, for scholastic universities had not included all disciplines, specifying focal points. For Paris, King Philip the Fair reconfirmed that tradition in 1312: as had been the case since the papal decree of 1219, the Sorbonne was further to forgo its proposal for a faculty of civil law; for the king of the legists, this was no easy decision, but it allowed Paris to retain its position as the heart of theological education 'for the entire world'. On the other hand, universities specializing in juridical disciplines, such as Orléans, were not allowed to award theological degrees. The new universities, however, fought for autonomy and a wider scope of subjects, even if that involved a lowering of standards – it was an indication of the tendency of the time to create small, distinct circles of thinkers parallel to the Catholic community. The Popes were fighting for the unity of *christianitas*, but opted to give in to local movements. They compensated by either expressly or unofficially disallowing the study of theology in Lisbon, Lérida, Rome, Avignon, Grenoble and Verona. In that way, the universal pre-eminence for theology was reserved for Paris; now, the new local foundations really depended on canon and Roman law, which was and remained indispensable for the education of the provincial upper classes, the episcopate and bureaucracy.

A similar attempt to compensate can be seen in the papal stipulations deciding whether teaching permission earned at one university would be valid at another, the *ius ubique docendi*. Since 1233, the Curia had occasionally decreed that the academic degrees of a newly established university would be valid at all others without the necessity for additional examinations. In 1292, Nicholas IV even awarded this privilege to Paris University, a privilege that, for an institution like the Sorbonne, would never have been questioned only shortly before. Now the Popes tried to withhold universal examination recognition from the newly founded schools. The early foundations of Lisbon and Avignon received the *ius ubique docendi*, but the schools founded later, Rome and Perugia, did not, and the later ones only with characteristic restrictions. According to Pope John XXII's bull of 1332, graduates from the University of Cahors were permitted to teach anywhere except in Paris; in 1349, the university of Florence was instructed to hire masters who had graduated in Paris, Bologna or in any of the other famous general education institutions. The provincial, yet untested institutes were obviously not intended to flood the West with graduates; the standards and prestige of the old universities had to be defended. Students' freedom of mobility was not restricted. Shortly after their foundation, nearly all new universities were freed from the stipulation that clerical scholars should take up permanent residence in the district where they were studying. This freedom was important for financial security, since scholars often had to live on the income of benefices in their home dioceses. It is notable that both Italian urban universities, Treviso and Florence, strove for this papal exemption but did not receive it. Accordingly, all their students came from the cities' territories.

At any rate, these papal decrees were meant to extend the universal education system of Christianity by means of new local universities. They were meant to provide for the needs of the local area but not disturb the old centres of education, which were still organized not according to geographical restrictions, but thematic focal points. This was a reasonable concept of reform for a stage of growth, but it was impossible to realize. The great number of new universities and the speed at which they were founded excluded systematic guidance; the newer schools did not want to be organized according to the papal bulls, they wanted to achieve the sovereignty of their rights and faculties. The intentions of the founders clashed with the Pope's plans.

VI

In only one of the twenty cases did the Pope himself initiate the foundation of one of the universities, acting as authorized territorial lord, that was Rome in 1303. On that occasion, Boniface VIII proclaimed that the university would benefit foreign students who came to the papal residence from elsewhere as well as the interests of local residents. Though universal and local aspects were balanced here, the Lisbon petition to Pope Nicholas IV of 1288 made the emphasis clearer: education in foreign countries could not be expected of residents of the kingdom of Portugal, due to the difficult journey and high expense. King James II of Aragon wanted to found a university in Lérida so that Catalan nationals would not be forced to study abroad. Arguing in favour of a university in Dublin, the Archbishop there, John Lech, argued in 1312 that without one Irish scholars would have to cross the ocean and risk grave dangers at sea to gain a higher education. In 1314, Treviso wanted to provide for the intellectual nourishment of its own countrymen. The same rationale, first introduced in 1224 by Emperor Frederick II for the national university of Naples, was also used in 1348 by Emperor Charles IV for Prague, in 1349 by King Peter IV of Aragon for Perpignan and again in 1354 by King Peter for Huesca. Lérida and Florence, and possibly others, carried their autonomous mentality as far as Frederick II had, forbidding their nationals to study abroad. This means that the sovereign founders of early-fourteenth-century universities saw the ecumenical charters differently from the way the Curia in Avignon saw them: they were not meant to further the universal Christian system of education, but territorial educational politics; papal consent was necessary to found a sovereign university in their own countries equal to foreign universities and attractive to foreign students, yet not chase away domestic ones.

The leaders of the universities furthered the politics of their princes and modified papal stipulations. More than anything else, they championed a wide range of disciplines and faculties. Around 1330, Oxford University was still in a position to boast of being 'more universal with respect to the diversity of our sciences' than any other general education facility in the Latin world; this was where theology had been taught from the beginning, despite the Parisian monopoly. But soon Oxford no longer stood alone, and step by step the Popes gave in. At first, they granted occasional permission to certain students to take their theological examinations outside Paris, which meant at a university without a theological faculty. There was then no logical reason to refuse the occasional civil law student permission to study in Paris, though Paris had no civil law faculty. Finally, in 1332, John XXII conceded to his home city Cahors the unrestricted right to teach theology right from the beginning. Pisa followed in 1343, Prague in 1348, Florence and Perpignan in 1349 and Huesca in 1354. Behind this concession, which destroyed scholasticism, might have been the disappointment of the popes about Paris, which had been intended to embody the unity of theology and which now wanted to betray it. After 1360, the new universities received their own theological faculties, as did the older ones: Perugia in 1371, Lisbon in 1411, Avignon in 1413 and Lérida in 1430. The pluralism of theological schools was thus institutionalized; the results became visible in the Great Papal Schism of 1378.

At the same time, the restrictions of the *ius ubique docendi* began to fall, which until then had ensured Paris its exceptional position. In 1317, John XXII refused to grant the University of Oxford the requested equivalence of academic degrees with Paris, apparently because of his irritation with Oxford theology; yet as early as the following year, he granted Cambridge the *ius ubique docendi*, and in 1333 cancelled the University of Salamanca's restriction favouring Paris and Bologna. After that, in 1339, Pope Benedict XII quickly granted the newly founded Grenoble university automatic recognition of its academic degrees at all other universities. Greater freedom of movement for the masters was also granted; but that privilege was largely ignored. The Aragonese kings had not been interested in the *ius ubique docendi* from the beginning, since they wanted to bind their masters to local universities; and this was the general tendency. As early as the beginning of the fourteenth century, the University of Paris complained that its academic degrees were not being accepted in Oxford and Montpelier without additional examinations. Even the French universities of Orléans and Angers would not accept graduates from other universities without additional testing, probably in order to protect themselves from the competition of Italian universities. With that, the very provincialization of the Western educational system, which the papal reformers had wished to avoid, began.

VII

Did the newly founded universities, after the popes gave in, become something completely different from the Curial reform universities they were meant to be, namely the educational institutions of local principalities, like the ones that shot up everywhere in the fifteenth century? Did the universities comply with the central movement of the period, the shift 'from an open system to a structured consolidation' (Peter Moraw)? This conclusion would be rash. The territorial lords of the fourteenth century were actively involved in founding universities in their territories and liked recruiting the clerics and jurists educated there into their political and administrative services; yet they hardly attended to the legal order or, most importantly, to the financial support of these schools. Only Peter IV of Aragon tried to support his University of Huesca through a tax on meat and tribute from Jews, and the attempt might not have failed had the state offices enforced it. Necessary facilities of that kind, however, were available only to the papal church, which alone could have provided the financial support of the teachers and scholars, as it could for its charters.

However, it no longer performed this service voluntarily. Bishop William of Angers complained vehemently at the Synod of Vienne in 1311 about the 'slackness and slow destruction of the universities, which in our time are deteriorating throughout the world', and said that the reason for this deterioration was that scholars were not sufficiently supported by the benefice-holding prelates of their home cities. And in 1316, Pope John XXII observed that the bishops were neglecting this duty of theirs and, as a result, the number of scholars attending Paris from all over the world had severely shrunk. The Pope was aware of the financial aspects of the university crisis and demanded that the episcopate help Parisian masters and scholars by granting benefices. We already know his intention: he meant to strengthen the universal pre-eminence of Parisian theology, for when the University of Oxford, which at that time was a breeding ground of unrest, requested the same considerations for its own scholars, the Pope did not react. The indirectness of going through bishops, however, became unfeasible for Paris; thus, in 1342, Pope Clement VI received from the Sorbonne the first *Rotulus beneficiandorum* known, an index of those who were to receive church benefices. In so doing, the university was, as an entity, requesting and receiving directly from the Pope the income allocation to which they were entitled. After that, Sorbonne scholars lived independently of the papal economy of benefices that, during the time of the reform councils, was denounced as mismanagement. Other schools, too, soon made similar requests; if our historical sources do not mislead us, the first were the universities closest to the Avignon Popes: Angers, Cahors and Grenoble in 1343, Avignon and Toulouse in 1353 and Salamanca and Prague in 1355. That means that the others, mainly the newly founded universities, were left financially to themselves in their early years. Although the theory recognized them as equals of the University of Paris, papal financial politics did not extend that far.

The young universities were also abandoned by local financial patrons. That is why they did not participate in another result of reform of the time, perhaps the most important: the formation of discipline-specific colleges. Those provided support and funds for masters and scholars that served more than just financial necessity; they renewed the old intellectualism of the universities and provided students of theology, mainly the poorer ones, with homes. The intensification of education by living and working together came through monastic custom; institutionally, therefore, theirs was a more conservative nature; at the same time, it conformed to the tendency of the time, which was to re-order life into smaller, compact groups. The founders of colleges were mostly clerics, among them two Popes of Avignon and many bishops, no kings and only few burghers. None the less, the colleges of Paris, where twenty-seven were newly endowed in the first half century, were open to the influence of the world. This is where the Collège de Navarre with Buridan and Oresme, its brightest lights, became the focal point of the new physics and economics disciplines, and Oxford's Merton College, with Bradwardine and Burleigh, promoted the study of mathematics and astronomy. As far as we know, among the new, early-fourteenth-century universities there were no financial patrons who endowed colleges. When students did not come from far away, they had no need of such colleges as places to live in any case. Thus, those schools lacked the basic points of crystallization for a theology of the future as well as for the rising empirical sciences. When, in 1362, fifty years after its founding, the first of the new universities, Perugia, finally received a college, it was in no way meant to pro-mote Italy's modern jurisprudence, which would only contribute to the destruction of the soul; yet it became the base of theological concentration, as did the endowments elsewhere. The majority of colleges were formed in the two biggest and most lively university cities of this group, in Avignon in 1379 and in Prague in 1366. Florence took until 1429, Lisbon until 1447 to acquire their first colleges. Thus, in this sense too, the newly founded universities were abandoned to a dangerous vacuum.

VIII

The underdevelopment of the new schools was a kind of opportun-ity too, for the propagation of colleges was accompanied by a fragmentation of the whole, and encouraged social discrepancies and tensions. The newly founded universities, however, were not able to use this opportunity to experiment with organizational sys-tems because the coveted papal licences limited them to scholastic models, and their flexibility was restricted by their territorial lords. That their written statutes were dictated in such a hurry was pecul-iar in itself: Lérida's was completed the same year as it was founded, in 1300, Coimbra's in 1317, Cahors' in 1367, Perpignan's about 1389 and Dublin's in 1320, when no academic community was yet present in the city. Even more surprising is that they retained the 'nations', the student organizations that had been formed at the end of the twelfth century in Bologna and Paris to help foreign scholars. In 1274, when the influx of foreigners had dissipated, the University of Oxford (which, incidentally, had no written statutes) disbanded its 'nations'; they had become little more than excuses for neigh-bouring clans to brawl with each other. It was little different in Paris, as became obvious during the fights in 1328 between the

Picard and Norman 'nations', that is, between French students; in this case, however, they were retained in order to preserve a pretended universality. Among the new schools, only Lisbon-Coimbra and the southern French group of Avignon, Cahors, Grenoble and Perpignan parted with the obsolete subdivision of 'nations'. But since Paris still had them, Lérida, Pisa and Prague had to have them too, though the principle of national subdivision hardly fitted the discipline-based organization of these geographically autonomous universities.

And because it did not fit, Prague had to pay with the only exodus of masters and scholars that ever occurred among the new universities. Migration in protest was hard to reconcile with that kind of local national university, but so was the students' uprising against hostile city populations, which shook the foundations of the old universities of Bologna in 1321 and Oxford in 1355. Among the new universities, student unrest occurred only in Lisbon and Lérida at the beginning of the century, then in Avignon and Prague, where students resisted the Parisian organization model in 1367 and 1372. The fact that the old organization was met with active protest in those cities alone was connected to the number of students: Avignon and Prague were the only new foundations that already showed a student population of more than 500 students by the late fourteenth century. They were so well attended because they were the only universities in cities of court residence. Permanent court residences were just beginning to form in early-fourteenth-century Europe; the papal court in Avignon became, like 'golden Prague', the early model of a capital city. Most new universities were established in isolated and peaceful locations. In the case of Lisbon, following student unrest in 1308, the King asked the Pope for his consent to relocate the university to the quieter location of Coimbra; by 1380, it had no more than eighty-one students. That case shows that provincialization, which the Popes had to some extent intended, was making rapid progress, because the dynamic political and social powers of the day, monarchy and the bourgeois, had abandoned the new universities. For them, universities were still the responsibility of the church.

Such insecure conditions were not conducive to the encouragement of intellectual exertion. In the field of philosophy and traditional theology, none of the new universities had made contributions worth mentioning; only three Italian universities became significant for the modern disciplines, and that because conservative-minded Bologna rejected them longer than Paris. In Perugia and Pisa, the Roman law school of commentators revolved around Bartolo and Baldus about 1340; unlike the Bolognese commentators, they went beyond text analysis of the *corpus iurus civilis* and referred to currently valid statutes and traditions to create a practical, contemporary law. In Florence, humanism gained a foothold around 1360, mainly thanks to Boccaccio's influence, which relied not only on classical Greek and Latin texts, but was also open to the literature of the modern vernacular. The great renewers of the century did not arise in the new universities, however, but in the old ones: John Duns Scotus and William of Ockham, Marsilius of Padua and Peter of Abano, Meister Eckhart and Petrarch, the men of the Collège de Navarre and Merton College, Oxford. Their movement of anti-Aristotelian, even anti-intellectual thinking made the Popes of Avignon smell a crisis of the old universities; in reality, the papally sanctioned reform movement of the new universities was ending in resignation.

The way the new universities would grind themselves down in the no-man's-land between crisis and reform gives a preview of their coming fates. No wave of new universities ever left so many ruins behind as this one. Of the twenty schools, six never got past the planning stages: Gray, Pamiers, Alcalá, Dublin, Verona and Cividale. Three soon collapsed: Treviso, possibly in 1339, at the latest in 1407; Grenoble before 1452 and Florence in 1472. Five had to be re-established after a short time: Lisbon in 1339, Coimbra in 1355, Perpignan in 1379, Rome in 1431 and Pisa in 1472. Two had such low enrolment figures that they were considered dead: Huesca in 1358 and Cahors in 1371. Thus, of the twenty universities, sixteen had major troubles, nearly all for political and economic reasons, that is, because they were not supported by anyone in power. Despite the plague, starvation and wars, four universities managed to survive, and those had been carried by local powers: Lérida thanks to the support of the Aragonese kings; Perugia as part of an independent commune; Avignon because of the papal aid there; and Prague as a favourite project of Charles IV. They survived; but the obscurity of the ideas behind their establishment haunted them for a long time. The future belonged to the truly national universities, which had been taking shape since 1364 in Cracow, Vienna and Heidelberg.

IX

To summarize: the crisis of the early-fourteenth-century universities did not have its roots where the Popes were looking for them: neither in the old universities' process of growth, which led away from scholasticism, nor alone in the tendency to found smaller and more compact communities. The crisis matured in the new universities themselves, which were intended to support the reform but became caught between two different concepts, the papal vision of a united Christianity and the territorial idea of concentrated monarchies. Both powers were strong enough to found many universities, but both refused to support even one of them fully. They failed because they could not answer clearly the central question of the century: What is church, community, *universitas*? Is it the Christianity of the papal church, the territorial monarchy, the municipal seigniory, the republic of scholars, or the class of intellectuals? The new universities, founded in the twilight of incomplete ideas, developed amid the confusion of chance and neglect and escaped neither the rut of tradition nor the chaos of reform. No one found an answer to the question as to where the line should be drawn between service to the whole and freedom of the individual.

One solution to the problem was proposed, in a desperate, radical way, by the rector of a new university, John Huss in Prague. His followers wanted a society that could not be found in existing conditions, so they sought it in a concept of society that was as intellectual as it was huge, which attacked Christianity religiously, socially and nationally. It was not until the Great Schism that the crisis of some of these universities merged with the crisis of the Late Middle Ages; but even before then, the harm had been done. In their hurry, they had not given a clear answer to the question: what type of institution would have the power to stabilize intellectual movements and to mobilize them at the same time? Perhaps we can speculate that in one way the crisis of the Late Middle Ages started with the initial process of growth, grew past half-hearted reforms and developed into a real crisis with no solution, because the question that encompassed all the others was this: in what kind of community can men live together as committed members and yet in an unconstrained manner?

Part VII
Experiences with Art

11

Women and Art
in the Middle Ages

I

In our century, art without women is unthinkable, even in a German city like Constance, which learns so slowly and forgets so quickly. 'After all, Christa Wolf has been here, and Anne-Sophie Mutter is coming soon!' And that is not all: the directors of the municipal art gallery are women; women from the local university have even been given permission to put on an exhibition, though one has to admit that that particular show had already gained acclaim in other cities. The initial impulse for that exhibition was inspired by the unanimous opinion of art historians that the Middle Ages were much different from modern times, that in those days women could certainly inspire and appreciate art, but almost always had to leave the practice of creating art to the men. Can it be that this idea is not only based on a tremendous prejudice, but also ignores the motivations and purposes of art in the Middle Ages?

The question is not easily answered. For the history of art in Constance, the common consensus may be accurate. In the fourteenth century, for example, the wood-carver Heinrich of Constance and the writer Heinrich Suso both received more applause from the women of that town than imitation. This impression might change, however, if the influence on neighbouring convents were also examined, but as long as one relies solely on the inventory of the local museum, proof of female creativity will forever remain out of reach. None the less, in other places, scattered across Europe, in the Middle Ages numerous women were active in the creative development of art. The names of three artists of the first order should suffice: the Spanish book illuminator En of Tavara in the tenth century, the German musician Hildegard of Bingen in the twelfth century, the

French poet Christine de Pisan in the fourteenth. It is easy to see what these women meant for the art of the Middle Ages, even besides the fact of their sex. In fact, it would be difficult to find traces of their sex in any of their masterpieces.

The difference in sex has another significance altogether when we turn the question around and ask it from a social and historical perspective: what did art mean for women in the Middle Ages? 'Less than for men', is the answer reached by the latest general studies on the subject of women in the Middle Ages, by Shulamith Shahar in 1983 and Edith Ennen in 1984. Both convincingly show that their legal situation kept women isolated from many experiences of the outside world; restricted to the internal activities of marriage and family, they took only a passive part in public life. When art was designed to influence society, women, as in social reality itself, were granted merely ornamental significance, not creative influence. In the most important and ambitious art forms, for example, in the construction of cloisters and cathedrals, of castles and palaces, women were wanted neither for design nor for realization. They were permitted only the fleeting game of luxury and fashion. The more sensitive women rejected such façades and turned to religious introspection, to a half-monastic, half-heretical women's movement on the far side of the priestly church.

Shahar and Ennen note the great attraction of such religious alternatives for women, but explain it by the longing for the company of peers. In so doing, they describe only the visible, the exterior structure. The main goal of medieval religiosity, however, was not the satisfaction of social needs, but the striving for the absolute, the 'unbound', the salvation from all earthly things, 'emancipation' in a figurative sense. Even if not all women considered the structure in which they lived a prison, where would they find homes of their own, if not in the intangible world? And did not the freedom of the heavenly world offer them experiences with the world of imagination, even with the earthly world? Was this detour really merely an escape from reality, or did it offer women another, better reality? These are the questions I would like to investigate by examining, in five examples, how and why art had an influence on the lives of medieval women.

II

First, an important qualification. Most people in the Middle Ages, men as well as women, received neither encouragement nor time for their artistic efforts; daily life exhausted their resources. A typical example of this is my first example, the female hermit Liutbirg. In the 820s, a widowed Saxon countess visited a Franconian convent. Among the maids serving her was a young woman named Liutbirg, who caught her attention; the widow inquired after her descent and class. Liutbirg was a peasant's daughter from the surrounding countryside; had she been a noble, she would have been singing in the choir with the nuns, not working in the kitchen and pantry. The countess liked the girl, and took her back to the Harz region. In the foreign Lower Saxony, the Franconian girl proved to be skilful, advancing beyond her allocated labours into less certain areas. Soon she was singing psalms and leafing through Latin Bibles; as her biographer later wrote, 'She would have been capable of learning if the weakness of her sex had not hindered her.' Since intellectual education was a man's concern, Liutbirg used her gifts for what that same priest called 'feminine activities': embroidery, knitting and weaving. During the day, she managed the countess's household independently and prudently, and later did the same for the young count, his two wives and their eight children.

Not until Liutbirg turned sick and weak, some twenty years later, did she ask the lord of the house to liberate her from the turmoil of community life and let her find God and herself as a hermit. The surprised count fulfilled her pious wish. For another thirty years she stayed in Wendhausen, in Harz, locked into a cell next to the church, provided with the bare necessities by the farmers. Even then, she gave more than she took. At the window of her cell, rebellious serfs as well as learned bishops came knocking, seeking counsel. From as far away as Bremen, daughters of high-placed nobles journeyed to learn those feminine arts in which Liutbirg had long been skilled, handicrafts and the singing of psalms. When she died in 880, advanced in years, she was missed by all. She had been able to help others because she had been granted what most farmers and farmers' wives were denied: retreat from daily burdens into a peaceful cell, where she could make her own rules. Yet even for Liutbirg, artistic activity could not be realized. Had she learned singing and composition in school, she might have been a part of our literary history today, like her more aristocratic and younger contemporary, Roswitha of Gandersheim.

III

Her life, the second of my examples, certainly disproves the common preconception that at least noble women had easy access to art. As the high-born Saxon Roswitha lay in her cradle in 935, no one guessed she would grow up to be Germany's first woman poet. Certainly, she was welcome in the highly cultured convent of Gandersheim, which was directed by a niece of the Emperor, but she was offered no artistic education. Benedictine convents were meant to serve God, and when they used architecture, sculpture, music and book illumination to do so, they were portraying a heavenly order, not earthly misery. In her early years, Roswitha managed to transfer what she had learned from neglectful school masters to temporal themes, which the monks avoided: she wanted to rewrite the vulgar comedies of the heathen Terence in a Christian version. Neither the abbess nor her fellow-nuns helped her; she worked secretly, fearing the reprimand of the older ones and the criticism of scholars, and her discarded attempts and mistakes constantly reminded her of what she called 'feminine frailty'. Nevertheless, this self-taught woman did not give up, and in the end she was even able to recommend her Latin poetry to the abbess as playful recuperation from the cares of the day.

Roswitha's chamber dramas, however, were anything but frivolous games: they discussed the most ticklish of subjects, including, most often, the conversion of immoral women. Roswitha confessed that she herself had often blushed while writing the brothel scenes, yet she was not embarrassed before her public, for that was the best way to improve the decadent society they all lived in. Take the drama *Dulcitius*, the story of a late Roman judge who sentenced beautiful Christian women and tried to rape them. Blinded, he groped around a dark kitchen embracing sooty cooking pots; this turned him so black that even his servants thought he was a demon. On the other hand, when they tried to tear the devout woman's clothes from her back before the tribunal, the judge was already too tired: he fell asleep on stage. Masculine justice was of little value, as was masculine wisdom. In the drama *Sapientia*, the woman of that name, embodying wisdom, faced the philosopher-emperor Hadrian. When he asked the ages of Sapientia's three daughters, 'Faith', 'Hope' and 'Charity', she answered with a mathematical puzzle based on the number theory of Boethius. This confused the emperor, who knew nothing of mathematics. Sapientia loved the knowledge of numbers and measurements because the pure order of the free arts led beyond the rule of untamed force.

On the other hand, the hermit Pafnutius, who thoughtfully explained the musical harmony of the spheres according to Boethius, easily convinced a whore that her sense of the beautiful was easier to fulfil in the convent than in the brothel. Earthly life could be more meaningfully structured when it was not confused by power-

mongers and fools; in Roswitha's own words: 'May feminine weakness triumph and masculine power be defeated.' For the time being,
only convents could provide equality for the weak and refuge from
the power of the sword. Yet, from within this refuge, cloisters might
have been able to alter the untamed present of Ottonian laymen. For
humanity, said Roswitha, is like a metal. As long as it rusts in the
darkness, it remains worthless; only hard hammering can make it
ring. It takes art to make of human beings what they, as God's
image, could be.

IV

Three hundred years later, aristocratic women no longer needed the
protection of convent walls; God was replaced by nature. My third
example is an account of the first French woman poet, Marie de
France. This surname suggests that she did not live in her native
France but abroad, probably at the English court. She composed her
most important writings for a venerated king, probably Henry II of
England, as well as for a certain Count William, whom she praised
as the paragon of chivalry, scholarship and manners. She liked to
refer to her own name, 'Marie am I, and come from France', yet
made no detailed confessions. We do not even know if she was
married, or how she lived. Her descent, undoubtedly aristocratic,
committed her to a life of dignity, not of labour, and certainly not of
literary labour. Yet she composed poetry day and night, without
tiring, perhaps, as she hinted, so that her difficult occupation would
comfort her through personal cares; at any rate, she did not let
mockers discourage her, the men who rejected her works as the
clumsy attempts of peasants. Since she was educated, she composed
her literature in Latin, French and English, and saw it as the duty of
the learned, of 'philosophers', to teach their fellow-men moral and
natural codes of behaviour. Her central theme, unlike that of Roswitha, was the cultured sociability of both sexes.

In her collection of fables, Marie mercilessly described just how
brutal the sexes could be in reality. Once upon a time, a wolf met a
pregnant sow and promised to spare her if she bore her litter quickly
and gave up her young to him to devour. She insisted on decency,
saying it was a disgrace for a female to bear her children in the
presence of a male. When the wolf crept away to wait expectantly,
the clever sow escaped. Marie concluded: 'all women should know
and remember this example.' The uncontrollable, natural law of the
strongest was still valid; the sow was practically predestined to fall

victim to the wolf. Yet she saved not only her own life, but that of her young, by fooling the greedy wolf and insisting that he conform to rules of decency. By expressing such teachings in French verse, Marie was preaching the value of social graces for the protection of the weak to her contemporaries.

Courtly convention rapidly deteriorated into a pleasing façade. Marie described that too, around 1160, in one of those verse novellas intended to be sung to the accompaniment of the harp. It featured an exemplary knight to whom nature had given only one fault: his life was dedicated exclusively to the arts of war and the hunt, and he had no interest in love. During a hunt he was badly wounded, and learned that only the love of a woman could heal him. The first woman he chanced to meet lived in a tower by the sea, where she had been locked in by her jealous husband. A painting in her chambers portrayed the goddess of love; the lady was also familiar with Ovid's poetry about the art of love. But aesthetic fiction could help neither of the dispirited characters; the only remedy was the healing pains of the most natural of all sicknesses, love. It was only with the aid of fantastic adventures and miracles that Marie's poetry could create such an imaginary world of ideal natural behaviour and mutual trust. The poet knew she was presenting new themes in unusual forms; she hoped that her art would not be forgotten, and that, in the course of time, it might even help establish more subtle ways of thinking, and more sensitive ways of living in a society.

V

A further 300 years later, bourgeois women no longer expected so much from art or nature, and even less from society; since the church, too, had failed, they once again invested their faith in the dialogue of the lonely soul with God, as the hermit Liutbirg once had, but this time the dialogue was not with their Creator, but with the crucified Christ. My fourth example illustrates this: Caterina Vigri, the daughter of a court jurist in Ferrara. At ten years of age, in 1423, she was sent to be the fellow-pupil of the prince's daughter, Margherita. In the humanist circles of the Este family, the girl acquired a variety of abilities, and not only feminine ones: she learned to read and speak Latin in both prose and verse, to create ornate manuscripts, to play the viola and sing folk songs in the vernacular. When her father died, the thirteen-year-old abruptly left the cultural centre of the court and joined a group of Beguines, burgher women living together in Ferrara and serving others with feminine handicrafts and devout poverty. Artistic sense was not in demand there, only the ability to work. When the older Beguines were caught up with enthusiasm for the contemplative humanitarianism of the Augustinians, young Caterina became mad with rage; she decided that the insecure life of the Beguines was too lax and demanded the establishment of a convent of the Order of Poor Clares with tougher asceticism and discipline: enough of this trifling.

In 1431, following numerous heated conflicts, she had barely reached her goal when her pampered youth caught up with her. She could no longer combat the demands of the senses, not even by the most radical methods. Because her attempts only led her around in circles, in 1438 she began secretly transcribing her doubts and fears. She had no private cell, not even a drawer to herself, so she would sew her diary into her bed-cover. When the other nuns found out what she was doing, she threw the book into the oven which they used to bake bread for the convent and started writing again from the beginning. At first, this spiritual autobiography disdained all artistic form, but as Caterina gained distance from herself by writing, she noticed that her loathing of the physical was injuring her soul. It was an insult to the divine Creator and crucified Saviour; He had after all affirmed His physical nature with the endurance of pain. Only by making herself into an empty body did she create room in her soul for God and her fellow man. This conviction gradually lent her a self-assurance and cheerfulness that became contagious. In 1455, she was transferred to another convent of the Poor Clares in Bologna, to which she gave the significant name *Corpus Domini*, Body of the Lord. There she worked as abbess until her death in 1463.

It was not until she was forty, in the last decade of her life, that she returned her attention to art in full, not merely to a humanistic decoration of mortal life. For example, she wrote and painted a breviary with austere portraits of her spiritual idols, the apostle of poverty Francis of Assisi and her courageous patron saint, Catherine of Alexandria. She also produced large altar murals picturing female saints. Her most important literary work, which to this day has been reproduced only in fragments, consists of nearly 6,000 Latin verses, in rhymed free verse, about the rosary. A sentimental subject, it seems, but at the very beginning she poses an unexpected question: 'What am I? Let subtle minds teach me this. Run back down the slopes, you who are reaching for the mountain tops; fly back down to earth, you who are moving between the sky and the stars, you philosophers who seek the secret foundations of nature. Tell me why you hesitate now, when your chance has come to witness the greatest thing on earth?' From incomprehensible nature, from the thin air of science, no answer can be found to the question of humanity. Its dignity is not in the claims of artificial terminology, but in the readiness to receive many visions, images and sounds.

Caterina used art as a means of leading her fellow-humans to God, to their peers and eventually to themselves. As she lay dying and the nuns dissolved in tears, Caterina ordered them to sing once more the Italian song in which she had answered the questions of her life. It brought close the suffering of the crucified Lord, yet returned again and again to a joyful refrain: *Anima benedetta/Dall' alto creatore,/Risguarda il tuo signore/Che confitto ti aspetta* ('Blessed art thou, spirit, of the High Creator; look upon thy lord, how he anxiously awaits thee'). When the nuns had finished singing and again began to weep, Caterina told them that if they wanted to be her daughters, they should stop sobbing and take the future of the convent into their hands. We usually call the religious art of Caterina Vigri 'mystical', but we should add that she herself never considered her art a budding flower in the garden of the soul, but an aid in mastering contemporary society.

VI

Nearby, in fifteenth-century Italy, the famous art of the Renaissance was flowering, a superior aestheticism that became, now and then, an end in itself for many aesthetes. My fifth and last example will illustrate how a clever burgher woman in Florence, the capital of the Renaissance, viewed the Medici's artistic cultivation. A contemporary of Caterina, Alessandra Macinghi, born in 1406, was the daughter of a Florentine citizen and married a merchant of the Strozzi family in 1422, at sixteen years of age. At twenty-nine years, in 1435, she became a widow with five under-age children on her hands. Their well-being became her life for the remaining thirty-six years, until 1471. When the Medici took power, they banned the men of the Strozzi house from Florence; from then on, the mother, sitting at home with spectacles perched on her nose, could do nothing but write long letters to her sons abroad, wait for their belated and brief replies, and fight, with petitions, for the honour and property of her children. Alessandra thought soberly and acted boldly; she scolded her sluggish sons as much as she did her ill-humoured daughters. In 1465, she counselled one son in Naples:

female creatures with simple minds had to be bridled by their men, but on the other hand, men often bought women as they bought goods. Thus, men should spare no expense in clothing their brides, to show what they are worth, as the Medici did for their women folk, putting on exuberant feasts at the expense of the taxpayers.

The widow Strozzi did not care for art as luxury. In 1461, one of her sons in Bruges sent several Flemish tapestries, which were used to make Italian homes more comfortable. His mother replied in a letter: 'Of the two colourful tapestries I received, one portrays the three wise men of the Orient, who brought gold to our Lord. Beautiful figures. On the other is a peacock, which I think is pretty, surrounded by all kinds of foliage. In my opinion they are beautiful. One I will retain, as you wish, for contrary to what you told me in your last letter about their market prices, they will hardly fetch three gulden here, as they are small pieces. However, if I find an opportunity to sell them at a good price, I will sell both. I will keep the "Sacred Countenance", for it is a pious portrayal, and beautiful.' The Strozzi lady was quite capable of appreciating beauty, but the exotic themes of the tapestries did not appeal to her; this was useless finery. Other things were more important: not only household money for physical subsistence, but the portrait of the crucified Christ, for example, for the salvation of the soul. Like Caterina, Alessandra felt His touch without intermediaries. In other ways, too, the patrician woman near the end of the Middle Ages resembled the hermit near the beginning: for both, as for the majority of women, art provided a glimpse of heaven, on which they otherwise had little time on earth to meditate. And since art could not change their daily lives on earth, it was at best an activity for leisure.

The others too, Roswitha, Marie and Caterina, having been given the opportunity to practise art by convent, princely courts and bourgeois communities, preferred to create an alternative to the daily experience of real life. Whether this situation was general or not is a question one would have to ask the men of the Middle Ages; it is possible that medieval art in general, not only that of women, had always tried to produce a radical alternative to reality, something more than a simply purified reflection of it. I cannot pursue this question further here, but only point out that the art of men tended to exaggerate the real instead of principally questioning it. In some way, this was connected to the fact that men had different, far more effective ways of getting a grip on their world, of dominating and changing it. We need only think of the hierarchical sermon, priestly counsel, theological systematics, medicinal therapy, juridical decisions, political action, military reputation, prudence in trade, precision in craftsmanship. Women were no more than polite observers in all these fields, if they were granted access at all, even those who belonged to the privileged groups of nuns or ladies.

VII

For women, then, artistic creativity was one of the very few alternatives to submitting to the unavoidable. Even within female communities, which were often religious, artists were only minimally supported and mostly had to rely on themselves. They had to learn, at their own risk, what no traditional school would teach them. In this way they were forced to be original. Yet what they had to say was more or less the same, for overworked women as for busy men. It was, incidentally, the more rational of the men who expected an alternative from women, so that they themselves would not wholly fall victim to their environment. The message of medieval women artists was, more or less, that reality is not all there is to life, nor is the present the end to history. Imagination is necessary to make a different, better reality. Art, capable of creating such an alternative world, is more than the pretty games of the *artes liberales*; it illuminates the ugliness of reality with the glimmer of hope.

Those who object that this medieval scheme has been out of date for a long time are partly right. Since the Renaissance, the artistic portrayal of reality has relied less and less on the longing for heaven that dominated the Christian Middle Ages. The more often the attempt to portray this life failed during the modern period, the more decisively did the art of men turn from the transfiguration of the existing world to the alternative of another one, which, in the Middle Ages, had been promoted mostly by women. Despite historical fluctuation, a constant relationship between women and art has asserted itself from the Middle Ages to this day. In Göttingen in 1983, the graphic artist Monika Loh formulated it like this:

> Reality, for me, corresponds to people, to life in a society, to things that happen in a human society, and, most particularly, to women in this society, the reality that we experience daily. And so much of that is dreadful! Because this is so complex, it is also difficult for me to explain my work in this respect. But my work is an attempt to create my own reality for myself, or at least a better one.

12

Science and Games

I

For us, the contemporaries of Michel Foucault and Umberto Eco, the world has come more and more to resemble a system of puzzling symbols to be deciphered. It would seem that we are meant to make the attempt, while we play archaeologists or criminal lawyers, as though we had nothing better to do. In the light of this post-modern attitude, the humanities, following the natural sciences, appear more and more a game. As stimulating as is this new perspective, it leads us to hasty conclusions, when, for example, historians following in Foucault's tracks interpret *'Kulturgeschichte als Schachspiel'* – cultural history as a game of chess – as Hans Petschar did in 1986; or when they ask: *'Ecos Echo – ein "Anstoß" für Mittelalterhistoriker?'* ('is Eco's resonance a stumbling-block for medieval historians?') – as Jürgen Petersohn did in 1986. Whether impulse or stumbling-block, it can only become productive when it is applied to the entire scope of human existence, and to the details of history. Until now, a wide gap has divided the world we expect from the pressing matters of existence; I will here attempt to make that gap smaller.

During the two-and-a-half centuries of known history, the equation of science and play was never taken for granted. And when the attempt was made to connect the two, history as it was experienced was banned to the fringe, to the hands of Foucault and Eco. A connection between science and play was certainly suggested at the very beginning of the European tradition of thought in two philosophical-theological statements; until recently, however, both statements overtaxed the understanding and behaviour of suffering people. The first phrase was formulated by Heraclitus of Ephesus: 'Existence is a child playing at a board game; a child holds the sceptre.' This might have implied that the world, from primitive times onwards, was meant as a game of divine wisdom and childish innocence; it might also have meant that life proceeds arbitrarily, according to childish rules. No matter how that phrase was interpreted, it allowed little room for the structuring of existence by human knowledge and action.

The second statement, from the biblical Proverbs of Solomon (8:29–31), sounded similarly obscure. Wisdom, the first-born of God, is speaking here: 'When He laid the foundations of the earth, I was a child at His side. I delighted and played before Him, I play day in and day out on His earth and take pleasure in man.' Wisdom might certainly have appeared to God and man as play, but it was hard for people of earlier times to reach out to wisdom's paradisiacal joys when pondering over their earthly relationships to each other. It seldom appeared as a charming game of children, performed for benevolent spectators and proceeding according to mutually accepted rules. Practical history was much more a desperate struggle for existence among a diversity of adults, each inventing his own rules and none able to foresee the malicious moves of the other.

Participants in this deadly game, which God observed only from a great distance, usually underestimated the more childish, relaxing and useless games. To master the earnestness of life, one needed something more than the pleasure of the game, it would seem: discipline, thoroughness, science. It was apparently impossible on earth to reconcile life with wisdom and art; later, perhaps, in heaven, before the countenance of God. That was how the scholars of the Christian Early Middle Ages thought. Between 620 and 636, however, their most important encyclopaedist, Isidore of Seville, realized that entertaining games could not be ignored in explaining the things man needed to know. In his *Etymologiae*, he mentioned it neither under the heading of sciences nor of arts, but under the heading of war, which the bishop feared. He warned of the sinful games in the theatre and the circus, of gladiator battles and obscene dances. Other, more childish games did not occur to him, and neither did more reasonable ones.

In the High Middle Ages, in his guide for students of 1125, *Didascalion*, the Parisian theologian Hugh of St Victor proposed an independent science of games, *scientia ludorum*. Hugh did not think them as useless as had Isidore. According to Hugh, the seven *artes mechanicae*, the learnable crafts, provided the bare necessities of life: clothing, shelter, nourishment, trade, hunting, health and entertainment. This is where he carved out a niche for games, here in the cellar of the encyclopaedic house. He confessed that as a schoolboy he had enjoyed playing with the abacus and the monochord, that is, with scientific instruments, though as an adult he strived for higher goals. It did not occur to him that the seven supporting columns in the temple of wisdom, the intellectual seven *artes liberales* themselves, were games of wisdom, or could become so.

Around 1250, the most important encyclopaedist of the High Middle Ages, the Dominican Vincent of Beauvais, included games of every sort in his *Speculum doctrinale*, categorizing them, as Hugh had, under *artes mechanicae*, but rating them as unfavourably as Isidore had, as accessories to war. Vincent ignored the rising popularity of social games in courtly circles and scholarly games in learned circles, but the popularity of gambling, which encouraged greed, alarmed him. He discussed it in the context of criminal law, between theft and cheating. Bourgeois society behaved more peaceably than the aristocratic one, but not less foolishly; the new games of economic influence drew man into as much injustice as the old games of military prowess. Digressions such as this prevented the elevation of the soul to theology.

The Late Middle Ages set it back even further. Here, play was categorized among the *artes liberales*, but only after depriving it of its basic value and of the claim that it reflected the world. The wisest thinker of the time, Nicholas of Cusa, as cardinal of Rome, classed certain instruments and games under mathematics and music in his *De ludo globi* of 1463. On the other hand, he also believed that philosophy could be found in all decent games of entertainment, such as chess, which he thought worth consideration; he even invented a game of skittles to illustrate his speculations about spirit and nature. What bound science and games together was nothing more than the scholarly ignorance of man, whose artistic guesswork circled around the wisdom of God in a process of trial and error, never reaching the heart of it.

Thus, modern natural sciences were able to develop in play and experimentation just outside the holy halls; in the seventeenth century, they unabashedly experimented with probability theory, using games of chance that had been forbidden earlier. In the humanities, poets had since the Renaissance been rising to the upper echelons, joining the philosophers and gaining the authority to determine what had meaning and what not, and they used their scholarly knowledge in their own games, as described by Hermann Hesse in his *Glass Bead Game*; however, the disciplines of the fine arts and the forbiddingly difficult sciences remained separate. No one was interested in agreeing on a unified terminology of the 'artistic' game.

For example, the bible of the Enlightenment, Diderot's *Encyclopédie* of 1765, carefully differentiated five kinds of games and game-playing: social games (*jeu*), natural games of anatomical and mineralogical anomalies (*jeu de la nature*), word games in frivolous literature (*jeu des mots*), gymnastic–scenic games of the antique (*jeux*), and modern probability theory (*jouer*). The second and fifth types came under the heading of the sciences, the third and fourth under art. There was a warning attached to the first, however, since games of entertainment furthered neither rational understanding nor emotional elevation, but merely pleasure, or, more precisely, greed and the hunger for thrills.

This differentiation between frivolous games and the serious arts and sciences continued until my student days, in the middle of the twentieth century. Especially in modern historical sciences, it was art scholars more than any others who stressed that history, including medieval history, had something to tell us not as an imaginative game, but as a mercilessly serious reality. Statements such as these, however, made me wary, for they contradicted each other as much as my own contemporary experience.

II

I believed without question what the idol of my early study years, Friedrich Schiller, had once proclaimed at the beginning of his lecture term in Jena in 1789: 'There are none among you today to whom history has nothing important to say.' Of the 'middle centuries', however, Schiller had only negative things to say: 'Crude feudal anarchy', 'clerical despotism', 'the idleness of monks', 'the repressive spirit of northern barbarians'. Either the only function of the Middle Ages in history is to frighten us, or it was not the voice of world history that spoke in Jena, but a historian making his own restricted perspective and standpoint absolute. Conflict with Schiller's ideas drove me further and further into the Middle Ages, though without dissipating the challenge of the present, for the Germany of the present day after 1945 was not ready to hear anything about the Middle Ages.

I survived the acid test thanks to the mentor of my final school years, Jacob Burckhardt, and especially to the central thesis of his lecture in Basle in 1868: 'Our base of departure is the only permanent focal point possible for us, the suffering, striving and acting human being, as he is, always was and always will be.' Burckhardt's position was just as applicable to the Middle Ages, and it rose above the prejudices of our times. What irritated this Swiss most was:

> our pretentious hatred for the diverse, various, for probing and
> for rights that are half or fully inactive, our equation of the

moral with the precise and of the inability to understand with
variegation and coincidence. The significance of history is not
retrospection, but understanding. Our life now is occupation,
life then was existence.

Yet my mistrust grew when, as Schiller had dismissed the Middle
Ages, Burckhardt simplified the modern period he rejected. Moreover, if we were really so confident of how we have been conducting
ourselves since Schiller, we would certainly be able to listen to what
the Middle Ages have to say with less irritation. If we were as
self-critical as we have grown to think of ourselves since Burckhardt,
we would rush to ask the Middle Ages for advice. If we demand of
the dead a mere affirmation of our own preconceptions about
ourselves, we will receive nothing in answer but the echo of our own
questions.

A third great historian whom I tried to emulate, Johan Huizinga,
led us out of this dilemma. His central message, delivered before the
Dutch Academy of the Sciences in 1929, still inspires me: 'History is
the intellectual form with which a culture accounts for its own past.'
That was less a definition of terms than a declaration of war against
the current American leisure-time activity of plundering any historical period, destroying one part of it and dragging off the other.
Huizinga's thesis also contradicted the opposite claim of many Germans today that history should give us an identity. History presents
us with a multitude of outlived identities, most of which did not
co-exist, but which fight each other to the death. The selection of
any one identity would force us, if we were to take it seriously, to
reject many others, and to repeat old massacres. If our life context
deserves the term 'culture', we have inherited a little from all historical identities; we must identify each part exactly, without identify-
ing ourselves completely with any of them. We are identical only
with ourselves. Not until we fully become so can we account for all
of history and prove to those who were once something, that we,
too, are more than fashion models or chess pieces.

III

Thus, we would only be able to hear what the historical Middle
Ages have to tell us if we were sure of our current, that is, our
political identity. Then we would understand the unfamiliar elements of the Middle Ages better than our self-fascination has permitted until now; at the same time, we would learn important things
about our modern existence that we might otherwise take for

granted. The common denominator would be found not in some final historical and political result, but in Burckhardt's anthropological premise. Of the many forms of human endurance, achievement and acts, there is only one I will discuss here: the game. I have occupied myself with this subject since 1982, when I saw that the reality of games described by medieval sources do not correspond to the ideals of game-playing described by modern authorities. In 1795, Schiller wrote in his letters, *On the Aesthetic Education of Man*: 'Man plays only when he is a human being in the most complete sense of the word, and he is only a complete human being when he plays.' Of course, Schiller was thinking of the game of fine arts that the ancient Greeks had designed and the German classicists had renewed; he believed the Gothic barbarians of the Middle Ages capable only of crude pranks.

Huizinga had something else to say in his late book, *Homo ludens*, of 1938. His opinion was that culture itself originated in games, in the purposeless, cultic, holy antithesis of the necessities of life, in 'man's feeling of being nestled in the cosmos', and in the contest of the noble of heart. Huizinga saw all medieval life as determined by this kind of game. Certainly, he underestimated the cruel streak in the medieval passion for games; the Middle Ages often used outsiders and the weak to recreate the game cats play with mice. Disgusted by Hitler, the Dutch scholar thought the twentieth century more capable of such perversions: when modern culture appeared at play, it was really cheating, thus fostering the childish element. It is true that the Germans have ruined the game of European culture so thoroughly that it has become difficult for them to play fairly with their opponents.

But as early as the Second World War, two brilliant Austrian Jews, living in Anglo-Saxon exile, revived the theory of games in two major branches. Since 1942, the mathematician John von Neumann had been designing a computer theory in Princeton that was applicable to the domestic card game as well as to global economy; the philosopher Ludwig Wittgenstein, living in Cambridge in England, discovered language games as a form of living in 1945. He was referring largely to games of speech that children use to learn their mother tongue, but included the fruits of poets, historians and philosophers: 'Reports on processes; hypotheses made about origins; proposals and proof of hypotheses.' Playing in this sense meant trusting one another, resolving differences according to mutually acceptable rules, checking the chaos of emotions, forcing games with others into non-violent forms. Though computer games and language games were not absolutely compatible with each other,

in recent decades the actual behaviour of adults in games has gained
recognition in other fields, far beyond scholarly circles.

In Germany, the recent performance according to game rules of
the most serious of transactions is only beginning to gain a vague
recognition. Here, traditional adherence to game rules is generally
attached to fields of non-responsibility like art and education, though
the uses of modern game theory are already permeating the central
concerns of contemporary civilization, economy and the social structure. If we were to examine the labyrinth of our current epoch with
a personal objectivity as intense as our current subjectivity, we
would be able to discern not only the way to the heart of the matter,
but also find there access to the catacombs of our past, blocked with
debris.

In 1973, Eco, perhaps the most sharp-witted analyst of symbols
and signals in language today, criticized Huizinga's narrow-minded
and vague comments, with this concept of playing in mind. Huizinga
had supposedly paid more attention to the behaviour of 'game-
playing' people than to the rules of the 'game played'. In so doing,
Eco stretched his definition of games too widely, to make it apply to
the complex systems of rules for whole cultures and epochs; only in
that way could he establish a correlation between the metagames of
medieval and modern semanticists, leading to his prediction of the
'New Middle Ages'. He would have thought twice had he found the
actual medieval games as exciting as modern football. I therefore
support Eco's own caution to study the rules of individual 'games'
first, before inferring from them the 'playing', that is to say the behaviour of the participants in general.

Here is an example. Eco's novel *The Name of the Rose* was filmed
in 1986 according to two guidelines. First, the sets had to be realistic; historical experts ensured that monks appeared authentically
dressed. Yet the plot had to be fantastic; historical experts would be
able to find conflicts in the fourteenth century far more tangible than
those based on treachery and detective work. Together, both guidelines or rules for making the film manipulate the reaction of the
viewer. The audience feels comfortable in its seats even during the
most gruesome scenes, for archaeological and criminalistic games
have no application to reality. A modern audience sometimes even
reacts to actual situations of the most horrible kind as if watching an
entertaining television show.

And here is a counter-example: in 1250, German missionaries
performed a stage play in the market place of Riga, using biblical
stories to convert Livonians to Christianity. They had no historical
experts to tell them how Old Testament warriors had dressed 2,000

years earlier; presumably, the actors performed in contemporary armour. When the dramatization of the war of Gideon against the Philistines began, the unbaptized spectators scattered in terror. It is easy to understand that they feared for their lives, as it is easy to understand the shame of the Christian chronicler, when we consider that other Germans had already tried to convert Baltic nations with the sword, and that medieval games had often been a part of a dangerous reality, the playing-field turning into a battlefield. When we sharpen our historical understanding of this connection with reality, we see contemporary games with other eyes, especially those less theatrical games in which the significance of all games surfaces even more clearly.

In the United States, for example, there is a computer game, 'Dueling Digits', which, since 1982, has been praised as being both relaxing and educational. It is the goal of both players to shoot down as many single, whole digits and basic calculation symbols as possible, all of which jump around on the screen; the players can also inflict losses on each other. A war game, then, as well as a game of profits, for winning is determined by how many points each player has. We recognize here the paradoxical dream-world of most computer games, where the goal is to shoot one's way out of the violence of war and to buy oneself out of the power of money. So much for the entertainment part: now for the education. The easiest way to win is to bundle together captured digits into multi-digit numbers and assign proper equations to them; profit multiplies mathematically. The player of this game is preparing himself for a life full of the sober business of calculation, and for a leisure time full of the intoxication of amusement.

There are some who say that both forms of behaviour are absolutely natural, that there is nothing we can do about it. But we do a great deal to support it, even applying rules to areas that Huizinga and Wittgenstein would not have considered game-related. Contemporary thought and action is almost entirely expressed in numbers. Using numbers, science formulates results, the economy formulates its yield, politicians count their votes, cultural guardians number visitors of exhibitions. The news measures public disasters and private happiness in numbers. I, too, count listeners and readers, assignments and prizes like factors of my existence. What is more, things appear important if we have to use a computer to deal with them; what can be counted on one's fingers is scoffed at, as if it were the milkman's bill. The astronomical number is always best, the one with countless digits, the overwhelming quantity. That is not the fault of the computers, but our own. Burckhardt would have considered his statements confirmed: we confuse the moral with the precise, being with having.

Huizinga and Eco are unaware of any comparable medieval games, and historians who examine and describe medieval reality are likewise unaware. According to them, the great lords of the Middle Ages beat each other to death with chess pieces, and the less important people drank themselves under the table while wagering their last shirt in dice games. A colourful life, certainly, gruesome and telegenic, but most viewers would rather lead a life of civilized business in front of a computer screen. It might be a different story altogether if there existed a medieval game that, contradicting Burckhardt's assumption, related the precise to the moral, mathematics to ethics and, in contradiction to Schiller's presumptions, merged the true with the beautiful and logic with music. A game of that kind would not only unsettle our ideological image of the Middle Ages, but would also do the same, in a healing way, for our technological self-confidence.

IV

There was such a game, and its name, the Battle of Numbers, was similar to our 'Dueling Digits'. Its inventor gave it the latinized Greek name *Rithmimachia*; later, others referred to it simply as the 'Philosopher's Game'. From the very beginning, its job was to teach something quite different from 'Dueling Digits'. Imagine a board game where the smallest values represented by playing pieces are made up of the natural numbers 2 to 9, divided into two opposing sides, one with the even numbers 2, 4, 6 and 8, the other with the odd numbers 3, 5, 7 and 9 (see figure on page 204 below). Whole numbers do not represent quantities in themselves, but elements of proportions: the smallest numbers are valid as multiples, that is, multiples of the number one, which does not actually appear in the game. In the rows behind the basic numbers n are groups of playing pieces representing larger numbers, the multiples of n, n^2: 4 to 64 on the even side, 9 to 81 on the odd side. These groups, in turn, are supplemented by groups of pieces with even larger numbers; these always have a ratio to the multiples of $(n + 1) : n$. That means $3 : 2$ ascending to $10 : 9$; that is, 6 to 81 on the even side, 12 to 100 on the odd side. Behind these, we place two further groups of pieces with the biggest numbers of all. Their ratio to the larger numbers are

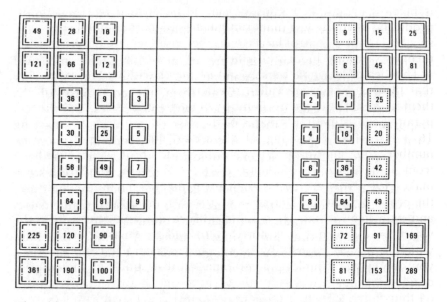

The oldest reconstructable formation of the Battle-of-Numbers game, taken
from an anonymous Liège manuscript of around 1070. (The pieces were
coloured: --- is white, – is black, ····· is red, ---- is green.)

generally $(2n + 1):(n + 1)$; they ascend from $5:3$ to $19:10$, in
other words, from 15 to 289 on the even side and from 28 to 361 on
the odd side.

This way of calculating is confusing for us, as we no longer think
in proportions. The same numbers appear more than once on both
sides. 49, for example, is n^2 when $n = 7$; it is also proportional to
42 with the ratio of $7:6$, which, in return, can be derived from $n =$
6; but it also appears in $n = 3$, for in its second derivation, 28 is the
ratio to 49 in $7:4$. The quantity of a number is never important, the
emphasis is always on quality: its various potential combinations
and how it leads back to the mother of all numbers, the hidden
number one.

Now imagine these 48 numbered pieces set up facing each other
on a board similar to a chessboard, the smallest numbers starting in
the front row, the next largest in the second, the largest of all in the
third. How do they engage? Identical quantities cancel each other
out. Larger quantities, however, succumb to smaller ones. For example, the 4 and the 8 can corner 12 and subsume it, because 4 and 8
together make 12. Even worse, if a 2 is eight empty spaces away, it
can capture a 16, as 2 times 8 equals 16. On the other hand, 16

is helpless against 2, because 2 cannot be divided by 16 without producing anything less than a fragment of a natural number. Thus, smaller numbers control larger ones, because they are hidden within them as seeds are hidden in fruit.

The idea in the game centres on two pieces with with a status like that of kings. They are called pyramids because one can think of them as a stack of square numbers. On the even side, the pointed pyramid consists of the squares of the first six numbers: 36 + 25 + 16 + 9 + 4 + 1, making 91 altogether. On the side of the odd numbers, the blunt-topped pyramid is made up of square numbers from 4 to 8, that is, 64 + 49 + 36 + 25 + 16, which together makes 190. Now all the insignificant number 7 has to do is aim at the proud pyramid 91 thirteen squares away, and the pyramid falls, and with it all its square numbers, which are simultaneously elsewhere on the board. It is not easy to find products or sums with which to topple the 190, but since every pyramid rests on its base, you only have to think up a combination that equals its foundation of 64; the simplest way is for the eight to snatch away the pyramid's 64 foundation from a distance of 8 squares, like David with Goliath.

This certainly does not resemble a game of profits, but it does resemble a war-game; in chess, too, the smallest pawn can defeat the highest king. In the original *Rithmimachia*, however, the winner is not the one to capture the pyramid, but the one to set up his mathematical sequence or harmonious sequence of three in the opponent's half of the board: for example, the simple sequence of 2, 4 and 6, or the less simple sequence 25, 45 and 225. The point of the game, therefore, is to create a harmony of numbers, optimally using those captured from the opponent, who, of course, interferes whenever he can. His wisest course is to concentrate his energies in setting up his sequence of three first, putting the opponent out of the game. This is possible even with weakened forces: a sequence of 3, 5 and 7, and the game is his.

The Battle-of-Numbers game was meant to educate the player in intercourse with numbers, things and people, using methods that were the philosophical legacy of the last Roman, Boethius, which the Middle Ages inherited. Many Latin instructions, using tables and diagrams, taught the player that the true unity of things in the countable world could not be achieved on earth, and took shape only in the beauty of equality. Conflict between equals only encourages fighting and results in inequality; yet they could also be bound together to make a good compromise. Since this situation will never end of itself, man must judge unequal numbers again and again, according to their inner structure, to their cross-references to other numbers, to their usefulness in longer number sequences. The mathematical game attempted to map out the order of nature itself by means of numerical relationships, using what Burckhardt called 'symbolic probing'. It even involved musical intervals and consonances, included geometrical figures and appeared finally as a condensed reconstruction of physics itself. Further, it forced the players to be precise and obey rules, to use their imagination and to experiment, to trust previous agreements and take responsibility. For the law of logical numerical order and natural intermeshing of effects was simply the law of a moral lifestyle. Thus, *Rithmimachia* demanded the same commitment and calm state of mind as did work and entertainment: to co-operate in search of the invisible pattern behind the fluctuating scores.

This game could provide cultural identity, if only to Latin speakers. It was invented around 1030 by a certain Asilo in Würzburg, probably in the cathedral school. Hermann the Lame joyously snatched it up around 1040 in the Abbey of Reichenau; his imitators in St Emmeram conscientiously expanded on it around 1090. But it would be a mistake to infer a national identity here; as early as 1070, the game went to Liège, then, around 1090, to Tournai, and from France it almost immediately went to England, later to Italy. It fascinated all kinds of people: at first the more open-minded of the school masters who wanted to teach their pupils mathematics, proportion and combination in a pleasurable fashion; afterwards the deeper thinkers among scholars, who were concerned with correlations between games and human existence, even John of Salisbury and Leibniz; finally, the more learned among the politicians, who wanted to reconcile thought and deed, Sir Thomas More as well as Duke August of Wolfenbüttel.

The specialists never liked the game, neither the humanists, from Abelard to Petrarch, nor the natural scientists, from Fibonacci to Oresme. The modern period turned up its nose at the game's artistic values. Thus, our epoch of 'two cultures' has lost all knowledge of *Rithmimachia*; mention of the game cannot even be found in the cult books of Hermann Hesse and Douglas Hofstadter, which attempt to reconcile those same two cultures. That this medieval game should still have something to tell us is something I noticed myself when my students in Constance experimented with it excitedly. It taught them calculation not as a mechanical task, but as a creative attempt at social life. But I must now leave the lowlands of game practice, and lead the reader up to the high peaks of game theory.

V

The people of the Middle Ages were unfamiliar with our cleanly divided branches of game theory: mathematical, economical, politico–military, biological, physical–chemical, pedagogical, anthropological, theological, speech-analytical, literary and sociological. But when modern game theorists search the modern age for the origins of their science, they come up short. The earliest theory of games is found in a book about *Rithmimachia* written around 1130. In order to reflect the necessary breadth of thought in the tradition springing from that first theory, I will restrict my examination here to a single generation, that between 1250 and 1285, and to a single institution, the University of Paris.

Scholars there were not able to talk freely of games, for the ruler living nearby, Louis IX of France, hated anything that had to do with them, as did his lieutenant, Vincent of Beauvais. On the crusade of 1248, it worried Louis to see his closest relatives indulging in oriental games, chess more than any other, but also the older game of backgammon and common dice games. On his way back, the king threw all game implements he could get his hands on overboard, and though he could not command the nobility to abstain from pleasure, in 1254 he did forbid his own court officials to participate in any amusement involving dice, board games and chess pieces. However, he only succeeded in the opposite of his intention, for now the methods and intentions of human game-playing became a basic question.

During his Parisian study years, the English Franciscan Roger Bacon had observed that bickering did little to further science. Thus, in Oxford he demanded the expansion of study beyond the restrictions of schools and disciplines; this he explained in his *Communia mathematica* of around 1258. Mathematics, he wrote, was neither the pure theory of numbers nor the practice of calculation, but both. Applied mathematics was not restricted to the use of the abacus, the instrument for calculation that had been in use for 300 years; one should also be familiar with the new Indian method, algorithm. Furthermore, one should be able to read planetary diagrams, know something of weights and mixture ratios, understand the procedures of buying, lending, exchanging and saving money, as well as measuring altitudes, lengths and widths. And because too much of this, carried out with utmost seriousness, only begets indifference, one should also play with numbers, especially in *Rithmimachia*. In some ways, he said, it is like chess, yet far more subtle and far more amusing, a game of true wisdom. Bacon took it for granted that Boethius' old theory of numbers, on which the game was based, was incompatible with the new methods of calculation involved in the decimal system. Yet the decision of right or wrong did not depend on which digit system was chosen; that could merely offer symbols anyway, not realities. He recognized the value of mathematic games for the orientation of man in nature two centuries before Nicholas of Cusa.

But its value was not generally accepted. The judgement of the German Dominican Albertus Magnus, who until 1248 had taught theology in Paris, was different from Bacon's. Albertus had barely arrived in Regensburg as bishop in 1260 when he wrote a commentary on the only statement Jesus had ever made about games. He referred to the gospel of Luke, which says that the men of this generation are like unto children sitting in the market place and calling one to another: 'We have piped unto you, and ye have not danced; we have mourned to you, and ye have not wept.' This biblical scripture, wrote Albertus, deals with the difference between good and evil men. The behaviour of the innocent was humane, their intercourse with others was social; their games, which liberated the spirit of all purposefulness, revolved around dancing and singing. (The partly musical *Rithmimachia* could be meant here.) Albertus did not think much of purposeful games men used to gain an advantage, horse exercises, for example, which served as preparation for battle. He denounced as evil cunning or lewd games, games of dice for money and shameless theatre plays. All games, good or bad, were actually preparatory games for children; they would never achieve the seriousness of an adult science. None the less, he conceived the value of pedagogical games for the moral education of man 250 years before Juan Luis Vives.

The Italian Thomas Aquinas, then master of theology in Paris, turned against his teacher and fellow-Dominican Albertus Magnus around 1270. In his *Summa theologiae*, he did not offer a *theologia ludens* in Hugo Rahner's sense; Thomas saw creation and salvation from the perspective of heaven, not of earth. Games, however, originated neither in God nor in the devil; neither animals nor children could really play, but only adults, and not scholars alone, either. Only a responsible being had the virtue of Aristotelian balance necessary for a sensible game. Because the powers at man's command were restricted, the tension between body and spirit constantly threatened to destroy him. To avoid exhausting himself in work, he needed games. In their value lay also their limitations.

They did not absolve one from the duty of social moderation; the man addicted to games was as immoderate as the spoilsport. Thus, for Thomas, what mattered was not the aesthetics of the rules, which conceded greater value to the wisdom involved in a game of logic than to the chance of a dice game; with one as with the other, a steadfast politeness was demanded of the players. Thus, Thomas would neither recommend the game of numbers nor damn the game of dice; he spoke in an equally unbiased tone of elite archery as of crude theatre. A great variety of games was necessary, according to the circumstances of the players, times and places. He founded the anthropology of games 500 years before Schiller.

That Thomas Aquinas stylized human society too academically and ignored its banality was the complaint of a Frenchman, the former priest and Bolognese student of law, Jean de Meun, in his Old French *Roman de la Rose* of 1275. In truth, he wrote, it is not we who play, but we are played with. Take the battle of Benevento in 1266, where the Frenchman Charles of Anjou predicted he would checkmate the Hohenstaufen Manfred; he did so 'by moving a pawn which had gone astray in the middle of the chessboard'. Common people, the pawns, knights and rooks, were in no position to be placed in check, like kings, yet they are in constant danger of being sacrificed by kings like ignorant boys, and Fortune, blind chance, rules over them all. The wise man of antiquity who invented the chessboard had been researching arithmetic and meant to write about numbers; but in so doing, he fell victim to a wonderful game, which he proceeded to explain, using examples – this could only mean *Rithmimachia*. However, chess is closer to real life, for one deals with people far less reasonably than with numbers. Jean de Meun understood that even the most logical and noblest game can develop into an instrument of foolish violence nearly 700 years before Stefan Zweig.

King Alfonso X of Castile, nicknamed 'The Wise', protested against so much scepticism. Alfonso had not studied in Paris, but supported the University of Salamanca; he wrote his book of games in 1283 in Old Spanish, intending it for aristocrats and peasants, not for scholars. God, Alfonso began, wanted people to be happy together, so they could more easily endure their worries and hardships, no matter of what kind. This is why they invented various kinds of games to comfort themselves. All three game types originated in the Indian Orient: he did not exclude games of chance, so vehemently tabooed by the Western church, for by throwing dice one could learn to come to grips with good and bad luck; it was best to practise logical thinking with logical games like chess; wisdom was best learned by mixing games of logic with games of chance, for example dice and chess. Thus, one can master the daily ups and downs of logic and chance in a social gathering when the working day is done. The more artistic Battle-of-Numbers game was inaccessible to non-scholars, but with his other games Alfonso managed to incorporate equally the rational and emotional needs of man; here, games were already what Ludwig Wittgenstein, nearly 700 years later, would call forms of living.

This brief review shows that Europeans in the Middle Ages did not consider themselves 'nestled in the cosmos', self-confident in a holy contest. It was as an epoch of overwhelming toil that this period was constantly searching for a human game with many variations; in doing so, it uncovered most of the aspects of modern game theory. However, it did not hope, as we do in modern times, to use work or play to classify our whole existence. Out of the confusion of facts and utopias, the *Homo ludens* demarcated only a few areas for orderly thinking and doing: incidentally, temporarily and with incomplete rules. He kept conflicts and harmonies within bounds, yet gave reason and imagination better chances than bloody reality permitted. Games like this were not world-shaking, but they were the beginnings of a change in existence.

VI

This conclusion displaces modern opinions, but does not negate them. Schiller separated games too definitely from the productive realm of active forces and from the sacred realm of law, shifting them into the pleasant realm of appearances that liberated man from compulsion and duty, physically and morally. Huizinga, too, relegates *Homo ludens* too quickly into a festive zone of cult life, far from the toils of *Homo faber* and the tribulations of *Homo sapiens*. Schiller and Huizinga both overlooked the fact that *Homo necans* is a game-player; torture for the fun of it and killing as a sport is part of the theme, in our modern period as in the antique age.

Eco, however, who sees all this, shifts the present too close to the Middle Ages. It is true that games now are becoming more and more frequently what they often were then, possible threats, realistic anticipations of the future – and that might well be reason for alarm. But – and this is doubtless a welcome sign – we are still fascinated by fictive games that the real world can only barely succeed in grasping, like masquerade balls in historical costume which no epoch has ever staged as perfectly as the period between Schiller and

Eco. Yet Neumann's theory of numbers cannot be seriously replaced by that of Boethius, the computer cannot be replaced by the abacus, and as far as the capacity of natural science to explain and illustrate goes, the Battle-of-Numbers game of the Würzburg cathedral school student Asilo is still inferior by miles to the static ball games of the Nobel prizewinner from Göttingen, Manfred Eigen.

The old *Rithmimachia* only reminds us that a physical–chemical 'glass bead game', which could be organized by a computer in seconds, excludes important matters from our lives: the social framework and historical perspective of institutions, the individuality of people and the risks of their lives. If one considers the present timeless, one will see in it the unchanging game between whim and compulsion. By including a future we cannot predict and a past we cannot change, it becomes something else, a game that is always different, somewhere between preliminary free will and after-the-fact self-justification. What the Middle Ages has to tell us could hardly change our current thought and actions, but it can change our perspective.

I will summarize the four general thoughts which my examples have all too briefly illustrated:

1 The solutions to the problems of our time would be just as incomprehensible for people who lived with other solutions as the solutions of the Middle Ages are for us. We need only consider the profound differences between medieval and modern number theory. If we could grasp this difference, we would no longer take any contemporary condition for granted. What was once accomplished in one way will have to be accomplished in another. On the other hand, the problems of our time are not as unique as our self-awareness makes us believe. Think only of the far-reaching commonalities of medieval and modern cultivations in games of killing. The study of related tasks with which the past occupied itself would deepen our self-understanding. What was once mastered will have to be mastered again.

2 The history of the modern age has been, until now, largely part of a dice game subject to the laws of probability; we Europeans were mostly just lucky. Survival, however, demands that we change the further course of this history into a game of logic, in the manner of the dialogue game invented by the philosopher Paul Lorenzen in 1958, following in the footsteps of Wittgenstein, and which German logicians and physicists have expanded on since then; this comes closer to *Rithmimachia* than any other 'glass bead game'. Not only our future descendants, but also our ancestors can participate in this dialogue. They would know even less than we of the intractability of

thought, but they would know more than we of the intractability of chance. Then, historians like us would no longer have to play the wrong role, defending or prosecuting the past; we could be what we are, interpreters and nothing more.

3   Such interpreters were not necessary before the French and Industrial Revolutions. The historian Schiller saw himself as a judge of all times, since what he knew of the past was similar to what he expected of the future. Our grandparents would not be able to communicate with our grandchildren, for time is changing faster and faster, the confusion of voices of those living at various periods is getting louder and louder. I do not know if the laborious extension of time can defeat momentary resistance; I believe that, in the long run, the post-modern escape from time, as temporary as it may be, will be a revolution only in the medieval sense of the word, a turning in circles that could quickly end in post-human silence. It is not modern man of the last 200 years, as Foucault prophesied in 1966, but the post-modern man of our days who has the best chances of disappearing 'like a face drawn in the sand of the seashore'.

4   The minority of the living who run back and forth in the arena, intoxicated or stunned by their own noise, should not forget that a massive majority is watching them from the spectator stands. The dead cannot give orders, cannot sue for their inactive rights: we are the ones who decide. Only their silence asks the question: 'We have piped unto you, we have mourned to you – did ye not hear?' Our humanity should be stable enough, our imagination flexible enough to answer them: 'Because our games are faster than yours, we have nearly forgotten your most prudent rules. But you are right, we will let you teach us: only he who talks with his past dead and trusts his future descendants gains his own history.'

Part VIII
Experiences with Mortality

13

Three Studies of Death
in the Middle Ages

I

If death had a history as we do, we could put an end to death as it
has put an end to us until now. But we did not invent death and will
not be able to stop it; it does not even change. Man's attitude
towards death has changed throughout the centuries, of course, but
not profoundly. Humanity is constantly caught up in the same
conflict, that all must die, but that for many the time has not yet
come. This gives rise to three relatively unchanging cares: one's own
death drawing closer, the presence of the dying, and the dead of the
past. Active history occurs one floor deeper, in the variety of changing forms with which the living avoid these concerns. This is the
subject examined by the monumental history, *Western Attitudes
Toward Death: from the Middle Ages to the Present*, by Philippe
Ariès, which was finished in 1974 after twenty years of research,
appearing in English that same year and in French the year after.
Why a history of death? It is a kind of analogy when Ariès recreates
a parade of 'death' throughout history; what he means is the history
of the customs and institutions of the living, the provisions they use
to protect themselves against death, the memories that insulate them
against the dead. According to Ariès, this history progresses from
wisdom to helplessness. In older times, specifically expected conduct
was clearly defined: they 'domesticated' their relationship to death;
in the modern period, man has lost his self-confidence and become
hopelessly confused, his relationship to death has 'run wild'. In the
end, the historian must put distance between himself and his subjects, like an astronaut on an orbital voyage of observation; the
earthly inhabitant left behind cannot return to his former condition,
nor does he want to perish with the advent of the future. He

asks himself what advantage is a history of his attitudes towards death and the dead, whether it is not actually just another way for historians to waste time.

Such a history would have meaning for all if it were to shift to the periphery of attention the process of dying itself, the actual transition of a man from death to the companionship of the dead. This fringe phenomenon points beyond history and yet right at its centre. In the process of dying, the unity of body and soul, which creates the reality of man, is dissolved. The body, which turns to dust, will doubtless never return to earthly history. The possibilities that await the soul can only be judged by religion, not by historical experience. There are many interesting things for historians to discover in the broad field surrounding death. They can consider the earthly fate of the body as a reflection of society's attitudes towards aging, as Rolf Sprandel did in his *Altersschicksal und Altersmoral* in 1981; they can investigate the conceptions of the fate of the soul after death, as Aaron Gurevich did in *Categories of Medieval Culture* in 1981 (English version, 1985), or like Jacques Le Goff in *The Birth of Purgatory* in 1981 (English version, 1984). In these works, much is said about the growing fear of death on one hand and increasing hope for the dead on the other, but almost nothing about the process of dying itself. That appears to be exempt from history.

At the same time, the process emphasizes history as a realization of human possibilities on the stage of time. Dying occurs in a time-span that is unpredictable beforehand and which cannot be put into perspective until afterwards; it is influenced by many expectations and the experiences of the living, and it determines once and for all the entire scope of the dying man's life. Dying is thus less a moment in the flow of history or an object to be observed than a test of the humaneness of man and his association with history. Ariès himself, who does not pursue this angle, provided the idea for it in 1969. In the preparatory research to his major work, he attempted to write the history of dying, in a way that was involved and moving, by contrasting two examples of dying almost without commentary, a modern case 'run wild' and a 'domesticated' one of earlier times. For his example of a modern death scene, he quoted the report of a French Jesuit visiting a fellow-member of his order in the intensive care ward of a hospital. The visitor could observe the patient only through a glass pane and had to talk with him through a microphone. The dying Jesuit lay on a bed with wheels on its legs and was attached to tubes and devices all around him. The visitor told the dying man that he only wanted to sit with him for a few minutes without speaking. At that, the patient freed his bound arms, ripped off his breathing mask and said: 'I am being robbed of my own death.' Those were his last words. It was a disturbing scene, though Ariès could have asked how many people today also consider the artificial extension of their own lives as a cheat, as this Jesuit had. Ariès did not, but contrasted it with an archaic death scene, this time in his own words:

> If things continue to progress along the same lines, the day will surely come when we have forgotten how people died thirty years before. In our Western culture, it was once an exceedingly simple procedure. At first came the premonition (more than a feeling) that the hour had come. 'A rich farmer who felt his death coming on...' Or the old man: 'As he finally felt that his last days had arrived...' It was a feeling that never deceived: every man was the first to know that he would die. The first act of a familiar ritual. The second act was taken up with the official farewell ceremony, in which the dying person presided: 'He summoned his children and spoke to them without witnesses...' or, alternatively, in front of witnesses: it was most important that he say something, make out his will and testament, make amends for the damages he had done, ask forgiveness, express his final wishes and finally bid them farewell. 'He is holding all their hands, he is dying.' That is all. That was the normal way.

The normal way? The scene is touching, but Ariès should have investigated whether this fairy-tale atmosphere regularly appeared in the reports of actual deaths. Of the numerous early reports of real death scenes, Ariès does not examine a single one in his crowning major work. The two scenes, therefore, cannot be accepted as representative for their epochs.

Nevertheless, they do testify to a basic change in the process of dying. The question is, what were the reasons for the change? Ariès answers that question towards the end of his book, suggesting that the reasons lie in the attitudes to four basic factors: man's awareness of himself, society's defence against untamed nature, faith in an after-life and belief in the existence of evil. As basic as these factors are, I see nothing in either scene indicating any psychological attitudes to such philosophical principles. Instead, I see social behaviour in the face of predetermined physical conditions. The farmer is surrounded by his entire family, with whom he has always lived in his house; the Jesuit, who has passed through many stages in his life, has been lying in the final one only for a short time and is visited there by a companion from another stage. The farmer has much to say before he goes on his way; the Jesuit grows silent, for his journey is ending. The farmer knows what is happening to his body only by sensing it; the Jesuit is being monitored by specialists. The farmer is supported by the presence of others who can do nothing to prevent his dying; those surrounding the Jesuit can postpone his death, but the price is isolation. When a Jesuit of the twentieth century dies differently from a Benedictine monk of the ninth, the differences originate not in psychological attitudes towards philosophical principles, for they are both defenders of the same faith, and therefore agree. The deviations originate in social modes of behaviour in the face of specific physical circumstances, for they deviate widely even among peers of different epochs. A farmer of the eighteenth century will still die differently from a farmer of the twelfth. In the same epoch, say in the fourteenth century, burghers of a city died differently from monks in an abbey, because they lived in different communities under different conditions.

For now, this is no more than a simple assertion. To verify it, and at least to people Ariès' panorama of centuries with a cross-section of actual deaths, I will discuss three deaths taken from different periods, countries and societies. The principal persons are: an Alemannic monk of the ninth century, a Holstein farmer of the twelfth and a Florentine burgher of the fourteenth. In all three cases, eyewitnesses gave their reports in a disturbingly sincere and detailed way. They did not deal with death in general, making no mention that others had been carried to the grave before and that we, too, must die some day; they wrote only of the presence of their dying subjects. They observed the conduct of the dying and of the survivors starting from the point when death seemed certain and continuing to the point where the man had actually passed on. The authors did not write out of curiosity, nor out of diversion, but to share something important with the living. The best thing would be for us simply to listen, to see whether there is something in history which we can apply to our conduct towards the dying, and as mortal beings ourselves.

II

Ariès calls dying in the Middle Ages 'domesticated death', since the living were confronted with death every day and because the dying were calmed with simple rites and bolstered by public compassion. That is true in general, but there is more to it than that. Ariès substantiates his theory of domesticated death with examples taken from poetry, especially with the death of Roland in the Old French *Chanson de Roland*. But that romance relates the behaviour of a stylized personality depicted with a didactic intention; it was dying as dying was supposed to be. Even on this normative level, the historian must be able to differentiate. Roland represents the heroes of the vernacular epic, the noble lord dying in battle as bravely as he had lived. Before his end, he reviews his past deeds, then turns to his inheritors; his death is an earthly one and concerns more the community of living than the future of the soul. But can the hero of a Latin legend die like that? Take a simple case, the death of St Gall, as described by the Benedictine monk Wetti of Reichenau around 820.

Near the beginning of his missionary assignment at Lake Constance, around 612, Gall became very ill. He was about fifty years old, already at death's door according to medieval standards. Though Gall must have seriously counted on dying, Wetti's legend makes no mention of such thoughts. Gall's abbot, St Columban, thought sickness was an excuse to get out of work: Gall was pretending he could not travel because he did not want to continue his journey with the other missionaries from Bregenz to Italy. Columban forbade him to read mass as long as the abbot lived, and left the feverish patient alone, unattended. Gall had to row himself across Lake Constance from Bregenz, and was nursed back to health in the commune of Arbon. Wetti forgets that Gall would not have been able to make his historical achievements if he had died from his illness. His successors know that he was not to die yet: Gall had a lifetime of powerful influence before him, and he had yet to establish the Abbey of St Gall. God must have wanted it, Gall must have known it; a life of uncertainty did not fit the image of a saint.

Not until the 640s did Gall's life approach its end, after he had done all he could, when he was aged and prepared for it. He travelled once more from St Gall and his monks to Arbon, to preach to the laity. Wetti writes:

> On the third day, he wished to see his pupils again, but a fever incapacitated him. It became so violent that he could take not even his usual frugal nourishment. For fourteen days, his bodily suffering became progressively worse, and this vigorous fighter for the Lord prepared to see the face of Christ. Then the fourteenth day arrived, and we believe he received the reward for his toils. His weak limbs dissolved and he was consumed to skin and bone. None the less, he did not abandon the service of

the Lord, but continued to send comforting prayers up to heaven and to speak words of encouragement. And so, at the age of ninety-five, on the 16th of October and still tireless in the service of Christ, to whom he had dedicated himself, he returned his blessed soul to heaven.

Wetti's narration corresponds to Ariès' basic pattern, but with important differences. Death was not heralded by an inner premonition, but by external signs. Nevertheless, Gall was the first to know he had to prepare for death, long before others could properly interpret the wasting away of his body. In the meantime, the dying monk actually did preside over a ritual of dying, and it took place in public: he spoke words of encouragement and consolation to the survivors around him, and turned his prayers to heaven, in whose service he had always stood. His closest friends, his fellow-monks, did not stand around his death-bed, nor did they receive instructions; there is no need for final words and glances to be shared, for the death of a saint is not of this earth, but concerns more the community of saints. His death is only a transition, the liberation of the blessed soul from an imperfect body. Nor is it necessary to note the year of death: the date is sufficient, so that survivors may pray to the deceased saint in the liturgy of the church year. Since Gall was already a saint during his lifetime, he died a pious death. Wetti did not witness that death himself, since it had taken place six generations before he recorded it, but it must have taken place in that way.

Such normative reports influence average behaviour. If you knew how to die, that was how you tried to die. However, we should not confuse what was meant to be with what was, as Ariès has. For example, how did the Benedictine monk die who narrated the exemplary end of St Gall? The death of Wetti was described almost immediately, at the end of 824, by Heito, the former abbot of the Abbey of Reichenau who had returned to his home cloister from an illustrious career at the Carolingian court, to prepare himself for his own death there. Heito assumed that he would die before his friend and pupil Wetti, who had also led a full life but was not yet fifty years old. Wetti had officiated as master of the Reichenau monastery school for twenty years, and his novices thought him an ideal monk. How one should die was something the pupils knew as well as their teacher; he had impressed it upon them only recently with his example of St Gall. Much would happen, however, before he would have to follow his own example.

On Saturday, 29 October 824, during the monks' common meal, Wetti was not able to hold the drink in his stomach, and he refused the food served him. He did not waste a thought on mortal danger and was able to eat and drink again the next day, though listlessly; on Monday and Tuesday his appetite returned. Tuesday, 1 November, towards twilight, Wetti was sitting with the others in the dining chamber when he said he could not wait for the end of the meal. They brought him to a small room next door where he lay down on the bed, intending to wait until the other monks had finished. The monastery did not take the indisposition seriously, and neither did Wetti. He closed his eyes but did not fall asleep. Suddenly, he saw a cleric standing beside the bed with an ugly face and no eyes, holding devices of torture in his hands; he let Wetti know he was going to torture him tomorrow. A host of evil spirits crowded around Wetti with spikes and shields, trapping him. It was crowded and hot: he thought he was going to die that instant. But that feeling was not infallible. All at once, worthy monks appeared in the room, sitting, and one said in Latin: 'It is not right that these idle souls should act that way, for this man will regain his health. Send them away.' The evil spirits disappeared; it seemed that the presence of the community of monks at the table next door had dispelled all danger. But Wetti was wrong again. A shining angel stepped up to the bed and said in a friendly manner: 'I am coming to you, dear soul.' Wetti saw that it was serious. He answered with a Latin confession of guilt and asked for the aid of the heavenly hosts. He hoped for direct communication between earth and heaven.

There is little need for psychoanalysis to deduce the condition of Wetti's soul from his first vision. He was torn between various possible ways of interpreting the symbols. He might die, he might get well. That depended not on physical conditions, but on spiritual connections. And if he were to die, he might fall into the hands of the executioner of souls, or he might be aided by the angel. At any rate, he knew what had to be done next. When he came to himself, he saw two monks sitting in his room; the abbot had sent them when the others returned to their cells. Wetti told them both of his vision, threw himself at their feet and begged them to pray for him with all their might. While he lay on the floor, they chanted psalms of repentance. The familiar liturgy began to lift Wetti's spirits, so he stood up and sat on the bed. Then he wanted to know how it was to continue. He was well-read and it occurred to him that the fate of the soul after death had been described in the dialogues of St Gregory the Great. His fellow-monks fetched the book from the abbey library and read the section aloud to Wetti, about twenty pages. The familiar scholarliness, too, calmed him. It was late at night, so he told his two attendants to sleep. They were to remain

in the room; Wetti did not want to be alone when the next
visitors came from the other side. He had hope in the aid of earthly
companions.

Wetti, too, fell asleep, and it was then that his guardian angel
reappeared. He admonished Wetti to continue his prayers of repentance and announced that he would start his great journey tomorrow; in the meantime, he led the monk out to a landscape featuring
a huge river of fire and high mountains of marble. Before him lay
heaven and hell. Now Wetti's second vision began, the most potent
we know before Dante's *Divina Commedia*. It was inspired by St
Gregory's writings, but extended far beyond everything the sober
Wetti had ever read or written about until then. His experience of
his pilgrimage through the after-life was terrifying: it was here he
saw how alone he was. There, on the other side, there were no
advocates from his Abbey of Reichenau to speak for him. In early
visions of the after-life, monks had always met hosts of familiar
faces, exchanged intimate words and received support. Here, no
one spoke with Wetti except his guardian angel. The most highly
esteemed members and friends of his monastery from throughout
the last century were paying for their sins in hell or purgatory. Not
even liturgy or scholarliness were granted to the Benedictine's credit;
the voice called down from the eternal throne: 'He should have
given others an example of edification, but he did not do so.' Wetti
felt that his life as a monk was a failure.

But the worst was yet to come. He was instructed to confess his
transgressions to all his pupils and friends and beg them to do good
and teach righteously in the future. Wetti now heard in detail, from
his guardian angel, just what was wrong with the life of the abbey;
Wetti was given a last reprieve to report this criticism to the brothers
of Reichenau, with the promise that if he preached it steadfastly, he
could still be saved. He knew this was a difficult mission and told
the angel that he was an unimportant man and unworthy of pro-
claiming such terrifying things to the earth. The angel rebuked him
sharply, saying he was still thinking of earthly prestige and was thus
gambling with his eternal salvation. The instruction of the angel
contradicted all familiar patterns: here, the living were not to pray
for the dying, the dying man was to preach to the living. Wetti could
not wait for his death, he had to race with it. He was not allowed to
finish his life's work, he had to destroy it. Only thus could he escape
punishment. These things had never appeared in legends before.
When Wetti awakes, he hears birds singing; Wednesday, 2 November, is just dawning. He wakes up the medical attendants and wants
to summon the abbot immediately. They resist at first, as it contra-

dicts the monks' daily schedule. The monks of the cloister are awake but praying alone in their cells; the silence is not to be disturbed. Now, Wetti sees how alone he is, even when he is awake. In his fear of running out of time, he dictates the second vision to the two monks, who inscribe it on wax tablets for others to read, in case Wetti loses his voice before he has a chance to explain. He has no time to lose because he does not know when his hour will come. Would the other monks know better?

Again he is wrong; his worry is unnecessary. After the second morning prayers, the abbot comes to visit the patient. When he hears of Wetti's unusual request, he sends the others out and summons the four oldest monks, the senior abbot, Heito among them. It is this abbey senate that listens to the narration of Wetti's experiences; he begs forgiveness of them and prayerful support, perhaps the support of the entire monastery as well. The dignitaries are surprised. He appears neither pale nor starved. When they ask whether he has pains anywhere, he answers in the negative. They feel his pulse; it is normal. They calm him down, assuring him that he will not die yet. They will have also counselled together whether they should allow Wetti to belittle himself before the other monks, especially before the novices and pupils. This would compromise the external standing of the entire abbey as well as its internal tranquility, and for what? The schoolmaster had, most likely, simply had a bad dream. Wetti, however, no longer hopes for understanding and companionship; he sees himself tossed back upon his own insecurity, which he should have been able to rise above, with the help of his liturgy and readings.

He is still unsure whether or not he must start on his last journey tomorrow, for the second vision had indicated that a long life awaited him. But did that mean life on earth or in heaven? The abbey leaves him to himself from then on, but he has no peace. He passes Wednesday in lonely prayers and discussions with friends. Early on Thursday, 3 November, he summons his favourite pupil, Walafrid Strabo, and dictates ten letters to various monks living in distant monasteries, all saying the same thing: he is in mortal danger, would they please send their help from other parts of the world to him in his weakness, by reading masses for him and reciting psalms. Walafrid, eager as he is, thinks it is a school assignment and wants to compose the letters in elegant verses. Wetti puts a quick end to that nonsense. Walafrid, who is less than sixteen years old, does not understand the seriousness of the matter; before the eyes of his teacher, the pupil falls asleep. The old man has lost his last audience. He lies down, gets up, walks around until it gets dark.

Then he asks a few monks into his room, telling them his life has come to an end and asking them to sing him psalms for the dying. He leads them in the music and lets himself be comforted by the rite of singing. After the final prayers, they administer the host to him and retire. Now it is time for Wetti to do what Ariès thought so properly medieval: lie in bed and wait for death. Instead, he wanders through the sleeping abbey, up and down, glowing with fever. Then he falls upon his bed and dies; Friday 4 November, 824, must have just begun. At what hour, with what words, from what sickness Wetti died, Heito does not tell us, because no one in the cloister knew.

In all, Wetti died the natural death of the Middle Ages, and also the tranquil death in the company of others. As a monk, he was able to die in peace; he did not have to provide for a funeral or dependants. As he had lived his life for death, so would he remain living, for the abbey, after his death. They would recite psalms for him, sing masses, perform his final will, copy down his visions and have Walafrid put them into verse. Yet his death was unusual; neither the understanding of fellow monks nor communication with angels domesticated his death. The survivors did not dare ask whether or not Wetti had gone to heaven, and what fate was in store for the proud Abbey of Reichenau now, if the things he told of the after-life were true. If they were true, then one could not trust appearances, one could not disregard feverish dreams, the world had lost its balance.

The island monastery had received many reports of visions of the after-life in recent years, but Wetti had heard and repressed them. Like him, most Reichenau monks thought similarly of descriptions of the after-life: 'feverish imaginings that cannot be taken seriously'. Now they knew Wetti's visions of the after-life had told the naked truth; his unexpected death proved it. In the first vision, worthy monks had told the dying man he would get well; following the second vision, the head of his abbey told him the same. But they had all been deceived. And his was not the only surprising death. The year before, in 823, a great plague had broken out in the Frankish empire that killed many men. Wetti appeared to bring the message from beyond death that this had happened because of the countless sins of the laity, and that soon the end of the world would begin.

Wetti was not as alone as he had assumed in his fears. If his fellow-monks had closely examined life outside the monastery walls, they would have long since known that every life was threatened. Among the laity, every fifth child died, and only every third survived its twentieth year. War, starvation and plagues made death commonplace, for the young more than for anyone. If any, it was only the aged monks, living on their protected island, who considered death domesticated. Medical experience was cultivated here more than anywhere else; monks could interpret a patient's pulse and the colour of his face. But now they were facing a puzzle. A modern doctor I asked would not venture a diagnosis of Wetti's ailment; the only obvious symptom was a delirious fever with lucid intervals. The other monks themselves doubted whether Wetti had even died from a physical ailment. They learned that even in the midst of life, they were surrounded by death. In 1977, Karl Schmid drew attention to the shock effect Wetti's death had on the entire cloister. The medieval monk knew no other way to domesticate death but with traditional rites, but now these were extended not only to gather together the monks of Reichenau, but all monks; it included calling upon not only guardian angels, but the saints as well.

In 824, the Abbey of Reichenau began keeping a fraternity book, an index of all their living and dead monks, including membership lists from fifty other European cloisters, a conspiracy of monks praying for the salvation of the dying. Wetti was entered among the first, and many monasteries prayed for him. Not long afterwards, before 830, Reichenau began gathering relics of early Christian saints from Italy and the Orient to gain potent advocates in the after-life. Fear of isolated death drove the Benedictines out of reclusion, into the realm of global Christianity and into the chronology of church history. Nevertheless, it remained uncertain whether a world-wide fraternity of mortals and saints could guide the individual monk past the final hurdle. For dying monks, the last hours had become a serious time crisis, as it had been for Wetti. Everything he had done and said in his life became questionable. His future, in heavenly paradise as in earthly memory, would be decided alone by what he did now. Thus, an extreme intensification of life was demanded of the dying, a demand no common ritual could satisfy. Public participation only worsened the crisis, for society confronted the dying with its own expectations, questioning their experiences.

Thus it was only with great effort that the ritualization of dying could bridge the gap between participants, or soothe the tension between the period's ideal and its reality, between the enticing intellectual world of religion and the threatened cultural world of the living. In the ninth century, dying became an opportunity for the society of the living to attempt communication with the society of saints, an attempt at personally surmounting the real contradictions, an hour of trial for the age's social and religious world systems. This new way of dying can hardly be called 'domesticated' death: a more fitting expression would be 'significant' death. In the crisis that was dying, the significance of life became obvious, for the individual monk as for his brothers collectively.

III

According to Ariès, from the twelfth century onwards 'domesticated death' was superimposed by another mode of conduct, which prevailed until the sixteenth century. Ariès calls it 'individual death', indicating the increase in significance of the individual since the High Middle Ages, parallel to the growing belief in an identical fate for all men, and thus the individual was given more attention at the time of death. This is fundamentally correct but not precise. The new significance of death was closely related to the changes in communal life, the increase in the European population, for example, making people live more closely together, but not as cohesively as in the Early Middle Ages. Small, tight groups were replaced with more abstract ties over larger distances. Added to this was the refinement of culture that improved the standard of living, making life freer and at the same time more sensitive and fragile. As a result of better medical knowledge and longer life-spans, life on earth gained a rising value and more deliberate care. These changes were, of course, not necessarily recognized as progress by contemporaries, especially not by the laity, for whom the gates of heaven were not open as wide as for clerics. The typical layman was glad to say farewell to the toils of life, yet usually left behind unsupported dependants and unfinished plans, from which he found it difficult to tear himself away. At any rate, the deaths of laymen seldom appeared as a transition, more often a caesura. It was not easy for them ascetically to scoff at pain; their physicality anticipated the bodily pain of dying. Sometimes medicine could postpone death, yet could not restore the full vitality of life. The hour of death was no longer predictable, nor could it be entered into with solemnity, and especially not in the case of laymen, who could never be sure whether or not they would die after proper preparation, in bed and in a circle of loved ones. The survivors' relationship to the dying was more reserved than before. They watched his physical ailing more clinically and often broke off their emotional ties in advance, as he was physically or mentally no longer a living part of their community.

In such circumstances, the normative image of the death of a hero also underwent basic changes. I will take the example of the death of Count Adolf II of Holstein in 1164, examining it in the form given to it by the priest Helmold of Bosau a few years after the fact, around 1171. Helmold was one of the founding monks in the episcopal cloister of Neumünster, which helped to Christianize East Holstein. As pastor of Bosau, he was familiar with the needs and desires of the newly immigrated Holstein farmers. Helmold judged the Holstein aristocratic society far more coolly than his parish and clerical peers. He appreciated their feudal lord, Count Adolf of Schauenberg, though also from a distance, for the count was not always friendly in his dealings with the church. Adolf had a literary and Latin education; when he started to colonize East Holstein in 1143, he tried as often as possible to use peaceful methods, coming to an understanding with the original Slavic population and their princes. New settlers streamed into the country from Flanders and Holland, from Westphalia and Friesland, but military conflicts soon arose, including some attacks by the Danish high nobility from the north. Around 1149, with only a few supporters, Adolf engaged in a battle with a superior Danish force in Rendsburg. He had admitted that his countrymen often accused him of having a womanly and cowardly heart, as he preferred to fight with the tongue rather than with the fist, but now the country's existence was at stake. No words were wasted on mortal danger, though the count was thrown from his horse during the fight. In the end, he won the battle and secured his claim to the country. More importantly, he tamed the stubborn and thieving Holstein inhabitants. He was a politician of peace, who seemed predestined from the beginning to have a contemplative death.

The end came as a surprise in 1164, when Adolf was about sixty-six years old. His duke, Henry the Lion, was warring against the neighbouring Slavs, and Count Adolf obeyed the ducal order to participate. His army, which consisted partly of Slavs, was negligent, as were the count and the noble lords, despite warnings from Holstein peasant leaders that Slavic spies were about. Suddenly, early one morning, on Monday 6 July, 1164, the Slavs attacked Adolf's camp at Lake Kummerov near Verchen. Only a handful of Holsteiners and Dithmarschers were out of their sleep fast enough to drive the first line of Slavs into the lake. When the second wave came, however, it buried everything under it like an avalanche. His counsellors urged Count Adolf to flee for his life, especially as his son and heir was only four years old. But Adolf remained, as Helmold tells us, faithful unto death: he dismissed the thought of flight and willingly died out of love for bravery, 'fighting with his fists and crying unto God', like the biblical hero, Judas Maccabaeus, in his struggle against the heathens. Helmold did not witness the count's death, but was sure he had received a foreboding of it; it was told that on the day before, he had repeated the psalm many times over: 'With fire thou hast tried me, and no unrighteousness didst thou find in me.' An obscure prediction, to be sure, and Helmold was aware that the count's death had come at a bad time, for afterwards the country suffered from the loss of the strong lord who had provided law and peace. Certainly Count Adolf died as an exemplary knight and hero; he died an 'individual death', but whether this death was meaningful for his fellow-man remains questionable, for the well-being of communities depended on their leadership.

The end of Count Adolf of Holstein was a familiar story to both the authors and the heroes of two documents composed in East Holstein a quarter of a century later, in 1190. The *Visio Godeschalci* is one of the few eye-witness descriptions of the death of a peasant of the High Middle Ages. Both reports were composed in Latin, one of them by a canon of the Chapter of Neumünster, a younger fellow-monk of Helmold of Bosau, the other by the pastor of a neighbouring village. Both were based on the statements of a farmer named Gottschalk from the county of Harrie, north-east of Neumünster. Gottschalk had known the old Count Adolf personally, had perhaps not fought in 1164, but was familiar with the exemplary death of his lord. Since Gottschalk's personal memories went back to the late 1150s, he was probably about fifty years old by 1190, certainly an advanced age for a man of his circumstances. The daily reality of a farmer was perhaps harder and more limited than that of a count, but his death was similar, nearly devoid of words and ritual, and so obscure that the question of its significance can neither be ignored nor answered.

Events that concerned a peasant all happened in the environment of the neighbouring villages, like the terrible story from the 1170s of the high-born nine-year-old orphan adopted by a sympathetic family in Emkendorf. Out of greed, the boy murdered the couple's only son, a seven-year-old, claiming afterwards that he had done it on the advice of a black man riding a black horse. The devil, it would seem, intruded upon village life too. To sentence the murderer, the farmers from the entire parish were called together; Gottschalk was there and, like most, he disapproved of the death sentence upon the boy – by the wheel – which was carried out immediately. Decades later, Gottschalk related the story in all its horrible details. That, too, was a form of dying: execution by merciless neighbours who did their best to anticipate the final judgement. In the next life, the boy-murderer's punishment would be less harsh, and God would not exclude him from heaven, of that Gottschalk was convinced. There was in general no mutual interest in the village; every man worked for himself and kept a mistrustful eye on his neighbours.

Who of them, for example, cared about Gottschalk? He was old, tired and sick; he had worked every day of his life, clearing away beeches and oaks, sowing fields, making swampland cultivable, erecting dams, bridges and footbridges. He was never allowed rest, especially since his wife was half blind and helpless, his only son weak and incapable of keeping house; he had probably married off both daughters into other villages. The survival of his family depended on the work-force of the old farmer and his only horse. To make things worse, high politics interfered in his life of hardship. Duke Henry the Lion, though banned to England by the German Emperor Frederick Barbarossa, had returned in 1189 when the Emperor and Count Adolf III of Holstein, the son of Holstein's colonizer, were absent on a crusade in the Holy Land. Henry the Lion took possession of the county of Stade and Holstein. Only the castle of Segeberg continued to resist the duke, so he laid siege to it. The farmers of the Holstein parish villages were forced to take up position before Segeberg in eight groups for two weeks each. On Sunday, 10 December, 1189, it was the turn of the peasants of Harrie, including the sick Gottschalk.

Gottschalk sympathized with the Schauenburg family and did not see why he should now fight against the count. He sought release from the responsibility on the grounds of sickness, but no one listened to him. His wife wanted to hold him back, fearing he would either not return at all or return so ill that he would not be able to work any more. These fears about her future were reasonable. Gottschalk had no choice but to follow the command: he fastened his knapsack in comparative silence, making no long speeches of farewell to his clamouring wife and stupid son. Though he felt wretched, he marched thirty-five kilometres to Segeberg with the other farmers. He collapsed two days later, on Tuesday 12 December, towards evening: he had a shivering fit and his limbs were weak, he had to lie down. The other peasants visited the sick man, feeling sorry for him, but they could not help him. There was no doctor around, only a priest who gave him Holy Communion. Very few words or prayers were uttered. After that, Gottschalk could not eat; his end appeared to be near, his family was far away, and no one summoned them to his deathbed. On Sunday 17 December, Gottschalk lost consciousness. His face was pale, his tongue limp, his pulse hardly discernible; these were the accurate observations of his neighbours. They also noted the following phase, from Wednesday, 20 December: Gottschalk no longer moved at all. They would have assumed him dead and probably buried him immediately, but a twitching of his mouth showed there was still some life in him.

So Gottschalk was still lying there on Sunday, 24 December, 1189, Christmas Eve, when the people of Harrie started returning home. They loaded their comrade onto a cart. When they arrived at Neumünster, they discussed whether it would not be simpler to carry Gottschalk straight to the church; the twitching of his mouth, they thought, surely would not last longer than a day, and then they would have to carry the corpse all the way back, seven kilometres, from Harrie to the cemetery in Neumünster. They were all as over-worked as Gottschalk; as long as he was still moving, they had compassion, but when he lay there stiffly, their thoughts turned again to their own exhaustion. Probably too they gave thought to Gottschalk's wife and children; at any rate, they did finally draw the cart all the way to his home village. Under the care of his family, Gottschalk recovered his strength. It was five weeks before he dared leave his bed, towards the end of January, 1190.

During this time, he remains sick and unsteady, plagued by unendurable pains. His appetite returns only gradually, constipation makes his stomach ache; even domestic work is too much for him. When his horse dies as well, no one does his work for him. No wonder Gottschalk is tired of this world and longs for the after-life; it will be better for him there than here, at any rate. During the five days before Segeberg, while he lay as if dead, Gottschalk experienced a vision of the next life which he now relates to his confessor, and, on request, to visitors. It was because of this vision that the clerics recorded Gottschalk's sufferings. The story of the dying man gives us an idea of the fears and hopes of a peasant who had worked all his life for others. Two angels appear, telling him to come with them, and when he asks where they are going, they answer his questions only in a general, soothing manner; they talk little to him and not at all to each other; they remain strangers to him, as would high-born people. His way to the next life, on a path which appears to lie south-west of Holstein, is as difficult as any road in his earthly life, and he walks it barefoot. He comes to a wide meadow full of thorns and brambles and though others are given shoes, he has to continue barefoot until he collapses, the soles of his feet torn. It is easier to cross the terrifying river that comes next; it is filled with iron blades and spear-tips, but he can balance on the narrow, long beam which crosses it because of his experience in building bridges in his earthly life. Then he comes upon a steep, sunken pass, so boggy and stinking that it makes his skull throb. Finally he reaches a burning plain of unbearable heat that causes him sharp pains in the sides. What Gottschalk sees in the next life is the earthly landscape he helped to clear for cultivation in his earthly life: that is his purgatory. For him, heaven is, and can only be, a city with wide and straight streets, a huge stone church, countless buildings and grand squares.

On his way, he meets numerous other travellers like himself, a few saved, even fewer damned, the majority lukewarm sinners. Gott-schalk sees many unfamiliar faces but learns no names or stories that he has not already known. Once in a while, he is overjoyed to meet someone from Holstein in the crowd, and mentions it to his accompanying angels. There are some aristocratic and clerical lords there too, good and evil, and at the head of the laity is old Count Adolf, whom Gottschalk is happy to meet on his way to paradise. More than anything, it is people of his own class, the nine-year-old murderer from Emkendorf, a worthy lay cook named Gottfried from the Chapter of Neumünster, and servants and maids. On the way back to earth, when the accompanying angels have already left him, he meets a farmer from his parish whom he had seen not long before as a wounded man at the siege of Segeberg, one of the many meaninglessly sacrificed. The man gives Gottschalk a message for his son, for he, too, has missed the farewell ceremony à la Ariès. Unfortunately, however, Gottschalk forgets the message by the time he has returned to his body, and so he cannot relay it. All his experiences in the next life were accepted passively. He did not question any of the heavenly messengers; no one predicted his future fate. Gottschalk hopes he will reach paradise again, but he must wait. He does not understand why he was pushed back into earthly life. In the short time he now has remaining, the sick farmer has no opportunity to change his lot in life, as did the sick monk Wetti: his fate appears to be out of his hands. Certainly, he should warn his fellow-men, who gather around this traveller from the beyond, but what good does it do Gottschalk in this life? Only when one of his visitors swears that he would give a huge pile of gold for such a vision does Gottschalk agree: he would not want to lose his heaven-ly vision for the greatest treasure of gold.

Every day, he feels what he took back with him from his journey: headaches, pains in his side, pains in his feet. He will not be free of them until he leaves his ailing body and this earthly vale of tears forever. He longs for that moment: early in the morning before seven o'clock, the sick old man sits out in front of his house looking to the east, where the sun is rising in the mist. Suddenly, he sees a huge light spreading, to renew the whole world. What still separates him from this light is his second death, and it is taking its time; the 'prison of the body' will not release him, he is desperate. The parish priest provides him with the consolation of the church, and relatives and neighbours in the village help out; but rituals of death do not change his fate. His fate will be determined according to criteria that a simple peasant cannot grasp. He does not know whether his soul will find companions after death or whether he will be alone. His 'individual death' is in reality an obscure death, one that cannot rely on the circumstances of his last hours, nor on the support of his fellow man.

The history of Gottschalk's vision illustrates how alone the farmer was. Except for the two writers who recorded the vision from his words, only a single Rhenish writer found it remarkable, the Cistercian Caesarius of Heisterbach; in 1220 he recommended it to his readers, together with Wetti's vision, only because it contained a message from the next life. It was Leibniz who rediscovered it, and the complete edition did not appear until 1979. Jacques Le Goff glanced over the text in 1980, Walther Lammers interpreted it in 1981 as a report of a journey into the next life, not as a study of dying. It did not serve as the norm for any society, did not provide the peasants with any cultural memories, did not make history. Emperor Frederick Barbarossa had begun his journey to the heavenly Jerusalem in the summer of 1190, on his crusade to the earthly Jerusalem, and that event was added as a marginal note to the manuscript, but when the peasant Gottschalk was finally relieved of his suffering is unknown. The next historian of East Holstein, the cleric Arnold of Lübeck, who wrote around 1210, made no mention of Gottschalk. That is the reverse side of 'individual death'; Ariès overlooked it, as have many other historians, who are so enthusiastic about socially rising groups in the High Middle Ages but blind to the devastating effects of the new individuality and mobility on social behaviour, and, above all, on 'obscure' death.

IV

The widest gap in Ariès' book must now be discussed: it concerns the changes in the process of dying in the Later Middle Ages, the fourteenth century. This period confronted the rigidly fixed, occupationally organized population of the continent with completely new phenomena, similar to those of the Early Middle Ages, which by now were long since forgotten. All that remained of the mobility of the High Middle Ages was its unrest: the hopefulness of that earlier period was nowhere to be seen. Changes in the attitudes towards death were most impressively described in 1976 by Werner Goez: protracted wars, recurring waves of pestilence and frequent crop failures led to mass dying. But society did not try to learn anything from it; no retrospective conclusions were drawn from the lives of the dead. The community of survivors retreated into more abstract institutions, feeling these to be immortal: the papal church, monarchy, specialized communes; man encountered death more tangibly, personified now as the skeleton, a kind of absolute ruler and merciless destroyer. Since no traditional pattern was valid any longer, and every mortal had to discover death anew, books about the art of dying spread like wildfire. Their most diligent readers were the burghers of large cities. Such literature helped survivors to assimilate the loss of loved ones and the fear of one's own coming death; it invested remarkably little effort in the contemporary process of dying, as if that lay beyond the realm of human effort. There were few city burghers who thought of their lives as a path leading to death. One of these, however, I will describe here: the Florentine Giovanni Boccaccio.

Initially, around 1350, he dispassionately and simply analysed the mass deaths of the Great Plague of 1348; he saw how a man's right to an individual death disappeared, and how neighbourly, community aid for the dying had deteriorated. Boccaccio's relatives fell victim to the epidemic, which was one of the reasons the thirty-five-year-old poet retreated from the idea of death and wanted to experience life as intensely as possible, as it was so short anyway, before it ended. After the first wave of disease had receded, Boccaccio began looking for something permanent in the midst of transience. He sought the answer in an exemplary figure, Dante Alighieri, whose life and death he recorded between 1351 and 1355. Few burghers, reasoned Boccaccio, would be able to match the norm of such a brilliant poet, but it might teach them that their existence was not wholly subject to the arbitrariness of death. In order to find the weak point of death, they had to know its strong point. Boccaccio generalized:

As anyone can plainly see, nothing in this world is permanent, and if any one thing is particularly easy to change, that thing is our own life. Just a little attack of cold or heat – not to mention the innumerable other, equally unforeseeable possibilities – can push us over the brink, without much ado, from existence into non-existence. Nobility, wealth and youth are exceptions to this as little as are any other worldly dignities.

Boccaccio returned to the convictions of Wetti's contemporaries, that death has unlimited power over bodily circumstances and cannot be tamed by social institutions. This was something anyone could learn, but almost no one wanted to believe. In the end, the omnipotence of death derives its power from mortals' blind lust for life.

Dante was one who saw further than the masses did. Boccaccio continued: 'Dante first felt the weight of this natural law on the death of another, long before his own.' What so disturbed the twenty-four-year-old Dante in 1290 was not a representative death somewhere in society, but the separation from his only beloved, Beatrice; he was not even able to be with her at her death. Boccaccio did not remark on the circumstances of the young woman's death nor on her behaviour in dying, but only on the reaction of the poet who survived her. Her death seemed to Dante as senseless as a life without love; he grieved so inconsolably that he physically and mentally deteriorated. His friends were afraid he would soon follow Beatrice. A few months later, however, Dante saw that no matter how many tears he cried, they would not bring back his lost companion. After a while, he even let his relatives talk him into marrying another woman. Life continued, and awaited Dante's contribution. His wife, to be sure, hardly supported him in his work at all. When he was banned from Florence, she shared neither his journeys nor his final exile in Ravenna with him. Practical life was to offer no sympathy for the poet, only worries about clothing, living space and nourishment, trouble with relatives, neighbours and housemaids; in other words, drudgery, aging and death, not much different from the life of the peasant Gottschalk. Dante found liberation in thinking about eternal principles, the movements of the heavens and the origin of life, and in 'creating things that would lend him life in the future, after he died, through the power of his fame'. With these words, Boccaccio formulated the new desire for intellectual permanence, which could overcome the power of physical death.

How did Dante die? Again, Boccaccio opened his report with a general statement: 'When the hour arrived which is appointed for every man, and as Dante was already in his fifty-sixth year, he became ill.' We learn nothing of the class, development or treatment of his sickness, nothing of his attendants or visitors in Ravenna, nothing of Dante's last hours or words. As if Boccaccio were consciously excluding any personal circumstances, he limited his description to the church rites, to Dante's receiving of the sacraments, to his date of death 'in the month of September in the year 1321 after Christ, on the day the church celebrated the elevation of the holy cross.' This brings to mind the 'domesticated death' of the legends of the saints, but Boccaccio's heaven was no paradise for ascetics, but an academy for the *beaux esprits*: 'There is no doubt in my mind that he was welcomed by the arms of the noble Beatrice. It is with her he is living now, in the sight of Him who is the greatest good.' All the characteristics that Ariès attributes to deathbed behaviour in the High Middle Ages were missing from Boccaccio's narration. Dante did not feel his own death closing in, did not take leave of his relatives, did not order his affairs; quite the opposite. Otherwise, his death would not have had such consequences.

Since Dante had not had time to publish the final thirteen cantos of his *Divina Commedia*, friends searched through his estate for it. It irritated them 'that God had not kept Dante in the world at least long enough to complete what little remained of his work'. Strange, for this final part of Dante's journey through the hereafter should have described his passage to the highest ranks of heaven, where he hoped to be eternally united with Beatrice. Was that part no more than dream and fiction? Had death destroyed both the work of the poet and his heavenly reward? Eight months later, Dante appeared in a dream to his son Iacopo Alighieri, dressed in snow-white clothes, to inform him that he had attained true life. Iacopo asked whether he had finished his work on earth first, and where it could be found. Dante led his son to his former bedroom and indicated a place on the wall. Iacopo woke up wondering whether his dreams were making a fool of him or whether he could trust the vision, for in the Late Middle Ages, the dead no longer appeared from the beyond very often. But the next morning Iacopo really did find the lost manuscript in the place he had been shown. Dante's appearance testified to his double immortality: that of a Christian saint and that of a poetic genius. The importance of greatness had already begun shifting from heaven to posthumous fame in this life. But again, Boccaccio bridged the gap between the two, for this was a connection that overcame the power of death.

Boccaccio wanted to live and die as classically as Dante had. He did not succeed, for his death was not as swift. It hounded him over two decades, launching surprise attacks, then retreating, nearing again and again. The only way Boccaccio could hold his ground against the enemy was by keeping a close watch on him. In numerous letters, he set down the observations of a dying man as no other author of the Late Middle Ages did after him. Death announced its coming to the forty-two-year-old poet for the first time during the hottest days of 1355. Boccaccio was much younger than Dante had been when he died, and was not thinking of death. A fever overcame him in Florence shortly before a trip to Naples, and he had to struggle. He saw sickness not as a natural process, but as a battle against death. After vehement resistance, he yielded to a further onset. 'I wanted to die, if fate had ordained it so. And I fell; I arrived nearly defeated at the portals of death, through which I would not have been able to return. Then I was frightened away by the horror of that gaping pit.' Whether he could have reached a heavenly shore there or not, Boccaccio did not know. He gathered up all the will-power he had and regained his health. On the eve of the year 1356, describing the new experience in Latin verse to a friend, he did not forget the danger he had weathered. Fighting death as if it were a tyrant – that seemed to promise life.

The next attack, six years later, came from an unexpected direction. Early in 1362, a miracle-working monk from Siena who disliked modern poetry lay dying, and he predicted that Boccaccio, too, would soon die. If he wanted to save himself, he should stop writing. Disturbed, Boccaccio wrote to Petrarch. If the monk were right, poetical work served nothing more than earthly renown, not eternal salvation. An early death could ruin all the artist's secular plans as well; Boccaccio was not yet Dante's age and still had not created a comparable masterpiece. Petrarch reassured his friend: anyone who thinks enough about it, he wrote, does not need predictions to be prepared for death at all times. Also, literary work could lead to sainthood just as well as a devout life could, and not only that, it could lend greater renown than the veneration of fools. Boccaccio was easily convinced. He would not lose his composure a third time. To await death calmly, no matter what form it might take, this was the distinction of a well-lived life, especially when death was not as easily recognizable or endurable as described in Dante's biography.

Three years later, death approached the poet once more, this time treading softly. Boccaccio had retreated from the noisy city of Florence to the country village of Certaldo, the home of his ancestors, when, in April 1365, he realized he was suffering from an abnormal weight increase. Immediately, he called on God's help and the help of his friends, but death, which had seemed inevitable, withdrew again, leaving behind only indications of its return. Boccaccio could read them plainly. His letter to Petrarch in July 1367 described his 'grey hair, advanced age and a body weakened by much too much fat'. He complained to a younger friend early in 1372 that his body's massive weight did not allow him to take walks. And with his grey hair, he no longer dared to ascend the peaks of academia; they were the property of younger minds now, while he must sink slowly into his grave. Obviously, he still enjoyed the game of metaphors and was looking forward to his friend's rebuttal. He was soon to lose this pleasure too, however, for the hardest crisis came just before his sixtieth birthday.

In the spring of 1372, his pains became more and more frequent. His body had become heavier still, and doctors today believe that he had dropsy. His legs were unstable, his hands trembled, his face had turned pale. To this was added scabies with strong itching, and more: stomach-aches, kidney pains, swelling of the spleen, gall infection, whooping-cough, hoarseness and a dullness in the head. His eyes still served him, his stomach retained food, sleep still granted him rest. But worse than the poet's physical condition was his mood. All desire to sing had left him, his memory was obscured, his spirit numb, he even felt no desire to read. It was a new experience that a creeping sickness could rob him of his mental powers, leaving only enough for him to observe the deterioration of his own body. The end was near, and Boccaccio's thoughts became seriously occupied with death and the grave. A few days earlier, he had regained a little strength, and now, on Tuesday, 10 August, 1372, he was able to communicate the cares of recent months in a letter to a friend. The letter took him three days, and he voiced no illusions. 'I desire death. It cannot be ill-timed, for I am in my sixtieth year. I have experienced enough, indeed much, and I have seen things my forefathers never saw. Even were I to live to be twice as old, I could never expect, with good reason, to see anything new.' This sounded cool, composed, but hesitant. The end was not expected to come quite so quickly: Boccaccio still had not put his affairs in order, nor had he called anyone to his bedside.

On Thursday evening, 12 August, when he had reached that point in his letter, Boccaccio was confined to his bed by a fever so violent that he believed he would fall prey to it and never be able to stand on his own two feet again. During the night, fever and headaches increased. As his present life was now reaching its end, he attended to his future life, to his many sins and the terrible judgement to follow. During his initial depression he trembled and wept, which was rare for him. The only one at hand was his housemaid, who had served him for decades. She thought her master was crying out in pain, and naïvely urged him to have patience. That made him laugh, and he regained his mental balance. He thought of distant friends, who would plead his case with God; in his mind he bade them farewell, saying they would meet again on the other side. There was little need for a farewell ceremony *à la* Ariès, for this was a poor man dying, one who had never married and whose illegitimate children, like his stepbrothers, had preceded him in death. There was little reason to think about the future; it was the present that demanded his full attention. At one point Boccaccio hoped that the inner heat he felt was straining to leave his body; then he feared that it would burn him from within. At times he longed for the end, then he resisted it again. In the course of this struggle he watched himself as if from a distance.

Finally morning came, and the housemaid fetched the neighbours. They urged him to summon the doctor. Until then, Boccaccio had trusted only nature, never medicine. So that no one would think he was trying to hoard his money, he agreed. The peasant doctor proved to be affable and prudent. He diagnosed the fever as a symptom of a liver infection and announced that he had to remove the poisonous juices as soon as possible; if he waited only one day, the patient might die in four days. Boccaccio agreed to the painful process of being bled and cauterized. He lost a great deal of blood, but the doctor declared him healed. And in truth, the fever disappeared, and the following night he could sleep. On Saturday, 28 August, Boccaccio was so much better that he was able to continue his letter of the 12th and add this new adventure. This was something he had not expected. There are times when the will of the patient and the mercy of God can be supplemented by the art of the doctor, to the extension of life. But what would happen next time? Exactly two years later, on 28 August, 1374, during a stay in Florence, Boccaccio made out his last will and testament, 'because nothing is as certain as death, and nothing less certain than its hour'. His housekeeper was to receive his personal estate, while two nephews would inherit the house in Certaldo. Several churches and abbeys received contributions so that they should pray for him. His most important legacy, his library, was to be installed in the Augustine Abbey of Florence and be accessible to all users. Permission to make copies of his manuscripts was to be granted to everyone. A scholarly Augustine friar was named as executor of the estate; he belonged to the circle of Boccaccio's humanistic friends and would care for both the salvation and posthumous renown of the writer better than all his relatives.

Soon thereafter, on 19 October, 1374, Boccaccio received a letter telling him of Petrarch's death. He postponed his reply to Petrarch's son-in-law until 1 November; it was to be his last comment on death, in fact, his last letter of all. He did not comment on the circumstances under which his seventy-year-old friend had died; he interpreted that death almost monastically, as a transition from earthly Babylon to heavenly Jerusalem. Boccaccio would have liked to say farewell to his friend at his grave, but for the last ten months he had been sick again. The symptoms were as usual, but this time his vision and digestion were suffering too. Florentine doctors with their medicines and fasting therapies had done nearly as much damage to his vitality as to his illness. Now he lay in Certaldo, weak from inactivity and, to his surprise, half dead from fear. He regained a little composure in his letter, as Petrarch's example had given him strength. In a short time, he wrote, we will go the way Petrarch went: Petrarch has made ready the path to the eternal mansions and is there helping his friends in heaven just as he thought of them in his will. We are all born to die, Boccaccio continued, but the poets will always remain together 'in a better life, after the transition we call death'. Only one earthly care remains: providing for his literary legacy. Boccaccio urgently warns that the works of Petrarch, all so important, should not be destroyed, and he requests copies, lest the immortal poetry fall into the hands of the stupid and jealous.

Thus Boccaccio came to terms with dying. The following months he spent thinking of his lost friends. He continued work on lectures about Dante, and when visitors came he spoke about Petrarch. What he had once tried to learn from the former, the latter now affirmed. Dying was simply a transition, a difficult one, perhaps, but not an important one. The community of humanists would hold together before and after. Poets who had gone before were preparing for their pupils to move into heaven; friends left behind were caring for the legacy of their masters. Dying could not break the ties of intellectual life, it could only destroy what is unimportant in man, and fully extinguish only unimportant people. The rest was silence. We do not know how Boccaccio felt in the end, who was with him in that hour, nor his last words. We only learn, initially from the letters of other humanists, that he died in Certaldo on 21 December, 1375. His biographer, who began writing in 1380, said nothing of Boccaccio's twenty-year ailments, and of his death only this: 'He died in the year of our Lord's mercy 1375, in his sixty-second year, and was buried at Certaldo in the collegiate church of St James.' The poet's renown broke the power of death even before his end: thus the details of that end were of little significance.

In the Late Middle Ages, few people died their own 'individual deaths'. A kind of precursor to modern death dominated, one which conforms to no context, either in the community of the living or in the life of the individual. This death, which made life unrecognizable, became shapeless. It was no longer a part of public life; many learned of it only through books and letters. Though its malice was plainly visible, its victims' defence remained haphazard. This misshapen death was most successfully resisted by a circle of creative people who harvested their crops in time and passed it on to their descendants. This kind of mastery over death succeeded earliest among Italian humanists. Their work consisted of written pages that could easily be lost, but could also be stored long; their community consisted of individualists who lived apart but worked in the same spirit. This abstract society was the first to make death something completely different: a death without significance.

V

Gall and Wetti, Adolf and Gottschalk, Dante and Boccaccio illustrate only three of the countless changes in the process of dying in the Middle Ages. Yet these three are sufficient to draw seven general conclusions.

1   In the course of the Middle Ages, and according to historical experience, attitudes towards dying changed. In the Early Middle Ages, dying, like history itself, was considered a transition from the eternal society of the original paradise to that of the last days. In the High Middle Ages, dying, like history itself, lost its timeless context. In the Late Middle Ages, dying, like history itself, became more and more relative to the perception of contemporaries. The better people mastered earthly life, the less they thought of the consolations of heaven. But with the affirmation of life, the fear of death grew too. None the less, it was death that repeatedly established the connection between the before and after of history. Practical reality categorized human existence into individual moments, into the diversities of events and circumstances. Dying summarized it, one might even say that death presented life in its most condensed form, a life that would outlast the brief moment of dying: with Wetti, it lay more in the heavenly continuation of his personal striving, with Boccaccio in the earthly traditions of his circle of contemporaries. If you prepared for death, you could achieve the idea of a fulfilled life, for yourself and for others. If, of course, you were dependent on others as Gottschalk was, you could not.

2   The history of dying depended for the most part on the circumstances of the various social classes. There was a world of

difference between the practical reality of monks, of peasants and of burghers. Few people in their lives ever looked beyond the walls of their abbey, their village or their city; the living preferred to interpret death from their own short-sighted perspective. Yet death provided, again and again, the relationship between all elements of existence. It liberated the essence, not necessarily by uncovering the lies of life, but by inviting men to make their lives beyond the scope of their occupations into a meaningful whole. More than any others, the challenge stimulated intellectuals, scholarly monks like Wetti and bourgeois men of letters like Boccaccio. They wanted deeds to seal their proposals in the end, deeds that would be representative for all, that would be exemplary for both counts and peasants.

3   The history of dying cannot be understood only by examining norms, it derives its life from the conflict between norms and facts. Expectations as to how one would have liked to die seldom coincided with the circumstances under which one died in practice. This conflict was never denied in the Middle Ages, only reformulated. Everyone knew they had to go through it; most people tried to learn it in time. That is why Wetti described the death of Gall, Boccaccio the death of Dante. If we were to read only these writings, we would hardly see half the picture. In this way, however, death repeatedly revealed the relationship between a period's ideal and its reality. It showed how close the individual, Wetti, Gottschalk, Boccaccio, was to the ideals he championed, or how distant from them, and how well or how poorly the supposed community, the Abbey of Reichenau, the village of Harrie, the city of Florence, held together. Dying shows how people come to grips with their history.

4   The possibility that their deaths could go wrong put terror into the hearts of the people of the Middle Ages. Ariès, however, claims just the opposite when he criticizes the modern age: 'Until then, I dare claim, people, as history shows them, were never really frightened of death. Surely they had respect for it, feared it to some extent, and were not afraid to admit it. But their fear never crossed the line into the inexpressible, the unmentionable. It was translated into pacifying words and channelled into familiar rites.' This is wrong. Real fear came upon Wetti, and the monastery could not comfort him with pacifying words. Gottschalk crossed the line, and his confessor could not interpret the symbols for him. Boccaccio was filled with horror of the inexpressible, and his neighbours could not support him with familiar rites. Death in the Middle Ages was more difficult than today, for no one knew an answer to the questions that were most important to the dying: whether their soul would go forever to heaven or hell, whether their body this time would give

birth to life or to death. They all had to gather up enough vitality to overcome their dual fear, religious and physical. By transfiguring their torment, we fail to recognize their accomplishment.

5 In the Middle Ages, no one died in order to go down in history. Even survivors were cautious about turning deaths into history, those who had passed away into the permanent dead. The modern historian is a survivor of the dead by profession; because he knows how the story went on, he could easily categorize the deaths of Wetti, Gottschalk and Boccaccio, as a doctor might. All he would have to do is suppose, with Ariès, that a host of scholarly monks in the Carolingian period had laid the liturgical foundation for a transition in the High Middle Ages from 'domesticated' to 'individual' death; that an elite of humanists in the Renaissance used literature to introduce the transition in the modern period from 'individual' to 'gradual, personal' death. Wetti's death was an early 'individual' death, Boccaccio's death was a pioneering 'gradual, personal' death. The diagnosis is not wrong, it simply misses the point and ignores the dying of the masses, like that of Gottschalk. In the Middle Ages, it was not the responsibility of death to draw lines on a historical medical chart. It demanded that you think back on how life was lived, and make provisions for enduring coming lives. To extract a history of the dead from an example for the living, you have to use force.

6 To put it briefly: for the Middle Ages, as for all ancient advanced civilizations, dying was considered to be one stage in the middle of existence. Only the modern age of Europe jumps to conclusions, passing facts off as norms, means as ends. Technical and medical achievements have reduced the dangers to life, increased the quality of life and at the same time extended our expectation of life and worn out our vitality. The remedies are indispensable and beneficial; they have made modern death far easier than archaic death. But they should not be allowed to prescribe to us the purpose of life. Even critics searching for new norms are dominated by facts. Psychologists and sociologists who make death seem humane, as if it were nothing but bidding farewell to a happy life and a friendly society, have put their trust in the wrong ally. Theologians and historians who demonize death, as if it were punishment for recurrent evil and modern progress, have identified the wrong enemy. The mistake of today is not so much the modern attitude towards death alone, but our fashion-oriented association with time itself.

7 Our task of making the moment of dying a part of our lives again has failed for the present because of our period's basic convictions. Our leisure-time age still believes that happiness consists of enjoying the here and now, and that enduring transience can bring

us nothing but suffering. Certainly, everyone talks about providing for the future and remembering the past, but let us not deceive ourselves: neither is accepted as one and the same responsibility that the living minority has for the majority of unborn or deceased: at best, they are merely two ways of passing the time. Transience as a basis for the present could not be endured; it is in this, viewed in the framework of the time assigned to man, that we could find the conditions for happiness. The moment of satisfaction, which is impossible without the pains preceding and following, is priceless for the simple reason that it does not last. If we, each of us individually and all of us collectively, were to take experiences with mortality more seriously, we could live more cheerfully. Then the people of the Middle Ages would speak to us more personally. Their mental and technical means are long since outdated, but their social behaviour in the face of the time granted them has yet to be matched. They provided a modest but lasting happiness: the compassion of those who were about to die for those who already had.

14

My Life

A speaker for the republic of scholars, Johan Huizinga, said in 1929, before the Netherland Academy of the Sciences, that history is a culture's intellectual form of accounting for its past. This definition contradicted with the pastime habits of modern barbarians who would plunder any past, partly ruining it and partly claiming it as a trophy. Before Huizinga's challenge reached me in 1945, I also saw history, if at all, as a toy one discovers somewhere along the way and later discards again. Since my birth in 1925, I grew up on the border of Lower Franconia in sparse hill country between the Spessart region and the Rhoen. The Catholic church in Brendlorenzen, which I attended as a pupil, was a thousand years old, an eternity I reverently lost myself in. From 1935, a good humanistic education by the Augustine friars in Münnerstadt expanded my horizons beyond the borders of the village. The secondary school, too, offered me a possession I could keep for ever: world literature from Homer to Schiller, and, at the secret centre of it all, Augustine. The classical canon fascinated me so much that I tried to expand it; at home I learned Italian in order to read Dante and practised the jargons of modern technology, mainly chemical formulae and Morse code.

History as a school subject bored me. But my father, an expert on local history and my first mentor, inspired in me a curiosity for my own origins. In 1938, I extracted our family tree from old parish records. The technology of historical investigation and the puzzle of origins excited me. What I discovered was all the more confusing. My oldest forefather was a peasant from the surrounding Kissingen countryside, and he first appeared in Würzburg documents in 1610 as a wood thief. Perhaps he had stubbornly refused to stop using the local forest after the prince-bishop Julius had claimed it for the state. Should I be proud or ashamed of this past? I preferred the alternative of exploring the ruins of Salz Castle, reconstructing knightly armour from the headstone of the Bildhäuser cloister-founder and poring over Wolfram's *Parzival*. But the complicated times of knights and monks were gone forever; Hitler took care of that. I wanted to study at the Julius Echter University in Würzburg, not history or literature but chemistry, and was admitted there following my graduation in 1943.

First, however, I was sent to another kind of school, the war: as an on-board radio engineer without a plane in France, as a parachute jumper on foot in Holland, as an aircraft sighter without radar in Italy. Berlin nights filled with bombs taught me how technical defects could ruin life and how chemical perfection could destroy it. In the spring of 1945, I was bewitched by medieval Bologna, by the stumbling pride of its aristocratic towers, the half-finished elegance of San Petronio, the cheerfulness of the bombarded citizens. Through the smoke of the bombings one could still catch a scent of the *Decameron*. If one wanted to survive with dignity, one had to embrace transition. I was completely liberated from the vexation of the moment by a series of lectures on the lives of ancient rulers, presented by Lothar Wickert in a prisoner-of-war camp near Rimini. The past of others opened new potential for us. At home, my father begged me remorsefully to forget the history we had abused and to follow Augustine's footsteps. But for the time being, I had made my decision. In the winter of 1945, I was accepted at the University of Göttingen, where Karl Brandi lectured on the Florentine sense of community, followed by Hermann Heimpel on Hohenstaufen chivalry. The university as a meeting place for survivors – that reminded me of Bologna and the promise of a future.

Heidelberg, where I wanted to attend the lectures of Karl Jaspers, rejected me in 1946. That freed me from the temptation of historical philosophy and I lost my heart in Göttingen. My girlfriend's studying art and being Lutheran encouraged me to think about the nervous asceticism of my mother and her historical religious motives. I seized the opportunity when, in 1948, Hans Heinrich Schaeder suggested the investigation of the largest sect in the Middle Ages, the world-rejecting Cathars in southern France and northern Italy. More specifically, we were to investigate the influences of Oriental Manichaeans and Byzantine Bogomils on the Latin Cathars, the influences of the oppressed heretics on the Catholic victors and the conflict between peace of mind and happiness of the senses (the results of which appear in my book *Die Katharer* of

1953). While Schaeder taught me universal historical perspectives, Percy Ernst Schramm taught me medievalist precision. Both doctorate supervisors inspired me with the sovereignty with which they accounted for their own pasts and forced their students to self-dependence. The English tradition in Göttingen also encouraged a certain nonconformity of research, as opposed to the warm comfort of a collective of classmates. After a quiet year in Munich's *Maximilaneum*, and after being awarded my doctorate in Göttingen, I pressed on, with unorthodox obduracy, to yet another teacher, the historian of heretics, Herbert Grundmann in Münster.

Grundmann summoned me to Westphalia as his assistant in 1951 and turned me in another direction. This cynic only took living or dead seriously if he could argue with them. I resisted him with a stubborn readiness for reconciliation, especially since I was now able to marry my girlfriend from Göttingen and, with her, bring up four citizens of the earth. We kept our distance from the absolute vivacity of the people in Münster; their joy appeared too grim as they rebuilt the Anabaptist cages in the Lamberti tower. We found more uplifting friends among fellow-assistants and learned intellectual companionship in their group of intellectuals, the *Mondkälberkreis*. Following Grundmann's footsteps, I reaffirmed the humanities as a field open to exploration, and the university as a step to entering into the unknown. My inaugural dissertation, about the origins and diversities of language, grew out of the euphoric atmosphere of the 1950s (*Der Turmbau von Babel, Geschichte der Meinungen über Usprung und Vielfalt der Sprachen und Völker*, 1957–63). The inspiration for this six-volume monster came from invitations abroad, to Spain, for example, where we were warmly received and misunderstood; the spirit and history of a person, even of a people, appeared to express itself only in the mother tongue. It was not a tower to heaven I wanted to build, but a bridge from person to person; I wanted all of global history to tell of the changing prejudices that drowned out the harmonies amid the diversity of languages and peoples. In principle, 'understanding' was not when people repeated foreign words, but when they held to their own words. My historical ideal was the academic group in which I lived. Disillusionment did not remain a stranger, however. While my friends, one after the other, were offered other appointments, I remained sitting in my tower for five years, as a lecturer without tenure.

My first offer, for a chair in Erlangen, almost took me home again in 1962, though Middle Franconia was set apart from Lower Franconia by reformation and industry. History was discussed more humbly here than in Westphalia, and the atmosphere of strangers was always present. I was amazed especially at the reverence that Nuremberg, modern and godless, showed to its medieval patron saint of the city, St Sebald. The book about it (*Die Sebaldslegenden in der mittelalterlichen Geschichte Nürnbergs*, 1966) shifted my tendencies from universal humanities to local and social history. St Sebald's reputation could be explained by the vicissitudes of the reality of life in Nuremberg; the community needed a permanent personification for their hopes. That my Erlangen Alma Mater also constituted a community and offered solidarity in growing hardship was proved by the circles of scholars around Helmut Berve and Walther Peter Fuchs, by efforts to reform the old faculty together with obliging colleagues, as well as by the devotion of many hard-working students. Just the same, discussions in Paris and Prague strengthened my impression that Erlangen was keeping too aloof from the rebellious 1960s. True, when I was offered a post at Bochum in 1965, the ruthlessness on the Ruhr river exasperated me more than the old Franconian modesty. But two years later, rejections first by politicians, then by students robbed me of my courage to stay in Erlangen.

It seemed easier to combine tradition and reform closer to Italy, at Lake Constance in the city of the same name, which still almost seemed a part of the Middle Ages, yet supported a progressive university. I was lured to the Alemannics by Waldemar Besson in 1968, and helped Gerhard Hess in his efforts academically to restrict encroaching politicization. In order to combine past European experience with the expectations for the future, which were almost American, I examined medieval universities for the motives and consequences of their contemptuous association with history (*Geschichte an mittelalterlichen Universitäten*, 1969). Historical thinking, I concluded, would neither retain everything present nor accomplish everything achievable, but would attempt some preliminary steps. I confidently joined Leonardo da Vinci in concluding that truth has never been more than the daughter of time. That statement betrayed me as early as 1970. As German cultural politics once again scorned their own constant, the coupling of expectation and experience, I resigned from the office of pro-rector and put the history of universities aside. Having become irrelevant among busy colleagues and limited to teaching a few students, I returned again to my desk at home.

From then on, I found comfort in a simpler way of dealing with history, far from the elevated institutions of states, churches and schools, in the circle of fellows, or, as Dante said, on the little threshing-floor of mortality, where association with one another instructs us, almost wordlessly, in our diverse duties. This book, an examination of European cultural forms in the Middle Ages, (*Lebensformen im Mittelalter*, 1973), attracted no interest among local colleagues, but much attention from far away, a kind of invisible, almost ghostly lecture hall and discussion group. Looking for a greater closeness to life, I applied for posts elsewhere. But Münster was encouraging more sects of specialized research rather than the individual heresies of the past. Along with the longed-for post in Würzburg, which the university offered in 1974, came strong and unwarranted expectations of church and state. The trimmed-down 'school' became uncanny: wind, sand and stars, but the kind of stars you might see on television, not in the sky: there was nothing between fellow-men but words. All that helped me get through the leaden seventies was the generous allotment of experimental freedom provided by the state of Baden-Württemberg.

At the same time, I was irritated by the German habit of fluctuating between exaggerated ideals and heavy-handed machinations; the Hohenstaufen exhibition in Stuttgart is a case in point. During its preparations, I abandoned the idea of writing the history of knighthood, which I had carried around with me since Münster. The difference between the dreams of chivalric poetry and the bare necessities of the noble castle were hardly to be bridged by a history of chivalry (*Das Rittertum im Mittelalter*, 1976). The shining Hohenstaufen themselves, it seemed to me, were victims of German one-sidedness. Though it is true that they had expected too much of their contemporaries with their high-flying plans, their influence deteriorated in the bickering of pre-judgemental scholars (*Reden über die Staufer*, 1978). It was then I noticed that the Alemannics at Lake Constance created more turbulence than they could master but had always resisted the impatience of outsiders with a decidedly non-German virtue, composure. I steeped myself in their local history, which revolved around abbeys, and found monastic life here more warm and companionable than I had believed I knew it to be in Franconia. Inspired by the rush of students, including those registered for part-time courses, I researched and described how much European influence the medieval monks of Lake Constance had spread with their collective humaneness. The book (*Mönche am Bodensee, 610–1525*, 1978) described a zone of moderation in the middle of the most volatile part of the earth, a continuing state of suspension among decisive changes.

Not that my wife and I felt entirely at home in Constance. In fact, it was because we have remained impartial observers that we have now decided not to leave. History helps us survive in that holiday area, like horse-riding over Lake Constance or a chat with far-away neighbours. Recently I have begun talking with an old mentor, Hermannus Contractus or Hermann the Lame, an eleventh-century monk of the Abbey of Reichenau. The crippled monk was not able to move from the spot, yet his scholarship elevated him beyond his island and his years. In his studies of universal history and contemporary criticism, poetry and music, chronological calculation and astronomy, he drew like-minded men of all ages into his discussion: antique poets, Christian church fathers and Islamic astronomers (*Ein Forschungsbericht Hermanns des Lahmen*, 1984). Though it is difficult for me to grasp the extent of Hermann's personal achievement, his handicap helps me appreciate all the more how lucky I was to find scholarly companionship in 1983. Gathered in the Heidelberg Academy are scholars of all the sciences with which I have briefly occupied myself during my life, as well as colleagues from all the universities of which I have been a part. Here, deceased peers such as Peter Classen or Werner Conze, whom I had met a generation ago, are remembered, and contributions are made to research projects that will last another generation, and survive my lifetime.

Because the Academy combined hard work with fanciful games, I felt encouraged to reconstruct a long-forgotten arithmetical and musical game, *Rithmimachia*, an invention of the eleventh century. It had aroused the enthusiasm of Hermann the Lame because it analogically depicted a universal order that one could see only fragments of in reality. Hermann, as could be expected, provided a glimpse into the relationship of arithmetic and music, and of science and art. I did not expect him also to provoke comparisons with the most demanding games of the twentieth century, however, with philosophical games of dialogue and computer games of natural science (*Das mittelalterliche Zahlenkampfspiel*, 1986). What took me most unawares were a circulatory collapse in 1986 and an accident in 1985; they dramatically reminded me of my own mortality and forced me to budget my time and energy more exactly.

In 1988, the German scientific foundation, *Stifterverband für die deutsche Wissenschaft*, made it possible for me to restrict my activities to further investigation of Hermann the Lame, and I was able to give up my university seat to a younger professor. The time has come to re-examine my thirty-five years of academic instruction, and to take another look at the subjects I discussed with students, to round them off. This is the intention behind this collection of essays, to summarize the most important of my old questions. And it is only the questions that have remained the same, not my answers, for in the course of my life I have rejected old ideas and gained new ones. The circle does not close. Of my dialogues with the dead, I can only report what a traveller might tell, retrospectively, tentatively, temporarily, that is to say, as a mortal can. Perhaps this attitude contributes most effectively to what Huizinga expected from the republic of scholars, and what our barbaric time most urgently needs: cultivation of the intellectual form that makes us peers of the present, past and future.

Bibliography

For every subject discussed in this book, the following bibliography lists about a dozen scholarly monographs, essays and collections, concentrating on the more recent secondary literature which combines loyalty to detail with far-sightedness, and which supplies references to particulars as well as indications of broader associations. I have ignored books unfamiliar to me personally, as well as unprocessed material on primary sources. Regarding those subjects which I have researched in greater detail in other cases, I have not referred to the older literature, only to my own publications and to the most instructive treatises following them.

Chapter 1 Barbarians:
The History of a European Catchword

Christ, Karl 1959: 'Römer und Barbaren in der hohen Kaiserzeit', *Saeculum*, 10, 273–88.
De Mattei, Rodolfo 1939: 'Sul concetto di barbaro e barbarie nel medio evo'. In *Studi di storia e diritto in onore di Enrico Besta*, vol. 4, Milan, 481–501.
Fichtenau, Heinrich 1986: 'Gentiler und europäischer Horizont'. In Fichtenau (ed.), *Beiträge zur Mediävistik: Ausgewählte Aufsätze*, vol. 3, Stuttgart, 80–97.
Gruber, Joachim, and Vismara, Giulio 1980: 'Barbaren'. In *Lexikon des Mittelalters*, vol. 1, Munich–Zurich, cols. 1434–6.
Jones, William R. 1971: 'The image of the barbarian in medieval Europe'. *Comparative Studies in Society and History* 13, 376–407.
Jüthner, Julius 1923: *Hellenen und Barbaren: Aus der Geschichte des Nationalbewußtseins*. Leipzig.
Koselleck, Reinhart 1985 (German version 1979): 'On the historical–political semantics of asymmetrical opposites'. In Koselleck (ed.), *Future Past: On the Semantics of Historical Time*, Massachusetts.

Lechner, Kilian 1955: 'Byzanz und die Barbaren', *Saeculum* 6, 292–306.

Nitschke, August 1981: 'Das Fremde und das Eigene'. In Werner Conze et al. (eds), *Funk-Kolleg Geschichte*, vol. 1, Frankfurt, 236–62.

Opelt, Ilona and Speyer, Wolfgang 1967: 'Barbar', *Jahrbuch für Antike und Christentum* 10, 251–90.

Schmugge, Ludwig 1982: 'Über 'nationale' Vorurteile im Mittelalter'. *Deutsches Archiv für Erforschung des Mittelalters* 38, 439–59.

Southern, Richard W. 1962: *Western views of Islam in the Middle Ages*. Harvard–Oxford.

Van Acker, Lieven 1965: Barbarus und seine Ableitungen im Mittellatein. *Archiv für Kulturgeschichte* 47, 125–40.

Chapter 2   The History of Languages in the Flux of European Thought

Arens, Hans 1969: *Sprachwissenschaft: Der Gang ihrer Entwicklung von der Antike bis zur Gegenwart*, 2nd edn. Freiburg–Munich.

Beumann, Helmut and Werner, Schröder (eds) 1978: *Aspekte der Nationenbildung im Mittelalter*. Sigmaringen.

Bischoff, Bernhard 1967: 'The Study of Foreign Languages in the Middle Ages'. In Bischoff (ed.), *Mittelalterliche Studien: Ausgewählte Aufsätze zur Schriftkunde und Literaturgeschichte*, vol. 2, Stuttgart, 227–45.

Borst, Arno 1957–63: *Der Turmbau von Babel: Geschichte der Meinungen über Ursprung und Vielfalt der Sprachen und Völker* (6 vols). Stuttgart.

—— 1966: 'Storia e lingua nell' enciclopedia di Isidoro di Siviglia'. *Bulletino dell' Istituto Storico Italiano per il Medio Evo* 77, 1–20.

—— 1966: 'Das Bild der Geschichte in der Enzyklopädie Isidors von Sevilla. *Deutsches Archiv für Erforschung des Mittelalters* 22, 1–62.

—— 1966: 'Dantes Meinungen über Ursprung und Vielfalt der Sprachen'. *Jahrbuch der Akademie der Wissenschaften in Göttingen*, Göttingen 15–24.

Brekle, Herbert Ernst 1985: *Einführung in die Geschichte der Sprachwissenschaft*. Darmstadt.

Coseriu, Eugenio 1970–2: *Die Geschichte der Sprachphilosophie von der Antike bis zur Gegenwart: Eine Übersicht* (2 vols) 2nd edn of vol. 1. Tübingen.

Koerner, Konrad (ed.) 1980: Studies in medieval linguistic thought. *Historiographia Linguistica* 7, 1–321.

Robins, Robert H. 1979: *A short history of linguistics*, 2nd edn (original edn 1967). London.

Wolff, Philippe 1971: *Western languages: A.D. 100–1500* (original French edn 1971). London.

Chapter 3   The Invention and Fission
of the Public Persona

Carrithers, Michael et al. (eds) 1985: *The category of the person: anthropology, philosophy, history*. Cambridge.
Cheyette, Fredric L. 1978: 'The invention of the state'. In Bede K. Lackner et al. (eds), *Essays on medieval civilization*, Austin–London, 143–78.
Gurevich, Aaron I. 1985: *Categories of medieval culture* (original Russian edn, 1972). London–Boston.
Hölscher, Lucian 1978: 'Öffentlichkeit'. In Otto Brunner et al. (eds), *Geschichtliche Grundbegriffe: historisches Lexikon zur politisch-sozialen Sprache in Deutschland* (vol. 4), Stuttgart, 413–67.
Kantorowicz, Ernst H. 1957: *The King's two bodies: a study in mediaeval political theology*. Princeton.
Marquard, Odo and Stierle, Karlheinz (eds) 1979: *Identität* (Poetik und Hermeneutik 8). Munich (esp.: Borst, Arno, *Barbarossas Erwachen: Zur Geschichte der deutschen Identität*, 17–60; Fuhrmann, Manfred, *Persona: Ein römischer Rollenbegriff*, 83–106; Luckmann, Thomas, *Persönliche Identität, soziale Rolle und Rollendistanz*, 293–313; Pannenberg, Wolfhart, *Person und Subjekt*, 407–22; Henrich, Dieter, *Die Trinität Gottes und der Begriff der Person*, 612–20).
Morris, Colin 1972: *The discovery of the individual 1050–1200*. London.
—— 1980: 'Individualism in Twelfth-Century Religion: Some Further Reflections'. *Journal of Ecclesiastical History* 31, 195–206.
Nédoncelle, Maurice 1955: 'Les variations de Boèce sur la personne'. *Revue des sciences religieuses* 29, 201–38.
Schmid, Karl 1983: 'Über das Verhältnis von Person und Gemeinschaft im früheren Mittelalter'. In Schmid (ed.), *Gebetsgedenken und adliges Selbstverständnis im Mittelalter: Ausgewählte Beiträge*, Sigmaringen 363–87.
Strayer, Joseph R. 1970: *On the medieval origins of the modern state*. Princeton.
Struve, Tilman 1978: *Die Entwicklung der organologischen Staatsauffassung im Mittelalter*. Stuttgart.
Ullmann, Walter 1966: *Principles of government and politics in the Middle Ages*. New York.

Chapter 4   Universal Histories
in the Middle Ages?

Brincken, Anna-Dorothee von den 1957: *Studien zur lateinischen Weltchronistik bis in das Zeitalter Ottos von Freising*. Düsseldorf.
Funkenstein, Amos 1986: *Theology and the scientific imagination from*

the Middle Ages to the seventeenth century (original German version, 1965). Princeton.

Grundmann, Herbert 1969: *Geschichtsschreibung im Mittelalter: Gattungen, Epochen, Eigenart* 2nd edn (original edn 1965). Göttingen.

Guenée, Bernard 1980: *Histoire et culture historique dans l'Occident médiéval.* Paris. (UK edn, 1985: States and Rules in Later Medieval Europe, Oxford.).

Kaegi, Werner 1954: *Chronica Mundi: Grundformen der Geschichtsschreibung seit dem Mittelalter.* Einsiedeln.

Krüger, Karl Heinrich 1976, supplemented 1985: *Die Universalchroniken (Typologie des sources du moyen âge occidental 16).* Turnhout.

Lammers, Walther (ed.) 1961: *Geschichtsdenken und Geschichtsbild im Mittelalter: Ausgewählte Aufsätze und Arbeiten aus den Jahren 1933 bis 1959 (Wege der Forschung 21).* Darmstadt.

Melville, Gert 1986: 'Der Zugriff auf Geschichte in der Gelehrtenkultur des Mittelalters: Vorgaben und Leistungen'. In Hans Ulrich Gumprecht et al. (eds), *La littérature historiographique des origines à 1500 (Grundriß der romanischen Literaturen des Mittelalters 11:1),* vol. 1, Heidelberg, 157–228.

Pannenberg, Wolfhart 1973: 'Weltgeschichte und Heilsgeschichte'. In Reinhart Koselleck and Wolf-Dieter Stempel (eds), *Geschichte, Ereignis und Erzählung (Poetik und Hermeneutik 5),* Munich, 307–23.

Randa, Alexander (ed.) 1969: *Mensch und Weltgeschichte: Zur Geschichte der Universalgeschichtsschreibung.* Salzburg–Munich.

Schmale, Franz-Josef 1985: *Funktion und Formen mittelalterlicher Geschichtsschreibung: eine Einführung.* Darmstadt.

Schulin, Ernst (ed.) 1974: *Universalgeschichte.* Cologne.

Zanella, Gabriele (ed.) 1984: *Storici e storiografia del Medioevo italiano.* Bologna.

Chapter 5 Historical Time in the Writings of Abelard

Braudel, Fernand 1958: 'Histoire et sciences sociales. La longue durée'. *Annales Economies-Sociétés-Civilisations* 13, 725–53.

Brunner, Otto 1980: 'Abendländisches Geschichtsdenken'. In Brunner (ed.), *Neue Wege der Verfassungs-und Sozialgeschichte,* 3rd edn, Göttingen, 26–44.

Chenu, Marie-Dominique 1964: *Toward understanding Saint Thomas* ... (trs. A.M. Landry and D. Hughes with authorized corrections and bibliographical additions; original French version, 1950). Chicago.

Elias, Norbert 1984: *Über die Zeit* (trs. from unpublished English *An Essay on Time*). Frankfurt.

Fumagalli, Mariateresa 1984: *Eloisa e Abelardo: Parole al Posto di Cose.* Milan.

Grundmann, Herbert 1977: 'Die Grundzüge der mittelalterlichen Geschichtsanschauungen'. In Grundmann (ed.), *Ausgewählte Aufsätze*, vol. 2, Stuttgart, 211–19.

Jolivet, Jean (ed.) 1981: *Abélard en son temps*. Paris.

Koselleck, Reinhart 1971: 'Wozu noch Historie?' *Historische Zeitschrift*, 212, 1–18.

—— (ed.) 1985: *Future past: on the semantics of historical time*. (original German version, 1979). Massachusetts.

Le Goff, Jacques 1960: 'Au moyen âge: Temps de l'Eglise et temps de marchand'. *Annales Economies-Sociétés-Civilisations*, 15, 417–33.

McLaughlin, Mary M. 1967: 'Abelard as autobiographer: the motives and meaning of his "Story of calamities"'. *Speculum* 42, 463–88.

Silvestre, Hubert 1985: 'L'idylle d'Abélard et Héloïse: la part du roman'. *Académie Royale de Belgique: Bulletin de la Classe des Lettres*, series 5, vol. 71, 157–200.

Spörl, Johannes 1968: *Grundformen hochmittelalterlicher Geschichtsanschauung: Studien zum Weltbild der Geschichtsschreiber des 12. Jahrhunderts* 2nd edn; (original edition Munich, 1935). Darmstadt.

Wendorff, Rudolf 1980: *Zeit und Kultur: Geschichte des Zeitbewußtseins in Europa*. Opladen.

Chapter 6   Heretics and Hysteria

Borst, Arno 1974: 'Häresie'. In Joachim Ritter (ed.), *Historisches Wörterbuch der Philosophie*, vol. 3, Basel–Stuttgart, 999–1001.

Cohn, Norman 1957: *Pursuit of the millenium: a history of popular religious and social movements in Europe from the eleventh to the sixteenth centuries* (rev. ed.: *Revolutionary millenarians and mystical anarchists of the Middle Ages*, London, 1970).

Grundmann, Herbert 1976: *Ausgewählte Aufsätze*, vol. 1. (esp. *Der Typus des Ketzers in mittelalterlicher Anschauung*, 313–27; *Ketzerverhöre des Spätmittelalters als quellenkritisches Problem*, 364–416). Stuttgart.

Koch, Gottfried 1962: *Frauenfrage und Ketzertum im Mittelalter: die Frauenbewegung im Rahmen des Katharismus und des Waldensertums und ihre sozialen Wurzeln (12.–14. Jahrhundert)*. Berlin.

Kurze, Dietrich 1979: 'Häresie und Minderheit im Mittelalter'. *Historische Zeitschrift*, 229, 529–73.

Ladurie, Emmanuel Le Roy 1978: *Montaillou: Cathars and Catholics in a French Village, 1294–1324*. (original French version, 1975). London.

Leff, Gordon 1967: *Heresy in the later Middle Ages: the relation of heterodoxy to dissent c. 1250–1450*, 2 vols. New York.

Le Goff, Jacques (ed.) 1968: *Hérésies et sociétés dans l'Europe pré–industrielle: 11e–18e siècles*. Paris–Den Haag.

Lourdaux, Willem and Verhelst, Daniel (eds) 1976: *The concept of heresy in the Middle Ages (11th–13th Century)*. Löwen–Den Haag.

Russell, Jeffrey B. 1965: *Dissent and reform in the early Middle Ages*. Berkeley–Los Angeles.

Töpfer, Bernhard 1964: *Das kommende Reich des Friedens: Zur Entwicklung chiliastischer Zukunftshoffnungen im Hochmittelalter*. Berlin.

Vicaire, Marie-Humbert (ed.) 1971: *Le Credo: la Morale et l'Inquisition* (Cahiers de Fanjeaux, 6). Toulouse–Fanjeaux.

Chapter 7   The Origins of the Witch-craze in the Alps

Cohn, Norman 1975: *Europe's inner demons: an enquiry inspired by the great witch-hunt*. London.

Gurevich, Aaron I. 1986: *Mittelalterliche Volkskultur: Probleme zur Forschung* (original Russian version, 1981). Dresden.

Hansen, Joseph 1964: *Zauberwahn, Inquisition und Hexenprozeß im Mittelalter und die Entstehung der großen Hexenverfolgung*, 2nd edn (original edn Munich, 1900). Aalen.

—— 1963: *Quellen und Untersuchungen zur Geschichte des Hexen-wahns und der Hexenverfolgung im Mittelalter*. 2nd edn (original edn Bonn, 1901). Hildesheim.

Honegger, Claudia (ed.) 1978: *Die Hexen der Neuzeit: Studien zur Sozialgeschichte eines kulturellen Deutungsmusters*. Frankfurt.

Kieckhefer, Richard 1976: *European witch trials: their foundations in popular and learned culture, 1300–1500*. London–Henley.

Meuthen, Erich 1985: *Das 15. Jahrhundert* (Oldenbourg Grundriß der Geschichte 9), 2nd edn (original edn 1980). Munich–Vienna.

Russell, Jeffrey B. 1972: *Witchcraft in the Middle Ages*. Ithaca–London.

—— 1980: *A history of witchcraft: sorcerers, heretics and pagans*. London.

Schormann, Gerhard 1981: *Hexenprozesse in Deutschland*. Göttingen.

Trevor-Roper, Hugh R. 1967: *The European witch-craze of the 16th and 17th centuries*. (originally in *Religion, the Reformation and social change*, London, 1967.) Harmondsworth.

Zacharias, Gerhard 1980: *The satanic cult*. (original German version, 1964). London.

Chapter 8   Patron Saints in Medieval Society

Delooz, Pierre 1969: *Sociologie et canonisations*. Liège–Den Haag.

Ewig, Eugen (ed. Hartmut Atsma) 1976–9: *Spätantikes und fränkisches Gallien: Gesammelte Schriften (1952–1973)*, 2 vols. Munich.

Graus, František 1965: *Volk, Herrscher und Heiliger im Reich der Merowinger: Studien zur Hagiographie der Merowingerzeit*. Prague.

—— 1975: *Lebendige Vergangenheit: Überlieferung im Mittelalter und in den Vorstellungen vom Mittelalter.* Cologne–Vienna.

—— 1980: *Die Nationenbildung der Westslawen im Mittelalter.* Sigmaringen.

Hoffmann, Erich 1975: *Die heiligen Könige bei den Angelsachsen und den skandinavischen Völkern: Königsheiliger und Königshaus.* Neumünster.

Petersohn, Jürgen 1975: 'Saint-Denis–Westminster–Aachen: Die Karls-Translatio von 1165 und ihre Vorbilder'. *Deutsches Archiv für Erforschung des Mittelalters,* 31, 420–54.

Peyer, Hans Conrad 1955: *Stadt und Stadtpatron im mittelalterlichen Italien.* Zurich.

Scholz, Bernhard W. 1961: 'The canonization of Edward the Confessor'. *Speculum,* 36, 38–60.

Schramm, Percy Ernst 1954–6: *Herrschaftszeichen und Staatssymbolik: Beiträge zu ihrer Geschichte vom dritten bis zum sechzehnten Jahrhundert,* 3 vols. Stuttgart.

Schwarz, Dietrich W.H. 1964: *Die Stadt- und Landespatrone der alten Schweiz.* Zurich (privately printed).

Schwarz, Marianne 1957: 'Heiligsprechungen im 12. Jahrhundert und die Beweggründe ihrer Urheber'. *Archiv für Kulturgeschichte,* 39, 43–62.

Chapter 9   Chivalric Life
in the High Middle Ages

Borst, Arno (ed.) 1976: *Das Rittertum im Mittelalter* (Wege der Forschung, 349). Darmstadt.

Bumke, Joachim 1986: *Höfische Kultur: Literatur und Gesellschaft im hohen Mittelalter,* 2 vols. Munich.

Duby, Georges 1980: *The three orders: feudal society imagined.* (original French version, 1978). Chicago–London.

—— 1986: *William Marshall: The flower of chivalry.* (original French version, 1984). New York.

Fleckenstein, Josef (ed.) 1977: *Herrschaft und Stand: Untersuchungen zur Sozialgeschichte im 13. Jahrhundert.* Göttingen.

—— (ed.) 1985: *Das ritterliche Turnier im Mittelalter: Beiträge zu einer vergleichenden Formen- und Verhaltensgeschichte des Rittertums.* Göttingen.

—— (Festschrift) 1984: *Institutionen, Kultur und Gesellschaft im Mittelalter: Festschrift für Josef Fleckenstein* (esp. Karl Leyser, 'Early medieval canon law and the beginnings of knighthood', 549–66; Hagen Keller, 'Adel, Rittertum und Ritterstand nach italienischen Zeugnissen des 11.–14. Jahrhunderts', 581–608; Thomas Zotz, 'Städtisches Rittertum und Bürgertum in Köln um 1200', 609–38; Werner Rösener, 'Bauer und Ritter im Hochmittelalter: Aspekte ihrer

Lebensform, Standesbildung und sozialen Differenzierung im 12. und 13. Jahrhundert, 665–92). Sigmaringen.

Flori, Jean 1983: *L'idéologie du glaive: Préhistoire de la chevalerie.* Geneva.

Goez, Werner 1978: 'Renaissance und Rittertum'. In *Geschichtsschreibung und geistiges Leben im Mittelalter: Festschrift für Heinz Löwe.* Cologne–Vienna, 565–84.

Jackson, William H. (ed.) 1981: *Knighthood in medieval literature.* Woodbridge.

Keen, Maurice 1984: *Chivalry.* New Haven–London.

Ruiz, Domenec José Enrique, 1984: *La caballeria o la imagen cortesana del mundo.* Genoa.

Vale, Malcolm 1981: *War and chivalry: warfare and aristocratic culture in England, France and Burgundy at the end of the Middle Ages.* London.

Chapter 10   Crisis and Reform in the Universities of the Late Middle Ages

Boehm, Laetitia 1978: 'Papst Benedikt XII. (1334–1342) als Förderer der Ordensstudien, Restaurator, Reformator oder Deformator regularer Lebensform?' In *Secundum regulam vivere: Festschrift für Norbert Backmund,* Windberg, 281–310.

Classen, Peter (ed. Johannes Fried) 1983: *Studium und Gesellschaft im Mittelalter.* Stuttgart.

Dieckhoff, Reiner et al. 1978: 'Antiqui – moderni: Zeitbewußtsein und Naturerfahrung im 14. Jahrhundert'. In Anton Legner (ed.) *Die Parler und der Schöne Stil 1350–1400, Europäische Kunst unter den Luxemburgern,* vol. 3, Cologne, 67–123.

Fried, Johannes 1986: *Schulen und Studium im sozialen Wandel des hohen und späten Mittelalters.* Sigmaringen.

Graus, František 1975: 'Vom "Schwarzen Tod" zur Reformation: Der krisenhafte Charakter des europäischen Spätmittelalters'. In Peter Blickle (ed.), *Revolte und Revolution in Europa* (Historische Zeitschrift, Beiheft 4), Munich, 10–30.

Ijsewijn, Jozef and Paquet, Jacques (eds) 1978: *The universities in the later Middle Ages.* Löwen.

Koller, Heinrich 1966: *Die Universitätsgründungen des 14. Jahrhunderts* (Salzburger Universitätsreden 10). Salzburg–Munich.

Lhotsky, Alphons 1976: 'Die Universitäten im Spätmittelalter'. In Lhotsky (ed.), *Aufsätze und Vorträge,* vol. 5, Munich, 34–50.

Seibt, Ferdinand 1973: 'Von Prag bis Rostock: Zur Gründung der Universitäten in Mitteleuropa'. In *Festschrift für Walter Schlesinger,* vol. 1. Cologne–Vienna, 406–26.

—— and Eberhard, Winfried (eds) 1984: *Europa 1400: Die Krise des Spätmittelalters.* Stuttgart.

Schubert, Ernst 1978: 'Motive und Probleme deutscher Universitäts-gründungen des 15. Jahrhunderts'. In Peter Baumgart und Notker Hammerstein (eds), *Beiträge zu Problemen deutscher Universitäts-gründungen der frühen Neuzeit*. Nendeln, 13–74.

Verger, Jacques 1976: 'Les universités français au XVᵉ siècle: crise et tentatives de réforme'. *Cahiers d'histoire* 21, 43–66.

Chapter 11 Women and Art in the Middle Ages

Baader, Renate and Fricke, Dietmar (eds) 1979: *Die französische Auto-rin vom Mittelalter bis zur Gegenwart*. Wiesbaden.

Bischoff, Cordula et al. 1984: *Frauen, Kunst, Geschichte: Zur Korrek-tur des herrschenden Blicks*. Giessen.

Doren, Alfred (ed.) 1927: *Alessandra Macinghi negli Strozzi: Briefe*. Leipzig.

Dronke, Peter 1984: *Women writers of the Middle Ages: a critical study of texts from Perpetua (+203) to Marguerite Porete (+1310)*. Cambridge.

Duby, Georges 1981: *The age of the cathedrals: art and society 980–1420* (original French version, 1976). London.

Ennen, Edith 1985: *Frauen im Mittelalter*, 2nd edn (original edn, 1984). Munich.

Ketsch, Peter 1983–4: *Frauen im Mittelalter: Quellen und Materialien*, 2 vols (ed. Annette Kuhn). Düsseldorf.

Menzel, Ottokar (ed.) 1978: *Das Leben der Liutbirg: Eine Quelle zur Geschichte der Sachsen in karolingischer Zeit* (original edition, Leipzig, 1937), 2nd edn. Stuttgart.

Pernoud, Régine 1980: *La femme au temps des cathédrales*. Paris.

Rädle, Fidel 1983: 'Hrotsvit von Gandersheim'. In Kurt Ruh (ed.) *Die deutsche Literatur des Mittelalters: Verfasserlexikon*, vol. 4, Berlin–New York, cols 196–210.

Schraut, Elisabeth and Opitz, Claudia 1983: *Frauen und Kunst im Mittelalter*. Brunswick.

Shahar, Shulamith 1983: *The fourth estate: a history of women in the Middle Ages* (original Hebrew version, 1981). London–New York.

Spanò, Serena 1971: 'Per uno studio su Caterina da Bologna'. *Studi medievali* III, 12, part 2, 713–59.

Chapter 12 Science and Games

Borst, Arno 1986: *Das mittelalterliche Zahlenkampfspiel*. Heidelberg.

Eco, Umberto 1985: 'Huizinga e il gioco'. In Eco (ed.), *Sugli specchi e altri saggi*. Milan, 283–300.

—— 1986: 'Living in the new Middle Ages'. In *Travels in hyperreality* (original Italian version, 1972) San Diego. 7–33.

Eigen, Manfred and Winkler, Ruthild 1982: *Laws of the game* (original German version, 1975). London.

Huizinga, Johan 1949: *Homo ludens: a study of the play-element in culture* (original Dutch version, 1938). London.

Illmer, Detlef et al. 1987: *Rhythmomachia: Ein uraltes Zahlenspiel neu entdeckt*. Munich.

Lorenz, Kuno 1978: 'Arithmetik und Logik als Spiele'. In *Dialogische Logik*, Paul Lorenzen and Kuno Lorenz (eds). Darmstadt, 17–95.

Neumann, John von and Morgenstern, Oskar 1944: *Theory of games and economic behavior*. Princeton.

Rahner, Hugo 1957: *Der spielende Mensch*. 4th edn (original edn. 1948). Einsiedeln.

Scheuerl, Hans (ed.) 1975: *Theorien des Spiels*, 10th edn. Weinheim–Basel.

Wilckens, Leonie von 1985: *Spiel, Spiele, Kinderspiel*. Nuremberg.

Wittgenstein, Ludwig 1981: *Philosophical Investigations* (original German version, 1953). Oxford.

Vorob'ev, Nikolai Nikolaevich 1973: *Teoriya ryadov*. Moscow.

Chapter 13   Three Studies of Death in the Middle Ages

Ariès, Philippe 1974: *Western attitudes towards death: from the Middle Ages to the present* (original French version, 1975). Baltimore–London.

—— 1981: *The hour of our death* (original French version 1977). London.

Braet, Herman and Verbeke, Werner (eds) 1983: *Death in the Middle Ages*. Löwen.

Dinzelbacher, Peter 1981: *Vision und Visionsliteratur im Mittelalter*. Stuttgart.

—— 1985: 'Mittelalterliche Vision und moderne Sterbeforschung'. In Jürgen Kühnel et al. (eds), *Psychologie des Mittelalters*. Göppingen, 9–49.

Goez, Werner 1976: 'Die Einstellung zum Tod im Mittelalter'. In Wolfgang Harms (ed.), *Der Grenzbereich zwischen Leben und Tod*. Göttingen, 111–53.

Lammers, Walther 1982: *Gottschalks Wanderung ins Jenseits. Sitzungsberichte der Wissenschaftlichen Gesellschaft an der Universität Frankfurt*, vol. 19, part 2. Wiesbaden.

Le Goff, Jacques 1984: *The birth of purgatory* (original French version, 1981). Chicago.

Schmid, Karl 1983: 'Bemerkungen zur Anlage des Reichenauer Verbrüderungsbuches: Zugleich ein Beitrag zum Verständnis der *Visio*

Wettini'. In Schmid (ed.), *Gebetsgedanken und adliges Selbstverständnis im Mittelalter: Ausgewählte Beiträge*. Sigmaringen, 514–31.

Sprandel, Rolf 1981: *Altersschicksal und Altersmoral: Die Geschichte der Einstellungen zum Altern nach der Pariser Bibelexegese des 12–16. Jahrhunderts*. Stuttgart.

Stüber, Karl 1976: *Commendatio animae: Sterben im Mittelalter*. Bern–Frankfurt.

Tenenti, Alberto 1957: *Il senso della morte e l'amore della vita nel Rinascimento*. Turin.

Chapter 14 My Life

Besson, Waldemar 1964: 'Die Friedrich-Alexander-Universität Erlangen-Nürnberg'. In Petra Kipphoff et al. (eds), *Hochschulführer*. Hamburg, 55–9.

Borst, Arno 1976: 'Herbert Grundmann (1902–1970)'. In *Herbert Grundmann, Ausgewählte Aufsätze*, vol. 1. Stuttgart, 1–25.

—— 1977: 'Geschichte an der Universität Konstanz'. In Hans Robert Jauss and Herbert Nesselhauf (eds), *Gebremste Reform: Ein Kapitel deutscher Hochschulgeschichte, Universität Konstanz 1966–1976*. Constance, 163–79.

—— 1978: 'Konstanz – Universität, Landschaft, Geschichte'. *Konstanzer Blätter für Hochschulfragen* 60, 69–80.

—— 1990: 'Verhaltene Annäherung'. In Gerd Appenzeller (ed.), *Mein Bodensee: Liebeserklärung an eine Landschaft*. 3rd edn (original edn, 1984). Constance, 30–5.

Fuhrmann, Horst 1987: 'Das Interesse am Mittelalter in heutiger Zeit'. In Fuhrmann (ed.), *Einladung ins Mittelalter*, Munich, 262–80.

—— 1987: 'Laudatio auf Arno Borst'. *Historische Zeitschrift*, 244, 529–35.

Heimpel, Hermann 1972: 'Königtum, Wandel der Welt, Bürgertum: Nachruf auf P.E. Schramm'. *Historische Zeitschrift*, 214, 96–108.

—— 1986: 'Neubeginn 1945'. In *Der Neubeginn der Georgia Augusta zum Wintersemester 1945–1946* (Göttinger Universitätsreden 77), Göttingen, 15–29.

Heß, Gerhard 1968: *Die deutsche Universität 1930–1970*. Bad Godesberg.

Huizinga, Johan 1936: 'On a definition of the term history'. In Raymond Klibanski and H.J. Paton (eds), *Philosophy and History: Essays Presented to Ernst Cassirer*. (revised; original Dutch version 1929). Oxford, 1–10.

Schulin, Ernst 1960: 'Einleitung'. In Grete Schaeder and Hans Heinrich Schaeder (eds), *Der Mensch in Orient und Okzident: Grundzüge einer eurasiatischen Geschichte*, Munich, 7–23.

Index